Living Poor

A PEACE CORPS CHRONICLE

MORITZ THOMSEN

Living Poor

A PEACE CORPS CHRONICLE

Seattle & London

UNIVERSITY OF WASHINGTON PRESS

For
STANLEIGH ARNOLD
and for
RAMON PRADO C.
ORESTES PRADO C.
ROSA VICENTA ESTUPIÑAN

Preface

FOR THOSE of us without fifty thousand dollars or so to invest in a pack trip through the Himalayan passes, the Peace Corps is perhaps the last great adventure available to Americans over eighteen years of age. The physical world has been mapped; but in the last analysis the Peace Corps is an intellectual exploration, the chance (if you are patient enough) to enter in some degree into the hearts and minds and feelings of alien peoples with exotic cultures. The final discovery, that we are all ultimately alike, is a hard-earned revelation. And it is well worth the trouble. The Peace Corps experience is, of course, more than intellectual. During my first year in Río Verde I think I read only two books; life was so full, so emotionally stirring, that reading seemed like a gray and tawdry substitute for all that surging life around me.

It may seem to some that this story is scarcely typical of the Peace Corps experience. Actually, there is no typical story to tell. The Peace Corps exists as a vehicle for acting out your fantasies of brotherhood and, if you are strong enough, turning the dream into a reality. One of the amazing things about being a Volunteer is that you sometimes go whole weeks without being aware of the Peace Corps at all. I used to wake up in the mornings to the noise of roosters in the town and the sound of waves and palm fronds clashing dryly in the wind, and think, utterly amazed and unbelieving, "My God, I'm in Ecuador." I was just another person in a poor village working out my own problems and frustrations, making friends and enemies like one more citizen of the town.

Yet even though each Volunteer makes his own story, the basic problems of fate, poverty, hunger, disease, and ignorance are pretty much the same. And the Peace Corps still exists as the great adventure and the great challenge for individual Americans.

A good part of the following material was first published in the pages of the Sunday *San Francisco Chronicle*. Why, I don't know. I got the idea of writing the pieces one morning as I was washing down a hog pen while I waited for my Peace Corps invitation, and I presented myself that same afternoon —still in Levis and jumper, and still, no doubt, exuding that subtle aroma so closely associated with my trade. I was very gingerly and at arm's length passed from desk to desk and ended up in the office of Stanleigh Arnold, the Sunday editor, who thanked me for my offer and told me that the *Chronicle* was buying no free-lance material. Thanks, but no thanks.

The rest of the story simply doesn't make sense. I went into Peace Corps training, began to write about it, and sent the articles to Stan—who published them.

One of the nice things that developed out of these articles, in addition to a friendship with Stan, was a communication with people in the Bay area. I began to get letters from people who felt involved with the town of Río Verde. Some of them were so involved that they joined the Peace Corps; some of them sent checks. This will, I hope, explain how we ended up with a farm and a tractor. It was through the goodness of friends I didn't know, have never met (and whose addresses, unfortunately, were stolen in a series of robberies before I left Río Verde).

One final word of explanation to any Ecuadorians who may tend to find this book offensive to their national pride. Ecuador, slashed and fragmented by the double chain of Andes peaks, fractured by canyons and rivers, separated town from town by mountain and jungle, is ten thousand different countries. Every village is a world entire; Río Verde in its Pacific isolation was one of those worlds—in no sense typical and in no sense untypical.

To my knowledge Río Verde has only been mentioned once in the literature of South America. I ran across this description of the Río Verde coast written by Agustín de Zarate in his classic, *The Discovery and Conquest of Peru*. It describes some of the impressions of Francisco Pizarro and his little band of cutthroats, and I hope it helps to explain my occasionally obsessive preoccupation with food:

The Spaniards also greatly suffered from hunger, for they found no food except the fruit of some trees called mangroves, of which there are great quantities on this coast. But these are very tough and tall and straight, and since they grow in salt water, their fruit is salt and bitter. But necessity compelled them to feed on this fruit and on the fish that they caught, and on shellfish and crabs, for maize does not grow anywhere on this coast. They rowed their canoes against the main sea current, which always runs north whereas their course was south. And all along the coast Indians came out against them, shouting and calling that they were "banished men." They taunted them with the hair on their faces, saying that they were the scum of the sea, and that they could have no other ancestry since the sea had thrown them up. "Why do you wander the world," they cried. "You must be idle vagabonds since you stay nowhere to work and sow the earth."

M.T.

March 4, 1969
San Francisco, California

Contents

Living Poor

A PEACE CORPS CHRONICLE

Part One: 1965

I GOT my Peace Corps application at the post office in Red
Bluff, California, put it on the table in the kitchen, and walked
around it for ten days without touching it, as though it were
primed to detonate—as indeed it was—trying to convince myself that for a forty-eight-year-old farmer the idea of Peace
Corps service was impractical and foolhardy.

I had read that a Peace Corps Volunteer would live at the
level of the people with whom he worked and that they would be
poor. Well, I could do that; I had been living poor for years. I
had read that the Peace Corps was desperate for agricultural
people. Good. That's all I knew. I had raised pigs, corn, alfalfa, beans, and pasture, had laid out orchards, leveled land,
and put in wells. And I liked farming. I liked being outside;
rows of growing corn, cattle grazing on green pastures, the
dusty excitement of a grain harvest—these things were like
music to me.

Finally I filled out the application and sent it to Washing-

ton. And I was accepted; Sargent Shriver wanted me to go to
Ecuador.

◻◻

Peace Corps training is like no other training in the world,
having something in common with college life, officer's training,
Marine basic training, and a ninety-day jail sentence. What
makes it paradoxical is that everything is voluntary; the schedule exists for you to follow if you wish.

At the State College of Montana at Bozeman where we
trained, there was only one rule, at first: it was illegal to bring
liquor on the campus. Later, toward the end of the training
program, they made another rule: it was illegal to throw cherry
bombs at the P.E. instructor. This one was promulgated
mainly for Joe Burkett, a twenty-year-old Texas goat farmer
who had a wild sense of humor and who, in the old tradition of
the wide open spaces, wanted to do funny things like stealing
the latrine we made and putting it on the lawn in front of the
girls' dorm. I don't know why he wanted to kill that certain
P.E. instructor, but he almost blew his head off more than once.
When you were talking to Joe, everything was as funny as "a
turd in a punch-bowl."

And you know how funny that is.

Our schedule began at 5:45 each morning and lasted until
9:30 at night. After that, if we so desired, our Spanish instructors were available to work with us. Actually, though, by 9:30
we were so tied up from being run around all day that we
usually headed for the nearest tavern where we drank pitcher
after pitcher of beer and sang songs.

It was a fantastic schedule—what they called a "structured
program"—and after the first three days we realized that it
was planned that way on purpose. If there were any psychotics
who had sneaked through the Washington screening and the

Treasury Department investigation (and there were a couple), the Peace Corps wanted to find out fast, and if we were breakable they wanted to break us in the United States. They told us the story about the Peace Corps trainee who had come to Bozeman the year before and who had learned the first sentence in the Spanish book—"The students arrive at the door," "*Los alumnos llegan a la puerta*"—and who had become deranged almost immediately from the pressures put on him. He went around repeating "*Los alumnos llegan a la puerta*" in answer to all questions put to him and screamed it all night in his sleep. We laughed at this story, but it was uneasy laughter because by the end of the first week we were all dreaming horrible stunted things in Spanish and screaming them in our sleep through those short, short nights.

We started taking psychological tests, and the laughter got a little raucous. "Have you ever talked to God?" "Do you think your private parts are beautiful?" But these damned things went on for weeks, tests so long, boring, and complicated that toward the end we were too confused and punch-drunk to lie. We listened to an endless series of two- and three-hour lectures by experts from all over the world who flew into Bozeman and crammed us with information—the geography, the history, the politics, the religion, the customs, the attitudes. It was interesting, but it was hard to keep our eyes open, and we felt that perhaps we should be spending more time in practical pursuits, like learning how to make a chicken coop or a latrine out of bamboo; unfortunately, there's very little bamboo in Bozeman.

We began to learn Spanish under a system based on tapes, a system so intense and concentrated that by the end of the first ten weeks we were using a vocabulary roughly comparable to that of Cervantes (1547–1616) and using it practically twenty-four hours a day. What was amazing was that with this tremendous vocabulary about all we could say with any degree of confidence was "*Los alumnos llegan a la puerta.*" We twisted and mauled that beautiful language into a million distorted shapes and watched our instructors, sensitive and dedicated people all, wither and age before our eyes.

The training program was broken into three different phases. At the end of each period, in a ritual compounded equally of drama and torture, we were handed envelopes, the contents of which held our futures. One envelope contained a mimeographed form which read: "Congratulations. You have been selected to continue training." The other envelope said something like this: "Good try, old man, but will you please report to Dr. Peabody."

Dr. Peabody was the dragon in our lives, a Peace Corps psychiatrist who evaluated all of the information about us and whose opinion was final. He was the only one at the college, for instance, who, theoretically, ever saw the Treasury Department reports. We did not especially like Dr. Peabody, resenting his power and feeling that if we were psychotic it was the Peace Corps's fault. Hell, we were all O.K. when we first got to Bozeman.

In all three phases of our training we were studied and appraised like a bunch of fat beeves about to be entered in the state fair. Men standing behind trees watched us; dark figures hidden in the grandstand at 5:30 in the morning as we staggered, groaning, around the track watched us. Our instructors watched us and filed daily reports; the psychologist and the psychiatrist watched us; mysterious little men from Washington in black suits whose names we never learned appeared from time to time and broodingly watched us. Each week end we went on camping trips where we were watched by our camp leaders. Boy, were we eager; we hauled in firewood by the ton. The doctor and his nurse watched us; our discussion leaders watched us; our athletic coaches watched us. Even the kitchen help watched us, and we were so naïve at first that we even thought that they, too, filed daily reports on our eating habits, or whatever it was they were watching.

The directors referred to their training program as a period of training and selection, but it might more properly be described as a period of deselection. Our group started out with thirty-eight trainees and ended up with twenty-four—almost a 35 per cent cut. It was cruel but efficient. In one sense the training period was basically not concerned with training at all; rather, it was a period of structured tension, of subtle and purposive torture in which it was calculated that the individual trainee would be forced to reveal himself. The purpose of the program was not to change your character but to discover it, not to toughen you up or to implant proper motivations for Peace Corps service but to find out what your motivations were. Many potentially good Volunteers have been eliminated from the program, a lot of them because they never figured out what it was trying to do.

The training was designed not only to reveal you to the Peace Corps but to reveal you to yourself. At any of the three deselection days, therefore, while the majority of those deselected felt the most terrible and guilty sense of failure (like the washed-out cadets of pilot training just after Pearl Harbor), a few felt relief. At Montana the sadistic little drama was arranged so that deselection letters were distributed on a Friday morning at 6:00 A.M., directly after thirty minutes of violent physical exercise, as we returned, panting with exhaustion, to our dorm. The girls must have arrived a moment or two before, because as I was handed the envelope with my name on it someone over in the girls' dorm began to scream. It was a scream of terrible heartbreak and disbelief, and though I had never heard this girl scream before I immediately identified her. She was one of the older trainees, a schoolteacher who, without realizing it, had brought a batch of personal problems with her.

The scream somehow made everything real; we were all trembling. We crept into corners and tore open our letters. "Congratulations, you are invited to continue," etc., but someone had locked himself in the toilet and begun to cry, and Gary from Oklahoma, with a feeling of relief, I think, silently handed us his letter and gave us back a blank look. While the winners ate breakfast and went to the first morning classes, the losers were whisked away like corpses in the old-age ward of the county hospital. No, it was more complicated than that, since we knew what was happening. We were a tightly knit and involved group, and when we lost one of our members it was like surgery; it had a crippling effect.

We were subjected twice more to the deselection process— once at the end of our training at Bozeman, and again in Dallas, Texas, as we disembarked from a jet after a final month's training in Pátzcuaro, Mexico. The system in Dallas was pure Grand Guignol; as we walked up the exit ramp some were told to walk right and some left. I was sent right just behind Ron Dudley, one of the biggest screw-offs in the group, and for a few minutes I was really shaken by the uncertainty of my position. But I was still with the winners. We were herded into a little office where, still tired from the trip and dazed at losing more of our friends, we raised our right hands and were sworn into the service. Talk about emotion! We were Peace Corps Volunteers at last.

We said good-by to Dr. Robert Dunbar, our director of training at Montana, and then, having been told to report in ten days to the airport in New York for our flight to Quito, Ecuador, we scattered to our homes all over the country. We

had ten anticlimactic days to rest and let all of those Peace-
Corps-training-engendered neuroses gradually drain away.

🔲🔲

Our group, Heifer 3, the third group trained for service in
Ecuador—twenty-four agricultural specialists, as we were
laughingly referred to—left New York from Kennedy International Airport one midnight and awoke about eight hours
later as we landed on the Quito strip. Five minutes before
disembarking we were all secretly struck with terror, not because of any hardships we might be walking into or because of
fear of homesickness or loneliness, but simply because we knew
that as part of the welcoming ceremony we were expected to
sing as a group the Ecuadorian national anthem. We had spent
endless hours in training sessions singing this song, at first with
the help of recordings of the Ecuadorian Army band and a
background chorus of about three thousand voices. Then later,
for at least five hours a week, we sang as a group, memorizing
the words line by line. The Ecuadorian people have an almost
religious respect for their national hymn, but it has so many
verses that it is only slightly less wordy than the Old Testa-
ment, and I seriously doubt if anyone but its author has ever
read the whole thing through to the end. Now, there is nothing
wrong with the Ecuadorian national anthem except for its
length and the fact that, like our own "Star Spangled Banner,"
it contains an impossible range of notes, high and low. The
truth of the matter is that we never did get it down so that we
could bring it off with any degree of aplomb. We trooped off
the plane convinced that in our first five minutes on Ecuadorian
soil we would precipitate an unhealable international incident.

As it turned out, though, our terrors were groundless. We
were met by a bunch of sweet 4-H Club kids who welcomed us

with incomprehensible speeches and great bunches of slightly
wilted flowers, and were greeted by all the Peace Corps brass,
some semihigh government officials from the Department of
Agriculture, and the old group of Volunteers who had arrived
from all parts of the country to look us over. Or, at any rate, to
look the new girls over.

Then we huddled together like a bunch of sheep about to be
slaughtered, took a deep breath, and swung into the Ecuadorian national anthem. Actually we knew the words much
better than the Ecuadorians, whose lips we were trying to read.
We were magnificent, rolling out the emotion, swelling in volume, gasping for breath in the ten-thousand-foot altitude.
Halfway through the song we discovered with a feeling of
exultant relief that the Ecudaorians were trying to read *our*
lips. After that everything was pure anticlimax; we had con-
quered the only obstacle to successful Peace Corps service in
Ecuador.

We spent two days in Quito being introduced to the country,
the Peace Corps staff, our doctor, and various officials from
AID, CARE, and the Departments of Agriculture and Development. The doctor was the most fantastic character of all,
chiefly because of the stories that the other Volunteers told us
about him. He was a New Yorker who had never driven a car in
his life, but when he arrived in Ecuador, the Peace Corps had
given him a jeep so that he could check out Volunteers in their
villages. The roads in the high Andes are, of course, the crook-
edest, most spectacular, and most dangerous in the world, but
Dr. Kaplan, with all the innocent nonchalance of a Barney
Oldfield, began setting new records for getting from place to
place as he began to learn how to drive. "Whatever you do,
don't get in a car with the doctor," we were all warned. "He
just cut forty-five minutes off the Tulcán-Quito run."

We were interested to meet these people, of course, but our

primary fascination was with the older Volunteers. They knew
things that we didn't know; things had happened to them that
we couldn't even imagine yet. We wanted to know what it was
going to be like, what it was *really* going to be like, but
actually they couldn't help us much. Peace Corps Volunteers
are no more articulate than any other group, and the essence of
the experience is as hard to describe as a Beethoven symphony.

They tried to give us hints. We went to a party one night,
for instance, and one of my new friends, pointing out three
Volunteers, intimated that they symbolized the whole thing.
The three included Gary Kinnett, who had just arrived with
my group and who was off in a corner giving an English lesson
to a young Ecuadorian. Another Volunteer who had been in the
country for one year was dancing a bolero with a pretty Ecuadorian girl; he was dancing close, eyes closed, very intense and
romantic. The third Volunteer was about to terminate; he had
put in his two years. He was standing on a chair with a glass
raised to the ceiling giving a toast. He was toasting Guayaquil.
"*Viva* Guayaquil!" But the party was given to celebrate Quito
and Quito's independence. After only two days in the country I
already realized that there was a brutal and uncompromising
competition between the two cities and that the third Volunteer
was mocking this irrational Latin attitude.

Before being assigned to a permanent site, we were each sent
to live in the village of an experienced Volunteer for two weeks.
Our permanent sites remained a secret, not, I think, through
any desire to confuse us but simply because no one knew yet
where to put us. I was delivered over to a Volunteer named
Byron Bahl, a twenty-three-year-old fellow from Lake City,
Iowa, who had been working for the last year in Cariamanga, a
town of about five thousand people near the Peruvian border.
Not only was he charged out with me, but he was also taking

back two eighty-pound feeder pigs, four hundred pounds of hog concentrate, and a cageful of rabbits. All of us together constituted a transportation problem that would strain the Ecuadorian bus system, so Byron went to the Department of Agriculture, where he was promised the use of a pickup for the trip.

Two days later, swathed in red tape like an Egyptian mummy, he gave up and took the problem to the Peace Corps office, where he was promised a Peace Corps pickup. A day later the offer was withdrawn, and we prepared to settle down in Quito for the duration. And then by chance Byron met a Staff Sergeant Billingsley from Chehalis, Washington, in the Bongo bar. He was working with the Ecuadorian Army in Accion Civica building roads in the southern part of the country. He was leaving the next morning in a 6x6 army truck for Loja, and he said that he would be delighted to give us a ride.

And so, four days behind schedule, we assembled at 5:00 A.M. on a lightly frosted street in Quito and began to pack the truck. What went into it included fourteen tremendous truck tires, three rebuilt truck engines, seven hung-over Ecuadorian soldiers, one hung-over American staff sergeant, two Peace Corps Volunteers, two complaining pigs, three uncomplaining rabbits, four hundred pounds of fish meal, a great bunch of freshly cut alfalfa, and our own personal luggage. To any ex-GIs who believe this is impossible, let me add that before the trip was over we also picked up three more soldiers, who were vaguely wandering around in the high paramo country south of Ambato, and the head truck-driver's brother-in-law from Latacunga, who decided to come with us just for the hell of it.

The Pan American highway from Quito in the north central part of the Andes to the Peruvian border is perhaps the most spectacular three-day automobile trip in the world. It has this in common with a great musical work: although it begins intensely with magnificent views of snow-capped volcanoes, ruggedly serrated chains of mountains, and spreading panoramas of farms and haciendas, it builds in intensity with each mile. About two-thirds of the way to the border, south of Alausí and into Cuenca, in a crashing climax of changing views which the eye can scarcely accept, the country opens up, explodes in ferocious splendor, as though, after countless subtle variations, the main theme were now being set before you. At the same time you become aware of a new motif in the bass section, a black, keening theme of desperate hopelessness, as the whole history of the Andean Indian begins to stab into your consciousness.

Hour after hour you twist and wander through three or four different worlds, each one separated by a layer of clouds, gazing paralyzed into bottomless chasms or across fifty-mile stretches of valley being farmed in small checkered squares with Japanese intensiveness. Or above the top cloud layer you are suddenly confronted by a series of mountain ranges—ten, fifteen, twenty mountain ranges—each one higher, more brutal, fading away from baked reds and browns to blue, purple, and violet. You become convinced that if Ecuador, like a crumpled handkerchief, could be spread out flat, it would cover the whole South American continent. Watching all this I thought of a story that one of my new Ecuadorian friends had told me. It seems that when God was making the Western Hemisphere He started out in Alaska and worked south; when He came to South America He went down the east coast with His building materials to the southern tip and then worked His way north again. But when He got almost to Panama He discovered that He had too much material, and in a fit of pique He threw it all down in a great pile. And that's how He made Ecuador.

It took us almost three days to travel 250 miles; the Ecuadorian soldiers were typical GIs, twenty-year-old crew-cut kids who giggled, wrestled, punched each other, and inces-

santly whistled at the girls as we sped through Indian villages
scattering livestock and children out of our path.

We climbed to eleven thousand feet over cold, barren, paramo plateaus where thin pastures supported a sparse sheep
economy, and an hour later we would have dipped down into
valley bottoms—lush, green, and steaming—a country loaded
with bananas, sugar cane, pineapple, and papaya. Two hours
later, freezing, we would be putting our sweaters back on as we
crawled up some mountain face toward another pass, the palm
trees having given way to eucalyptus, and the eucalyptus finally to the heather and the coarse clump grasses of the high
country.

Superimposed like a black shroud over this mountain area of
natural splendor is the situation of the Indians who, since the
time of the conquest, have been robbed, murdered, and exploited; now, centuries later, their situation is basically unchanged. Little by little they have been forced off even the
second-rate land, and they have moved out of the valley bottoms onto the slopes. Their little plots of two and three acres
cover the mountainsides on slopes so steep that sometimes animals cannot be used, and the men must tie themselves to their
fields as they hoe or harvest. Working this land, which is in no
sense agricultural, has speeded the erosion of the slopes to a
suicidal rate; great ugly gashes cut through the fields, and the
streams are a dirty red, saturated with the mountain topsoil.

The Indians have gathered together in tight little family
villages and live their lives out in hopeless poverty, suspicious
of outsiders, traditional, conservative in a resignation that
would be noble if it weren't so tragic. Since in the past all
change has been for the worse, they resist all change now.

A few weeks after this trip I asked a fairly important Ecuadorian agricultural technician what he thought was the best
way to solve the problem of the Sierran Indian. He made

machine guns out of his hands, swept them around before him, and said, "Da-da-da-da-da-da." When he noticed the expression on my face, he said with the bitterest sarcasm, "What are you looking so shocked for? Isn't that how you solved the Indian problem in your country? And don't you think we would be a rich country today if we had followed your example?"

At sunset on the first day as we crept up the mountainside, we passed what looked like a football field cleared out of the pasture. It was a day of fiesta, and several hundred Indians from that rural area were gathered on the field. The men and the women were dressed in pure black—black dresses, black ponchos, black hats; they stood in groups or individually, scattered over the field. Parked by the highway, an ancient Buick rigged up with a sound system blared out an incredibly sad song in the Sierran manner, orchestrated for hand harps and native flutes; the trunk was filled with bottles of *aguardiente*. Two Indians lay unconscious in the dust by the car, their wives kneeling at their heads and fanning the flies away from their open mouths. Everything was motionless, frozen, as though the group of villagers had been standing this way for a hundred years, as though those two patient women had been waiting for a hundred years for their husbands to awaken from this joyless celebration. I found out later that these dark-clothed Indians were of the Cañar tribe and that they had gone into a perpetual mourning four hundred years ago when the Spaniards murdered their emperor, Atahualpa.

More than four months had passed since I had started Peace Corps training in Bozeman, and at last I was getting to see a Volunteer in action. I began what turned into about a two-month internship. We had studied for the different projects in which we would probably be working—the construction of latrines, hog pens, calf stables—an endless list. But there was a difference between studying a latrine and coming upon one suddenly in the high Andes, its proud adobe walls glistening in the thin sunshine of altitude, proclaiming progress. It was a heart-lifting sight.

I spent the next ten days with Byron in his border town. I followed him around as he worked in the village and in the small rural centers in the hills, where the farmers gathered at the church or in a classroom on the days when they were to meet with the agricultural extension people. We inoculated pigs against cholera, introduced new types of vegetables in community gardens, and Byron gave talks on sanitation and animal nutrition. We visited small farms and a boys' club on the rocky slopes above Cariamanga. There we showed the farmers how to delouse pigs with old crankcase oil and how to treat sick baby pigs with penicillin. We hauled some bags of coffee out of one mountain valley for a farmer who had neither a wagon nor a horse.

In the background of all these activities, the small boys of the town followed us in crowds, chattering and kidding. The girls, who were too shy or too well-bred, stood in the doorways of their houses chanting Byron's name, "Meester, Meester By-ron, Meester By-ron," as we passed.

We spent a morning at a community garden that Byron had started after the hardest kind of sell. Finally, not because they believed in the garden or saw the need of one, but simply because they were tired of the pressure and because they liked Byron, the villagers agreed to plant a small plot of onions, lettuce, radishes, tomatoes, and cabbages at the bottom of a piece of steeply sloping communal land. Everything grew beautifully; the farmers were delighted to have a change from the steady diet of rice, yuca, and potatoes. They had tripled the size of the garden at the next planting. The day we were

there bringing them new seeds from Quito, about twenty farmers and their wives were working in the beds, weeding or stak-
ing tomatoes up on rows of string. Another group was breaking sod and prying boulders out of the ground to make the
garden even bigger.

They were very excited and proud; they planned to raise
enough cabbage so that they would have a surplus, a cash crop
to sell in the market at Cariamanga. Byron, listening to them,
decided that they were on their way at last, and instead of
giving them the seed this time, he charged them one sucre, a
nickel, for each package. Strangely enough, now that they had
to pay for the seed they even bought a package of a new type of
lettuce that they had been unwilling to try when the seed was
free. This involved a conference of about five leaders, who
argued together for twenty minutes about the risks and advan-
tages of such a dramatic innovation. The seed was from
CARE; Byron turned the money over to one of the newly
formed boys' clubs to apply toward the purchase of a volleyball.

I guess the most touching event was when we delivered the
two feeder pigs that Byron had picked up from our Heifer
Project organization in Quito for a group of farmers who lived
about ten miles outside of town. Months before the pigs were
delivered, the group had been coached in a series of weekly
meetings on the necessity of a balanced diet and a warm place
for the pigs to live. The farmers had organized a pig club and
had agreed to build a proper shed. They had done a good job,
much too good a job, I thought, constructing a two-room
building with five-foot-high walls and an outside pen, all of it
of adobe and tile and plastered with cement. It had a cement
feeder and a cement waterer, and it must have been built at
considerable sacrifice.

We drove out one morning with the extension agent in his

jeep, the pigs tied in gunny sacks with just their heads sticking out, both of them furious at this latest indignity. About forty families were waiting for us at the pigpen. It was not a town we went to but simply an open place on the slope of a mountain—a one-room schoolhouse, a football field slanting away toward the valley floor ten miles below, a couple of farmhouses, and a small cabin where the schoolteacher lived.

Wow, what excitement! What exclamations of disbelief as we dumped the pigs into their new home. Eighty-pound pigs at four months? It was incredible; they were as heavy as year-and-a-half-old native pigs, and their backs were broad, and there was meat on the hams. They were the first decent animals these people had even seen, and owning them now, the people lost their cool. Actually, they didn't own them yet. The two pigs were being loaned to the members of the community. The farmers had agreed to feed them properly and care for them according to rules set up by Byron; they were to be paid for by replacing pigs of equal value after the gilt had farrowed. These new pigs in turn would be loaned to another group or another farmer under the same conditions. In a nutshell this is the basic plan of Heifer Project, a nonprofit corporation maintained by private and church donations in the United States. This organization administers the agricultural projects of Peace Corps, Ecuador. Its plan is designed to get pure-blooded animals onto farms all over the world and into the hands of farmers who otherwise, because of poverty, would be unable to upgrade the quality of their animals.

Heifer animals are a powerful tool for a Volunteer, for they can be used to demonstrate the importance of breeding and diet in this protein-starved country. It is much easier to capture the passions of the poor when the Volunteer can bring them fine animals which minimize the inherent risks of the innovations that he constantly preaches. When Heifer–Peace Corps is most successful it expands into the areas of human nutrition. For instance, a *campesino* who feeds his hog a ration that meets the needs of that animal and for the first time sees normal growth can more easily accept the necessity for changing the diet of his children. The stunting of children through protein starvation may not show up for years, and then only after it is too late to do anything about it; the stunting of animals is sudden and dramatic.

My ten days with Byron, ten days in another world, were altogether fantastic, but I wasn't sorry to leave; it was his town, not mine. I was more uncertain than ever of my own role, but in spite of that more anxious than ever to get assigned to a site and start working on my own. There was also a sadness in this cold mountain country that depressed me; early-morning fogs lay fat and heavy in the dry valleys below us, and the thin-soiled rocky slopes, submarginal at best, gave no promise of production no matter what was done to change agricultural techniques.

Early one morning Byron left me at the bus station. "So long," he said. "I've taught you everything I know. Now go on out and save Ecuador." He was a good kid, but he was enveloped in the sadness that brooded over that dark country. As I waited for the bus to leave I suddenly realized with a stab of panic that for the first time there was no one sitting next to me who could interpret my needs to the restless natives; now I was going to have to start learning Spanish. I sat there rolling verbs around in my mouth. An Ecuadorian farmer sitting next to me said something; I didn't want to be rude, so I did the best I could. "*Los alumnos llegan a la puerta,*" I told him, smiling. That shut him up.

Until you ride in one for a short distance, there's something touchingly sweet and naïve about Ecuadorian buses. They all look as though they had been designed by six-year-old kids; they are short, fat, and perky, painted in the primary colors, striped like a layer cake; they look sort of feisty, sort of pregnant; some even seem to smile. One thing they don't look like: they don't look like they'd ever move.

Riding in one you undergo a personality change which is truly profound; you take on a degree of innocence lost since childhood, and you feel like a paper cutout, very simple and uncomplicated, riding in a bus drawn with red or green crayons. On long trips this feeling of innocence is slowly replaced by feelings of pain, then horror, then rage. Ecuadorian buses are not designed for people over five feet eight, and Ecuadorian women have learned how to fight with their bottoms for the limited space available and have perfected a technique by which with a subtle twitch of the rear end they can send an unsuspecting gringo sprawling into the aisle. The only alternative is to risk suffocation and ask for a seat by the window.

The reason the buses are so fat is that three people sit on each side of a twelve-inch aisle. When you are traveling in the rural areas (which is practically all of the time), this impression of riding in something conjured up by a first-grader is intensified by the fact that a good percentage of the travelers will be carrying improbable things—chickens or baby pigs or great bunches of bananas—things that only a child with a beautifully uninhibited (or beautifully neurotic) imagination would ever draw into a bus. I saw one bus south of El Tambo, for instance, with about twelve sheep, their feet trussed with ropes, riding up on top, and another dozen or so old ewes with dazed eyes riding with the passengers, their heads sticking out the windows. If Paul Klee had seen that bus he would have died with joy—or else given up painting for photography.

On another bus I sat next to a six-year-old Cayapa Indian kid who was completely naked except for a pair of pink plastic cowboy boots; next to him sat his mother, a beautiful girl from around Esmeraldas, who was bare from the belly button up; a nursing baby hid one breast. It is things like this that sweep the cobwebs out of the brain and send a gringo, grounded in the Puritan ethic, reeling in search of a new definition of reality.

One of the stories they tell about the Ecuadorian bus driver is that whenever he runs off the road and kills a few of the passengers without killing himself, he immediately goes into hiding in some distant part of the country so that the bereaved can't even up the score. There are rumors of whole villages down in the far reaches of the Amazon Basin populated almost entirely by retired bus drivers. This is probably apocryphal, but it is true that as newly arrived Volunteers we were briefed on the health hazards of Ecuador and given to understand that probably the greatest health hazard would be overconfident and wildly optimistic bus drivers who, filled with *joie de vivre* or perhaps a few shots of *puro*, had a tendency to plunge off cliffs into bottomless Andean gorges or crash headlong into banana trucks—or each other. I have never seen two Ecuadorian bus drivers who were friendly with each other, perhaps because there are so many competing bus lines.

But I am happy to report, after having traveled on several dozen Ecuadorian buses, that our Peace Corps doctor was unduly worried and that the bus drivers are almost invariably an overworked, underpaid, reasonably good-humored bunch who just have one hell of a lot of awful curves to navigate. At the same time I'd have to admit that the Volunteer who arrived in the country and was in three bus wrecks in his first three weeks may have a slightly different feeling about the transportation system.

Ecuadorian roads for the most part are graveled and wildly twisting, and if it's true that courage is simply a lack of imagination, I would guess that Ecuadorian bus drivers are the

most unimaginative people in the world. Certainly, their pro-
fession has built-in hazards that the Greyhound driver on the
run from San Francisco to Seattle, for instance, could never
conceive of—or, if he could, they would start him up screaming
from his bed at night.

The reason Dr. Kaplan was worried about bus drivers (although he probably had some traumatic confrontations that
he's not talking about) was that the last group of Volunteers
had barely arrived when two of them were in a bus which went
off the road and rolled over several times. They were both
injured, though not seriously. Of course, as Volunteers they
had been thoroughly briefed on first-aid techniques and what to
do in just such a situation—step one, step two, and so on.

"Now, what was the first thing you did?" Dr. Kaplan asked
one of the recuperating Volunteers, sitting on the edge of the
hospital cot, taking out his pen, and preparing to organize a
report.

"Well, Doc," the Volunteer said, "it was a real dramatic
scene: overturned bus completely squashed, bodies all over,
blood on the grass, all that sort of thing. To tell you the truth,
the first thing I did was take a bunch of pictures. Sure hope
they turn out; I was using Kodachrome."

That first long bus ride in Ecuador, twelve hours long, was
pure sensation, and I was new enough to the country to enjoy
at least the first nine hours. In a trip of steadily plunging
descent we ran the gamut of temperature variations. We
started out at 6:30 in the morning in chilly mountain country,
and we ended up that evening careening through equatorial
jungle beneath trees that dripped with orchids. And the whole
trip was down, hour after hour, until you began to feel a little
hysterical, convinced that by this time you must surely be
several thousand feet below sea level. This impression was en-

forced by a growing humidity which approached 100 per cent on the coast along a narrow, gently rolling stretch of farmland planted almost entirely to bananas.

On this trip to Machala to catch the coastal steamer for Guayaquil I made my first close emotional contact with a national. I might as well confess that this contact was not exactly sensational and that I did not project very successfully the Peace Corps image. He got on the bus someplace up in the mountains above La Toma—or rather he was poured onto the bus by some friends of his who, I'm convinced, were glad to see him go—a man of about forty with a foxy little black moustache and quick, black, buttonhole eyes. There was no place for him to sit on the bus, so he squatted in the aisle, put his head in my lap, and quietly passed out. The bus rushed down the mountain vibrating and pulsating, and my friend gradually sifted onto the floor, where he slept for a couple of hours. He awoke suddenly, after one particularly spectacular bump had thrown him about three feet in the air, and found himself staring into the face of a gringo.

He was thunderstruck. His face took on an expression of loving kindness; it was obvious he loved gringos. He began to pat my head. And he began to talk. He talked a torrent of Spanish at me, as though there weren't much time and he had a million things to tell me. But I could scarcely understand perfect Castilian enunciated clearly and slowly by some Spanish Richard Burton, let alone the coastal patois with its slurred and jazzy sounds, all well mixed with sleep and alcohol. My God, I couldn't understand a word he said, not one single word, and I had to sit there mile after mile, smiling like a dummy, surreptitiously wiping off the flecks of spit that he enthusiastically directed at my face. The other passengers were watching me with expressions of increasing pity as it slowly dawned on them, one by one, that the gringo was a half-wit. My friend

finally realized it too and gave up. He crouched in the aisle and
dozed, but he awoke from time to time to gaze at me and shake
his head with a baffled look on his face. It was a look of anguish
for me—for me, the escaped but harmless crackbrain, wandering lost, dazed, and speechless in a strange and distant country. To tell you the truth, for about three hours on that wild
plunge to the coastal tropics, this was also exactly how I saw
myself.

▣▣

One day in Peace Corps training at Bozeman they showed us
some color slides of typical Ecuadorian villages. One of them,
an air shot, simply made my heart stop beating; some psychic
intuition instructed me that I was gazing at the village where I
would live. It was a picture of jungle, of bamboo houses built
on seven-foot stilts, and it looked like it was about twelve miles
from the end of the world. The colors in that shot were pure
Rousseau, and the picture seemed to reflect a profound tranquillity. I even wrote letters home describing the place, for I
was convinced, though no one had told me, that I would finally
be stationed on the coast, in the rain forest, and in a village of
bamboo houses. It was going to be on a trail or on a lousy road,
without lights or water, a sort of jungle Walden Pond, where
life, reduced to its essentials, would reveal itself for what it
really was. It was a romantic conception, because at that time I
thought that poor people were somehow better, more honest
and more alive, than people with money, not realizing that the
absence of money in a society built around it could be as
corrupting as money itself. The little village was going to be
romantic as hell.

Well, this is exactly where I ended up, at least temporarily,
though I didn't realize it at the time. It wasn't magic; it simply

turned out finally that I got to pick my own village. I only missed one thing: my village wasn't romantic.

In Guayaquil I was assigned to a government experimental station called Puerto Limón. It was to be a new colonization project, and the government had asked for a Peace Corps Volunteer to help build an animal reproduction station where good types of hogs and cattle could be raised for distribution to the farmers. It sounded great. Tomás Guerrero, my boss, drove me to Santo Domingo one day to introduce me to the colonization officials and deliver me to my site, but we soon discovered that Puerto Limón scarcely existed. It was a twenty-five-mile hike from the end of a bad road, and the government hadn't actually got started yet; it was still a half-planned dream for the future. Tomás said I couldn't stay there, and that was great, too. I had a growing awareness of some kind of sickness, a feeling of lethargy and exhaustion, and the idea of walking twenty-five miles every week with a pack filled with groceries sounded like just a little too much of a good thing. The village that lived in my mind was at the end of the world, but, by God, you didn't have to walk twenty-five miles to get there.

Tomás told me to stay in Santo Domingo and work with the agricultural extension office, and to keep my eyes open for a village where I thought I could do some work. I rented a room in a small hotel on the plaza just over a froth of saloons, each with a competing jukebox, and across from the offices of six bus companies. In a few sleepless nights I had worked out the schedules of them all, since each arriving bus carried with it a small boy who stood in the street screaming destinations.

I was given a desk in the agricultural extension office. About every other day I went into the field with the extension agent to discuss some farmer's particular problem—there were great white worms eating the stalks of the bananas, the leaves on the pineapples were turning an unhealthy red, there were peculiar knotty growths on a bull calf's neck, a sow had eaten her litter. But my Spanish was still very bad, and about 80 per cent of the discussions went blowing past my head.

On the porches of farmhouses we would drink hot milk or a *chicha* made of the drainings of oatmeal and sugar or, if the farmer were a rich one, glasses of scotch whiskey, and I quickly became a sort of invisible party. I would think, for instance, not having opened my mouth since arriving, that the farmer and the extension agent were talking about the future of ca-buya as a marketable fiber and discover toward the end of the conversation that they had been talking about the bullfights in Quito or the latest disastrous drop in banana prices. At times like this, after listening for hours to a language which is badly understood, the brain goes into a paralysis; it closes the doors and shuts up shop. I would sit there trying to look reasonably intelligent but feeling completely useless, my eyes glazed, my mouth hanging open, slowly drowning in a flood of strange, soft sounds.

Of course, what was happening and what I didn't realize at the time was that I was getting some additional basic training. The first few months he is in a new country the Volunteer's biggest problem is simply communication, and especially on the technical level where he hopes to work. But after the months of training we are too impatient. The days go rushing by; we want to do something.

I began to develop stabby feelings of guilt. I couldn't speak enough Spanish to compete with the extension people in the office, and I spent most of my time reading old *Time* magazines. I would think about that eleven cents an hour that I was getting and feel like a real thief. About the end of the second week I began to sneak out of town on the open-air local buses and tour through the jungle looking for a place to move to. I had all the other Volunteers working for me, too. "Look," I'd tell them, "if you hear about a romantic village where fat white worms are eating the bananas or where the calves have strange growths on their necks, let me know, will you? I think I can help."

And rumors of lost villages began trickling in. The craziest rumor came from Elizabeth Mills, one of the new Volunteers who was teaching in a school twenty-five miles out of Santo Domingo. She told me about a village of eighty families some five miles by trail from the town where she worked. It sounded promising, and one morning I went out on the bus and finally found a farmer who said he knew exactly where the place was and that he would be glad to guide me there. We headed out into the jungle, up and down over hills and across streams on fallen logs, and we walked for about six hours. The trail was nothing but a series of mudholes, and from the beginning it didn't seem to be well enough used to indicate any great population center out there beyond us. We went out eight miles and along the way we saw exactly five farmhouses, each of them at least a mile apart.

Sometime early in the afternoon, an hour after I had given up, the farmer stopped in the trail and turned around; he gave me one of those Latin shrugs which indicated that fate was screwing him again. We stood there staring at one another, and then we both began to laugh. He was laughing because I was laughing; I was laughing because I suddenly realized that he had the face of Charlie Chaplin, with the same sweet, defeated, and baffled look of a man outraged by fortune. He had a little Hitler moustache that he began to twitch for me. I stood there, weak with laughter. He did a little soft-shoe shuffle out there in the mud; he twirled his machete like a bamboo cane and the effect was the same. After the performance we returned.

A couple of weeks later Ron Dudley and I hitchhiked up

the road toward Esmeraldas to visit John Generoux, who
had just been assigned to the town of Quinindé. We rode
in banana trucks or anything that came along. About forty
miles out of Santo Domingo, winding through solid banana plantings, we came to a bend in the road; in a little
clearing cut through by a stream, with a row of hills behind it
covered with undeveloped jungle, I saw something familiar.
"Look," I yelled at Ron. "There's my town." But it didn't look
romantic even then; the truth is that nothing looks romantic
from a banana truck.

It was fairly simple to get a clearance from Peace Corps to
move; the name of the place was La Unión, a newly organized
town on the newly built highway to the seacoast town of Esmeraldas. Tomás came out with me one day and we checked the
place out.

How did the town feel about having a Volunteer? Was there
work that could be done? The place was called La Unión. How
about it: was there actually any union among the people, any
chance of getting them to work together in community projects? Was there a place to live, a post office, a grocery store?
We walked around the town making calls, and Tomás, who
seems to know everyone in Ecuador, produced from a black
notebook the names of the town leaders. But none of the town
leaders was at home that day; they were both in Quito.

We found two rooms for rent in the town's best and newest
building, a plaster-fronted construction with two stores downstairs—a shoemaker's and a grocery—and window boxes in
front of the upstairs windows full of tomatoes and nasturtiums
hanging six feet down toward the street. The rent was one
hundred sucres a month, about five dollars.

It took me almost a week to move. I went to Quito first to

borrow a stove and a gasoline lamp from the office. I bought
great quantities of beans, rice, lentils, and macaroni in Santo
Domingo, plus cups, plates, and silverware. Then I got warmed
up and walked through the markets packing buckets full of
pots and pots full of buckets, and I picked up a couple of weird
frying pans that later refused to cook anything and instead
turned everything to ashes. I tried to keep it simple, but bar-
gaining for things was such good practice for my Spanish that
I ended up with enough stuff for a small, intimate hotel.

While I was moving into the rooms, I spent little time in
La Unión. I felt very out of place and uncomfortable packing
my stuff up the street to the house. I always took the next bus
back to Santo Domingo to the comfortable security of the
swarms of Volunteers who worked there; they were my friends;
they spoke English. In La Unión I was an outsider. I was by
this time much sicker than I realized with a lung infection
(contracted, incidentally, in California), and a growing exhaustion, which I was afraid to acknowledge even to myself,
colored this experience in La Unión with a depression, a feeling
of hopelessness.

The Ecuadorian in the jungle villages is reserved and
withdrawn; a resentful suspiciousness, a basic coldness toward
strangers dominates him. He will never say "Hello" to you
first. Walking toward him on a trail, for instance, you find that
not once do his eyes ever come close to you. Until you speak to
him, he never betrays by any expression the fact that he is even
aware of your existence. After you have committed yourself he
will always answer in a courteous and formal way, but at the
same time there is a startled look on his face, as though until
this moment he had thought himself invisible.

I had been in town a half-dozen times, and no one had said a
word to me or given me a smile or even seen me, except some of

the little kids who gathered in the hallway and peeked into the
room, grinning, as I staggered around unloading pots. At least
they were basically friendly, I decided, but more curious than
friendly. Finally everything was moved, and I had no legitimate excuse to visit Santo Domingo. I began to walk around

town trying to get acquainted. But what an effort of the will it was in those first days to open the door of that sweet familiar room and go down into the street. A month later, to leave my tight little world of books, letters, pots, and pans, and walk out into the country still required that one conscious decision to do it, like deciding to jump from a twelve-foot board into icy water.

Even later as I began to make friends and to look forward, for instance, to working with Vicente on his chicken house or Elvira in her garden, it was always wonderful to get back to that room, to spend the evening alone, not talking a word of Spanish, to read a chapter in an English novel or simply to sit and slowly reform myself into what I was, an American in Ecuador.

By the end of my first week in La Unión, the price of an egg had jumped from five to seven cents. I was pretty much living on eggs at that time, and my purchases used up all that were being placed on the local market. By the end of the first month the price had dropped to four cents as the news spread that eggs were a hot property since the arrival of a gringo. Farmers from a mile in each direction would bring in their eggs; shy farm wives knocked on my door at 5:00 A.M. with a few eggs in a hat for me to inspect; each day they got bigger and cheaper. Eggs, like all the protein foods in rural Ecuador, are a luxury, and for the majority of men who earn less than a dollar a day as farm laborers, a food that is scarcely ever eaten. Eggs are for holidays or for guests or for sick people. Well, I broke the market in La Unión, but I don't imagine that it did much good.

Because there was such an amazingly small amount of food in the village, I spent a good deal of time the first few days going from store to store. They all had about the same thing: rice, beans, cans of tuna fish, platano, and potatoes. At first I didn't believe it, but as a result of this semihysterical shopping

I did begin to get acquainted. I was about halfway through the process of losing thirty-five pounds, and the food situation was becoming obsessively interesting.

The people were suspicious and careful with me. They were about the same, I would imagine, as the people of a small town in Georgia or Mississippi. I discovered later that their near hostility had been partly due to a rumor that had started the day I arrived—that I was a rich gringo looking for cheap land to buy. Except for a few small boys who used to visit me after school, I was more or less ignored by the town. I talked several times with the director of the school about starting a school garden, but he was cool to the idea, since vacations were due to start within a couple of months. What he really wanted was a sleeping bag like mine. Couldn't I illustrate the friendship of a great rich country like the United States for a poor exploited country like Ecuador by buying him a sleeping bag or stealing one from the Peace Corps office? When I told him I couldn't, he seemed to lose interest in the idea of helping me work with the kids.

I talked with some of the farmers, trying to find out what they thought they needed. All their water was hauled from the little stream that cut through town, and they said that what the town really needed was a good well. I suggested that we begin to organize. I knew I could get a pump from CARE if the town would dig the hole and buy the three or four sacks of cement needed to seal the well off from the drainage of surface water. But this idea did not really enflame them. No, they said, the people in the town did not work together. In a mild way, apparently, everyone hated everyone else. Couldn't I arrange just to have someone give the town a well and do all the work? Then, quite by accident, I found a new well that the government had built for the community only a few months before I arrived; two months later some kids had broken the pump, and no one had even bothered to fix it.

I talked to the President of the colonization,* who kept promising that at the next Sunday meeting he would explain to the farmers who I was and how I could get CARE seeds for them or plans for inexpensive farm shelters for their animals. But every Monday morning when I went to check with him, and while we guzzled rum and orange juice, he would explain that he hadn't had time to bring the subject up. His daughter, a middle-aged woman built like a wrestler and with the deep voice of a man, began giving me hot looks. She wanted to plant a garden with me, she said. Out in back of the barn. Monday mornings about 10:00 A.M. always found me staggering back up the road toward town, softly humming to myself, superficially happy but with a growing sense of frustration.

I even got hot looks from one of the farmers, who kept grabbing at me one day as we sat together in his house looking through his long, boring photograph album. I began to feel that I had landed in an extremely screwed-up little town.

I had become friendly with a farm family that also ran a cafe out on the road where the buses stopped. The father was Chinese and the mother Indian, and their children—about a dozen of them—were extremely beautiful. The girls helped in the cafe, and the boys worked on a piece of land which they were planting to coffee and cabuya. I was always afraid to eat there; some of the dishes were pretty wild looking. But I went down almost every day for a cup of coffee and a talk with the farmer or some of his children. One morning I was sitting there drinking coffee and waiting for a bus to take me down to the

* With the opening of the highway between Quito and Esmeraldas, government land was made available to individual farmers in a way roughly similar to the United States system of homesteading. La Unión was one of the many "colonizations" that was formed in this way.

next village, where John Generoux and I had teamed up to plant a school garden. One of the farmer's sons and his wife arrived and sat down by me. She was holding a baby who was dying of pneumonia, and I sat there listening to that unbearable gasping for breath, that bubbling struggle to live, while the family calmly gathered around the child and watched. Only the mother seemed to be upset.

I could hear the bus headed for Quinindé coming down the road through the bananas. I was sure that they were waiting for this bus to rush the baby to a doctor, but as the bus came closer and finally lumbered into sight they made no move. Suddenly, using the most beautiful Spanish of my life, completely out of control with anger, I screamed at them, "Your baby's dying; get him to a doctor. Now. Now!" The mother began to whimper; her husband looked at his father, who simply nodded his head in a sort of permission without saying anything, and the young couple ran down to the road and stopped the bus. When I got back that night they told me that the baby was dead.

The next afternoon I was out on the trail about a mile from town buying pineapples from a farmer who lived just past the graveyard. As I was coming back I met the funeral procession, the toy-like coffin painted white and sprinkled with a silver dust being negligently packed on a farmer's shoulder. Behind him and strung out for a hundred yards the family and their friends followed. The men carried bottles of *aguardiente*, stumbling and reeling in the mud of the trail, a confusing scene of dignity mixed with slapstick so that you didn't know whether to laugh or cry. Some of the farmers stopped to offer me a drink.

The statistics, of course, I knew: in the country areas three out of five babies die before their third year. And I was also aware of the Catholic philosophy which makes these deaths

bearable to the country people. They hold the unshakable belief that when a baby dies, it dies in a state of grace and flies
directly to heaven. Within this framework then, the death of a
child is something to celebrate; he has been released without sin
from a life of poverty and suffering to become one of God's
little angels. But knowing all this I still could not accept it; it
was just too sinfully irrational. Later I would talk to farmers
who, when I asked them how many children they had, would say
sadly and as though cursed, "Oh, ten, I think. I've had bad
luck; not even one *angelito*."

Two mornings later, drinking coffee in the same open-air
cafe, and once more waiting for a bus, I had to leave and stand
in a drizzle of rain to keep from watching another dying baby.
The calmness with which they accepted his death was obscene to
me.

I began to develop a grudge against La Unión and to make
wild generalizations in my mind about the town and the people
in it. I pretty much decided that I really didn't like the people
and that it would be impossible to work with them. About the
only adult I had met for whom I had any feelings of friendship
at all was a young shoemaker who worked in a kiosk by the bus
stop, an Indian from the Sierra who had dared to move down
into the tropics. And God knows he wasn't really an adult at
fifteen.

When I seriously thought about what I was going to do in
this unrewarding spot for eighteen more months, it sent me
spinning into a real depression. I locked myself in my room for
three days and read Ian Fleming novels and drank about five
gallons of coffee. In the afternoons when the little kids knocked
at the door, I held my breath until they went away. I had
thought that I could move into a completely different culture
and, if not love it, at least accept it enough that I could do the
job I had been trained for. It came as an ego-shriveling shock

to discover after the first month that I wasn't doing much of anything but reacting naïvely and emotionally to the poverty around me.

Then little by little I began, however superficially, to become involved with the life of the town. The President of the colonization, who was a jolly old drunkard and who had treated me as though I were some exotic toy for the town's enjoyment, was one day voted out of office. The new President, a younger, more progressive man, called on me one evening and asked me to come to the next town meeting and explain why I was there. "What *are* you doing in the town?" he asked. "I've heard rumors; is it true that you are a technician from the United States and that you wish to aid us?" I told him, surprised that he didn't know, and when I used the words "Peace Corps," his rather cold, stern, struggling farmer's face melted with emotion.

The next day, very nervous and speaking very badly, I was introduced to about sixty farmers at their Sunday meeting at the schoolhouse. I explained it all again—that I was with the Peace Corps, a representative of the government of the United States, that I wished to live in the village, make friends, learn their language and their customs, and that I wanted nothing from them except their friendship and, if they wished, a chance to help them create a school garden and to organize an experimental nursery. I also wanted to show them some new ways of raising pigs, chickens, and cattle.

I sat down, trembling, and suddenly everyone was smiling; all the faces had softened. Old farmers sitting behind the tiny fifth-grade desks turned to catch my eye, and smiled and nodded their heads. The president made a formal speech welcoming me to the town. It was my town now, he said. "If you need land for a school garden just tell us how much you need; we are completely at your service." When he had finished, five or six other farmers got up and welcomed me. They spoke in a formal and gracious Spanish that was quite beautiful, and since they all said about the same thing, I even began to understand it. A couple of them, getting practical, exhorted the other farmers to show their appreciation by cooperating and working together for a change.

Someone suggested that a *minga* be formed immediately to clear the land for me and to build a fence against the pigs and chickens. A *minga* is a group of workers in which each family is represented; its members work together on community projects. Everyone wanted a *minga,* but no one wanted a *minga* with a definite date pinned to it. This was the Latin way, I already realized; it would take about four more meetings before the school garden became a serious project.

The meeting ended on an inconclusive note, but it was a fine encouraging day. A couple of the farmers came over to visit me that night, and we sat around by candlelight drinking coffee and talking about pigs. I think it was at this meeting that I asked a farmer if he would bring me a few bananas next time he came to town. He would be enchanted, he told me, and the next day he appeared in the street below my room leading a horse almost crushed beneath at least two hundred pounds of bananas, for which he charged me twenty-five cents. I hung them up on the porch, and the kids used to steal them and bring some of them to me as presents.

My relationship with the town changed quite suddenly after that meeting. It was as though I had to acknowledge publicly an intention to live twenty months among them before they could believe it or take it seriously. The last couple of weeks that I was there I had actually become so busy that I had to make appointments with the farmers three or four days ahead of time. I was happy and very tired (the words seemed to go together), and I realized then that perhaps my main frustration with the town had been all that free time without any definite obligations.

At one end of town I was helping to build a chicken house out of bamboo strips dragged in fresh from the jungle, and at the other end of town (behind the barn), I was planting home gardens. In between I was advising people about wells and latrines. At night a steadily growing stream of visitors appeared. They wanted to talk about life in the United States, how much my shoes cost, or John F. Kennedy. Some of them, many of them, could not talk about Kennedy without weeping, and I, who was really quite sick by this time without knowing it, exhausted, emotionally naked, couldn't keep from weeping with them. I had a perpetual low-grade fever by then, and at night I had sweats that soaked the bed, but since I had never lived in the tropics I didn't know what to expect. I thought perhaps you were supposed to feel this way in the tropics. As for the depression, I figured that it was a normal reaction to living among the very poor.

It was an intense, emotional time. I talked one young guy into staying with his wife. He was trapped and defeated by home life and wanted to run away, back to the happy days of childhood in Guayaquil. It took about three nights and six dollars' worth of beer to talk him out of it, and I guess this was my most successful project during those first four months in Ecuador.

On the last day of my life in La Unión, Eduardo Sotomayor, one of the Heifer Representatives, delivered three pigs to the village for me. I was getting a couple of hog projects started. One of the pigs jumped out of the pickup and ran wild through the village for thirty minutes, with the whole town finally involved in his capture. What else happened that last day? I gave my buddy, the little shoemaker, a copy of *Esquire* that I had bummed from Maurine Henry, a Volunteer in Santo Domingo. It was full of the latest shoe styles, and he was radiantly happy with it. I visited my friend, Antonio, the local carpenter (specialty: children's coffins), with plans for a wooden washing machine which was hand-operated but far superior to beating clothes on rocks. Then I took off for Guayaquil to buy chicken feed, promising to return in two days.

Thankfully, I don't remember the bus trip to Guayaquil; it was one of those eight-hour ordeals that spanned at least three lifetimes, and I went into a coma. The next day Tomás took me to a doctor who diagnosed bronchitis and sent me to bed. I don't remember those three days either, but finally the doctor sent me to Ecuador's best radiologist, Dr. Luis Blum, who took some snapshots of my chest and told me I had noodles in my lungs. From the way I felt, this sounded like a pretty precise diagnosis. But Tomás explained that noodles meant nodules, and Dr. Blum explained that nodules meant anything from benign tumors, as he so beautifully put it, to tuberculosis or a lung fungus. When I heard this, my true strength of character immediately asserted itself; I cut down to one pack of cigarettes a day. Tomás called the Peace Corps office in Quito, and after some discussion they agreed that it was cheaper to ship home a live body than a dead one. The next morning I flew to Quito where I said good-by to the director, Gene Baird. Ron Dudley, my friend from Santo Domingo, dropped by the office to have a dislocated finger x-rayed. Someone told him that I was dying of lung cancer, and as we said good-by we both began to cry. At one o'clock that afternoon my jet left Quito.

Just at dark the following day I found myself looking out a window from the top floor of the Public Health Service hospital in Baltimore. A few inconsequential snowflakes, black trees stripped of their leaves, the flat roofs and brick fronts of rowed apartment houses, a mad freeway of underpasses and over-passes—it was a strange city but completely familiar.

But later, in bed with the lights out and my eyes closed, I could put out my hand and touch the wall of my room in La Unión. Everything fell into place, the table with my books, the plank wall with the maps of Ecuador and California, the garden tools and the pile of seed in the corner, the windows with their boxes of tomatoes and nasturtiums that looked down into that sad street. Even the sounds belonged to that little town. The dry cough of someone in another room was the cough of the shoemaker's wife downstairs who was dying of tuberculosis. "Oh, man," I thought, beginning to realize where I was, "when I get back where I belong, and if I ever feel sick, I sure as hell won't tell Tomás."

Four weeks later I was still undiagnosed, though by this time everyone was pretty sure that it was not cancer or tuberculosis but simply a bad case of histoplasmosis, a lung fungus. A month to the day after entering the hospital, I received a visit from Joan Hero, an ex-Volunteer from Africa, who was working with the Peace Corps in Washington.

"I suppose you know," she said, "that after thirty days in the hospital you are automatically out of the Peace Corps."

"Yeah," I said. "I know."

"And it's better for you. You're making seventy-four dollars a week now under your Social Security instead of a hundred dollars a month."

"Yeah," I said. "I guess it's better."

"You can always reapply at a later date," she told me, doubtfully.

"Don't worry," I said. "I will."

Part Two: 1966

IN August of 1966, after about twenty collect phone calls from California to the Peace Corps doctors in Washington, I was reinstated as a full-fledged Volunteer. They sent me my passport and an economy jet ticket to Quito, and a week later, well fleshed out in baby fat (or a reasonable facsimile) but having forgotten practically all my Spanish, I found myself in Santo Domingo again, looking for a place to work. The Quito doctor had told me to stay away from La Unión and to look for a drier climate. Tomás had suggested Tulcán just before leaving for Montana to take part in a training program, so he wasn't there in Quito to insist. Everyone who had ever been to Tulcán told me that it was a high, cold, foggy town. I headed back for the coast.

I was staying with Ron Dudley and three other Volunteers, really feeling out of it, their Spanish was so fantastic, really feeling like a rookie again. Ron told me that an Italian priest from a coastal fishing village north of Esmeraldas had come to the Peace Corps office requesting that an agricultural Volunteer come to the town and start some animal projects and work with the people in agriculture. The village was reached only at low tide on an old bus that ran along the beach. But first you had to cross the Esmeraldas River in a canoe, and at the end of the bus line cross another river. I had never made the entire trip, but had seen the town once from a distance. I remembered standing on the beach looking north along that sweeping stretch of sand and breakers, everything softened in an ocean haze, and thinking that it was quite like paradise.

I talked to Tom Torres, the Peace Corps Representative, and to Eduardo Sotomayor about going to Río Verde to live. They had no objections. They suggested that I go out and look the place over, taking Ron along as an interpreter. The area was particularly interesting to them because, although not inaccessible, it was inconvenient for the agricultural extension people to visit, since there was only the one bus a day. The area had been generally neglected by the Ecuadorian agriculturists. Of course, this was one of the reasons why I thought I would like the place—I would be more or less on my own and could work with the teachers, the priest, and the local leaders without the complications of clearing everything with the extension office. Another reason was that the farms stretch along the Río Verde for three days by canoe, and I had this wonderful, gold-plated vision of canoeing for miles into the interior with a package of CARE seeds held high in one hand and a purebred Duroc gilt cradled in the other. In this vision I always saw myself lolling up in front of the canoe while my trusty, dusky canoeman stood in back doing all the work.

One of the complications of reaching Río Verde was that you had to cross the Esmeraldas River at high tide and then wait until low tide for the highway gradually to appear. Ron and I were lucky; we hired a canoe for fifty cents that missed all the main sand bars in a falling tide to arrive in Tachina just a bare

hour and a half before the truck left. This was cutting it pretty fine for Ecuador.

"When is the bus leaving?" we asked.

"*Ya mismo.*" *Ya mismo* is one of those idiot expressions in a country which has absolutely no sense of time or its passing; it can mean many things, "*ya mismo*"—immediately, in a little while, in two hours, in five hours. The expression is a wonderful conversation piece in moments of high frustration when it becomes imperative to fight back a little against the Latin way of doing things and lay down a light veneer of gringo rationality.

The road to Río Verde is the smoothest road in the country —twenty miles of wide, curving beach, completely rebuilt twice a day. It is bounded on one side by an unbelievably tranquil Pacific, over which float endless trails of pelicans, all in combat formation and engaged in practicing follow the leader, and on the other side by low, forested hills, pastures of Johnson grass, and miles of rowed coconut palms.

We got into the bus, which was really a two-ton cattle truck. Like most Ecuadorian trucks that have been translated into vehicles for hauling large segments of the population, the Río

Verde bus was pragmatic. Everything had been removed from the cab, which had been cut off, and a wooden cab extended back ten feet from the still-remaining windshield. Within this construction—which vaguely resembled a modern flat-roof cottage, painted red and blue and covered with drawings of palm trees and tigers—there were four rows of narrow wooden benches, each with about four inches of leg room, extending two feet out over the running boards. This part was crowded with people eight to the row, and we rode in back, which was also full of people, personal luggage in gunny sacks, piles of platano, sacks of rice, and cases of Pepsi Cola, beer, and other vital necessities.

About fifteen minutes out of Tachina it started to rain, and it rained so hard that in two minutes we were soaked to the skin. After it rained very hard for about ten minutes, it really began to rain—solid sheets of water. There was something so funny and touching about the people who sat through this deluge chatting and laughing as though it were perfectly normal, something so unreal and strange about hurtling up an Ecuadorian beach at forty miles an hour through a cloudburst that totally obscured the vision, that Ron and I both became hysterical with laughter and practically fell off the truck. A little Negro baby held in her mother's arms, her hair glistening with a million diamonds of water, slept through the whole catastrophe, never realizing what a bargain she was getting—a free bath and her clothes washed all for a half-price bus ticket.

We arrived in Río Verde in bright sunshine after about a two-hour trip, both of us dry and spotless. Ron and I had very different first reactions to the town. He was excited and (trying to sell me on the place) kept saying he would trade sites with me. I kept saying, "No, no," but I was half inclined to take him up on it. I was more sophisticated than Ron. I had seen the Joan Crawford–Walter Huston production of Somerset Maugham's "Rain," and I knew instinctively that any town as poor, exotic, and picturesque as this had to be full of lost souls. It was too exotic to be real.

Actually there were two towns, Palestina on one side of the river and Río Verde across the river on the northern bank. Río Verde was a town of about thirty houses, three of them cement and the rest bamboo. A proud little dock jutted out into the river; it was high and dry at low tide, and you reached it by walking through mud. A small hand pump stood in the middle of a sandy street; it delivered a brackish water that could only be used for washing. On a slope just above the town a new, bright blue schoolhouse assaulted the eyes. With the exception of the school and three or four houses, the whole town was no more than four feet above the sea at high tide, and if you walked the two hundred yards or so through town and suddenly came upon the ocean, breaking at the very base of the coconut palms, you experienced for a few seconds the panicky feeling that you and the whole plain were about to be engulfed by the advancing waves.

Along the beach just a few yard from shore, porpoises, the fishermen's friends, rolled and played in the gentle ocean swell. At sunset hundreds of frigate birds soared over the town and the river on the way to roost for the night in three dead trees in a mangrove swamp on the Palestina side. The sun was kind and was usually hidden in light clouds; except for an hour or so at dawn, there was always a fresh wind blowing in from the sea. Early in the morning, discounting those damned roosters, the world was completely tranquil.

As Ron and I walked through town, up the beach, and then back, we created a quiet sensation. It was a Negro town, and there didn't seem to be any of that Indian reserve, that hostility that had so depressed me in La Unión. A bunch of kids (as usual) followed us, but something new was added. A couple of cackling old women in the last house stuck their heads out the window and began joking with us; a granddaughter joined them and told Ron that he was handsome; the men on the street smiled and wished us a good afternoon. It looked like a wonderful place to work. We stopped at one of the three stores for a Coke and asked about renting a house. "But, *hombre,* I'll rent you the store," the owner said. "We just came out for the fiesta, my wife and I, and we're leaving for Esmeraldas in two days."

It was a two-room store built of cement, by far the best building in the town. With a patch or two it could be made completely rat-proof. The shelves that held Pepsi and *aguardiente* could be used for bookcases. The front doors opened to the street, and the back yard—a little collapsing patio of bamboo and *pambil*—could be repaired and used to raise chickens. Through the back door you looked out on a small grove of palms, clumps of wiry salt grass, sand, the sea, and the river. At six o'clock without fail there was a tropical sunset that blazed and burned with a spectacular vulgarity, each one more brazen than the one before.

We talked the owner down from the outrageous 200 sucres a month rent that he was asking to a more reasonable 150, about $7.50; we were all delighted with the deal. Then we met a guy named Alexandro Martínez who lived in a house across the town square. He immediately involved himself with my problems, and within half an hour I had arranged to take my meals in his house and had hired him to take me by canoe and horseback to the different villages along the Río Verde and the rivers to the north.

So, an hour after arriving in Río Verde we had settled all the major problems of living, and the next morning Ron hopped aboard the truck and left me on the beach. Once more I was alone in a strange village, but this time without that terrible feeling of having intruded upon an alien, a closed and secret, world.

I didn't want to get involved in any quick projects this time, and I spent the first few weeks traveling around the zone with Alexandro meeting people and trying to learn their names and the names of the little villages where they worked. I went to Santo Domingo and brought back some boxes of clothing and books. I met an American, an old man named Bill Swanson, who had lived just outside Río Verde for forty-five years in a beat-up sawmill, and when I thought that I was going mad from hearing only Spanish I would go up and visit with him. Mostly, I just sat around and listened.

Bill Swanson talking: "During the war I was an agent for the American government buying up rubber and bananas for the war effort. I was operating the balsa mill, too. My God, the money just rolled in.

"I spent a lot of time on the river, had a little outboard motor. When I was on the river I always had my bottle of 'Sure Shot' for treating the people for worms. You can't miss the look they have, especially the children with the blown up stomachs and the eyes all sunken and glassy.

"Going up, there was always one sight that I loved to see. It was a man and his son, a little nipper about six. They used to sit on the bank of the river fishing, both of them with big hats and both of them smoking pipes. The boy would copy all the gestures of his father. The father would cross his legs; the little boy would cross his legs. The father would knock the ashes out of his pipe; the little boy would knock the ashes out of his pipe. They would smoke their pipes and nod to me very solemnly when I went past, and it was always sort of a highlight of my trip.

"One day I went past, and the old man was sitting alone on

the bank puffing on his pipe. 'What's wrong?' I asked. 'Where's the little nipper?'

" 'Oh, holy sainted Jesus,' the man said. 'He's in the house; he's dying of a fever.'

"I went up to the house, and the boy had a very high fever; he was dying of worms. 'He's got worms,' I said. 'We'll have to give him some "Sure Shot." '

" 'Oh, no,' the father said. 'You can't worm my son with that fever; you have to wait until the fever dies.'

" 'Listen,' I said, 'he'll die before the fever does; it's the worms that are causing the fever.' We argued for half an hour; he was upset and really determined, and I finally had to make him go outside while I gave the boy a good double dose of 'Sure Shot.'

"Well, I came back down the river about a week later and, by God, there they were sitting on the bank fishing, the father and his little boy, both of them smoking their pipes and looking at the river. When the man saw me he rushed into the water to embrace me, weeping, crying that whatever he had was mine, his whole life was mine. Goddamn, he almost dumped me in the river with his kisses."

Swanson again a few evenings later: "They're a lazy shiftless bunch here on the coast, the worst in the whole country. I guess the worst in the whole world. The living is too easy. A piece of fish, a dish of rice, a platano, and their goddamned hammock, they don't want anything else. You're not going to change them; you're not going to change anything. They'll love you to your face, boy, but they'll hate you to your back.

"You know what's going to happen here the day after you leave when you go on back to God's country? I'll tell you what's going to happen. They'll take all those nice chickens you've promised to get them, and they'll have a big party, and they'll eat the sons of bitches. Yessir, a month after you've gone, nobody will ever know you were here.

"All they ever wanted from me was a chance to give me a good screwing. I swear, boy, I've been here forty years and can't honestly say I've got a friend in the bunch. Hell, I guess it's more than forty years. They'll rob you blind if you turn your back on them. But I never asked them for a thing, and in all my life I've never borrowed a cent of money, and I paid my men every Saturday; no one ever waited to be paid.

"But you know the way they are? They'll come to the house looking for a job and if I give them one, the first thing they ask is 'How much you going to pay?' Goddamn, boy, can you imagine it?"

Alexandro talking: "The gringo? A wonderful man. When he ran the balsa mill the whole town worked for him; there was money in the town then; things were very good. Now the only mill belongs to Nelson Estupiñan four miles up the river, and that's too far to help us much. Señor Swanson paid us every Saturday, and we never had to wait. He took care of us. For example, he had safety devices on all the machinery; in all those years there was never a single accident. Oh, but how he watched us. He was everywhere, and he really made us work.

"He has been a wonderful friend to the town, and we have all sought his friendship, but he is a very rich man and was very busy; I don't think he ever had time for friendship. I have known him all my life, worked for him for years, am related to his wife, and it's a strange thing that he still doesn't know my name or when I go to visit with him act as though he recognized me.

"He never drinks water, you know, only beer, about a case a day. Imagine being so rich that you don't have to drink water."

Alexandro's eighteen-year-old son Lucho, in revolt against

parental authority, spent a lot of time in my house, especially around eight o'clock when I was cooking up a little something extra to get me through until morning.

Lucho talking: "I've got to get out of this lousy town; there's absolutely nothing to do. My father's on me all the time because I'm not working. But working at what? Well, my uncle in Guayaquil says if I go there I can live in his house and perhaps he can even help me get a job. Now, I'll tell you, the idea of leaving this place where I was born is a little frightening, but with luck I could make as much as a dollar, a dollar and a half a day. Besides I have this serious problem of my two front teeth. Without them, you know, I am an ugly devil. No, truly, I have a terrible time with the girls; they don't like me.

"In Esmeraldas you have to pay cash to have teeth put in, but in Guayaquil there is a dentist who gives you credit. I read his advertisement in the paper; he makes a wire thing that goes behind your good teeth and holds the new ones in, and they look absolutely real. I mean a man with all his teeth, you know, could look real cool, real clever. He charges twenty dollars, which is a lot, but you don't have to pay it all at once. I think with my front teeth the girls would like me better, I really do. It's getting so that going to Guayaquil is just about all I think about."

And crazy little Ricardo, the carpenter's fifteen-year-old son: "I want to talk seriously with you now about what I have been thinking. I have been thinking that you are not going back to the United States for over a year and that if in that time I got a job someplace and had real luck I could save almost fifty dollars. Would that be enough to ride with you to California in an airplane?

"What I want to do is learn how to manage your car and drive it for you. I could manage your car and drive your tractor and be a real help. I'm a very serious type, very dependable, ask anybody. I could help you on your farm, driving your things around like they do and taking care of you.

"But there's one thing I've been wondering about, if on the airplane it would be possible to sit next to you. I have never been in an airplane, and I would like to sit next to you, at least at first, if such a thing were possible."

And finally, Ramón Prado, a twenty-two-year-old fisherman. About five months after I arrived Ramón opened a little *salón* across the street; before that he used to walk into town almost every night to visit with me: "What I really wanted all my life and most of all was that my father love me and to help him on the farm, that we work together. But he was so ambitious, just burning with ambitious plans, and when they went wrong he was wild like a crazy man. The farm was always more important to him than his children; that's all he ever thought about was the land, getting more land. When something went wrong he always took it out on us.

"One morning I spilled half a bucket of milk, and I was terrified. Walking up the beach to sell it in town I filled up the bucket with sea water; I don't know, it was stupid but you can't imagine how terrified I was of my father. Well, he found out, the whole town was complaining, and you know what he did, my own father? He tied me down on the floor with four ropes, like a hog, and beat me with bamboo.

"It was all over for me. I stole twenty pounds of tobacco that night and went to Esmeraldas, walking up the beach all night. I was about fourteen, my God, just a green kid, walking the streets and looking for a job.

"About a week later Carlos Torres ran away, too; he was just my age, and though I'm ashamed to admit it now that he's turned into such a complete bum, he was my best friend then. We slept on the beach and ate bananas out of the hog lots and stole. He used to cry all night. Well, I guess I did, too.

"We worked with machetes for a month up the river near Biche cleaning a banana planting; when we wanted our money the farmer said he was sorry, he had no money. A month of work, *por gusto*. Carlos was afraid; our clothes were all worn out, we were half sick with the food they gave us, and he had also stolen a watch out of the farmer's house. He ran away again and went back to Río Verde. I went back to Esmeraldas out to the beach at Las Palmas where the boats are anchored and began yelling out to the boats; telling about it now I sound a little mad; I guess I was. I was crying and yelling at the boats, 'Take me to Muisne with you,' and one day a captain who knew my family took me to Muisne.

"Now I've got to explain that before all this happened my father had caught my mother with this man and had told her to leave his house. I don't really blame my father, though at the time, when I was only six, I couldn't believe that my mother was evil. Now that I'm a man I realize it was a very bad thing she did, and even at fourteen I had a coldness in my heart for her for the excesses of my father and the sadness of my life.

"My mother cried every day I was in Muisne because of what she did. I think she realized that I didn't have too much feeling for her, and I think this made her cry too. One awful thing for me: she was living with this man, not even the man she had run away with. Well, she bought me clothes and shoes and many gifts; she even bought meat for the table. She wrote my father where I was, and he wrote back begging me to return to Río Verde, that he would never beat me again.

"O.K., so I went back to the farm. When my father saw me he cried and told me to stay and be close to him and help him, and I was crazy that my father would cry for me. Just imagine.

But little by little my father is more difficult. He says I don't help enough or have enough respect for him or take the right interest in the farm. I don't understand now why I needed his love so badly, that poor man. I would leave again but now there is no money to leave with, and now I must think about my wife. It is a difficult time, and I don't know what to do. I don't think I want to stay any more but the cities are crowded with farm boys looking for work; in the city a farm boy is just a piece of shit."

And Ramón talking again: "One reason I don't drink very much is because of my temper; I have a devil in me, and it really scares me. I've lost my temper twice in my life, once in Río Verde one Saturday night about a year ago. You can see the teeth marks here on my stomach.

"We were all drinking that night in Pablo's, and you know how it is. Crispín got in a fight with Lucho and began to beat him up. Lucho was very drunk, that's one reason why Crispín picked a fight that he knew he could win. He had Lucho down on the ground, unconscious, but still he kept kicking him, and I said, 'Come on, Crispín, cut it out; that's enough,' and tried to drag him away. When I felt him biting me on the stomach I just went crazy. I almost killed him. It took eight of them to hold me down, I was just insane with rage.

"Before that, one night I was drinking beer with my brother Orestes in a jungle *salón* and these strangers, very drunk, kept bothering us with sarcastic remarks, that we were just country hicks, you know. So I said, 'Look, just don't bother us, will you; just leave us alone, we don't want any trouble.'

"They went outside, and one of them went home and got his machete. When we came out into the darkness a little while later one of them swung at the head of Orestes. But he ducked and the machete came down on his hand where he was holding on to a railing. I have never been particularly close to my

brother, Orestes, but when I saw his fingers lying on the floor of
the porch and the blood gushing out of his hand, everything
turned red in front of my eyes, a perfect flood of red. I don't
remember anything after that except that I wanted to kill
those sons of bitches.

"Before they dragged me off I almost did kill one of them.
I'll say this: he was in the hospital a lot longer than my
brother, Orestes. When I came to I was tied up with ropes."

All of these conversations, terrible in their implications
about the quality of life in Río Verde, had an amazing effect on
me. I had never been an emotional sort of person, but now I felt
all my defenses against sadness being stripped away. And my
defenses against happiness, too. Those first months were fantastic ones, as I became involved with people on a new level of
awareness, completely vulnerable at last to the joys and horrors of this new kind of life. How could I keep from weeping
for Orestes, for instance, this fisherman from the beach, who
was almost destroyed as a producing person in one drunken
moment, and who now returned from a day's fishing with a
hand bloody from trying to hold a paddle?

□□

Late one afternoon Alexandro and I were returning from
Chungillo, which is three hours by horseback from Río Verde. I
had gone up that morning to talk to the school director about
starting a school garden. It was my first month in Río Verde,
and my first trip into this area, and everything was new,
strange, incredible, incredibly beautiful. It was all so unbelievable, so emotional, that since arriving I seemed to exist simply
as a vessel into which a million new impressions were pouring;
that old, boring personality that I knew as myself had disappeared. Of course, I had experienced this same thing before—in motor cars driving at a hundred miles an hour; in

bombers over German cities during the war, when your personality disappeared and you turned into something called pure terror; and also a few times in my younger years when I had been in love. But I had never been so transformed for such a sustained period of time.

Alexandro and I were riding through a ten-acre pasture of Johnson grass in the middle of which stood a giant, dying tree covered with very large dead leaves. We were almost under it when this amazing thing happened. A little gust of wind blew through the pasture, a chill gust completely out of place in that gentle fragrant air. It shook the leaves from the tree, and they rattled along the ground; that wind and the sound of those dry leaves filled me for a moment with an unbelievable sadness, an overwhelming sense of loss, disaster, and failure.

I figured it out immediately. It was that first cold fall air coming down from Mount Shasta and running through the valley, and the sound of dead corn leaves rasping and rattling in the wind on my farm in California. That old sadness which I thought I had escaped was the sadness I felt each year husking corn alone in the field, knowing that another year had passed, that the crops were all in, and that once more I had lost a little money farming.

In the village the saddest and finally the most infuriating expression to the average Peace Corps Volunteer, if my own experience is any guide, was that frightened sentence they pulled out of their hats when you were talking about change or when you were trying to push some slightly new idea. I was eating dinner one night with Alexandro, and he used the expression four times within a half an hour.

What he said four times was: "The people aren't accustomed to doing it that way." Each time it was a little more irritating, especially, I think, because finally it was even irritating to

Alexandro. The last time he said it he even blushed a little. The conversation offers some insights into both the problems of a poor town and the problems of a Volunteer working to change things in a poor town:

First we talked about orange marmalade. Elizabeth Mills, a Volunteer in Santo Domingo, had showed me how to make orange marmalade one Sunday afternoon. When I got back to Río Verde, I cooked up a batch and kept track of the expense. A quart of marmalade cost me about three sucres—fifteen cents —as compared to the commercial product in Quito at fifteen sucres. I had taken some of the marmalade over to Alexandro's house and had given an inspiring pep talk on how easy, cheap, and nutritious it was. Everyone tasted it; it really wasn't too bad except that the peel was overcooked and tough as leather. But the flavor was nice.

It was so nice that my own private jar was constantly being raided, most compulsively by Ramón Arcos, a guy of about twenty-three, the manager of the light plant. I'll never be able to prove it, but I think he used to turn out all the lights in the town just so he could sneak into my kitchen, where I would find him in pitch darkness, caught like a little boy with a spoon sticking out of his face.

To be honest, I had cooked that first batch of marmalade strictly for myself out of desperation, trying to find some way to disguise the taste of the bread. In its pure and pristine form Río Verde bread was absolutely inedible; it was made of flour and water only. Shortening was too expensive and eggs were out of the question, and the river water that they used gave the bread a slightly evil flavor of moldy moss. Marmalade disguised the bread to the point where it could be consumed in modest quantities. (Later I learned that if you took the baker three eggs and a little lard he would cook up a special batch of bread for you, but I didn't know this when I was going through my marmalade phase.)

Anyway, to get back to the dinner table: "When are you going to make some more *conservas?*" the *señora* asked me. "It was very rich and delicious."

"Why don't you make some then?"

"Lemons are very scarce and dear," she said.

"My God," I said, "it only takes two lemons."

"But the price of lemons," Alexandro cried. "A real *fandango*, pure gold, over a penny apiece."

"I can show you again how to make it, and you can show the women how to make it." I sat there visualizing all the women in town stirring up great pots of marmalade and stuffing the scrawny children with vitamins.

"Oh, the people," Alexandro cried, as though we were separate from them. "The people aren't accustomed to making marmalade."

We were having meat for dinner that night. In the four months that I had been in Río Verde, except for one chicken on Alexandro's birthday, one chicken that was killed by a little tiger, and an occasional fish, it was the first real meat I had eaten in the town. Well, no, come to think of it, I wasn't eating it, but at least there was meat on my plate, two little sausage-sized tripes filled with something black and grainy—blood, I think. I pushed them to one side and ate the rice.

"If you don't like *longanisa*," Alexandro said, "don't eat it; there are many people who don't like it."

"I'm not accustomed to tripe," I said, fighting back, while he neatly speared the little sausages off my plate.

He told me than that he had used the money I paid him for my meals to go up the river and buy a young pig; he had killed it that morning and sold the meat to the people in the village.

"There are no pigs here at all," he said, shaking his head in disgust. "It's a barbarous little hole; we never have meat to eat here; but tonight the whole town is eating meat. The nice part is that I made twenty-five sucres selling the hog, and in addition I have the head, the insides, and all the blood."

"It sounds like a good business," I told him, turning pale and visualizing with a nicely controlled horror the next few meals.

"A very good business," he agreed.

"And couldn't you go up the river every week and get a pig and sell it here in Río Verde?"

"No, the people are very poor, but every two weeks they would buy a piece of meat."

"Why don't you do it then?"

"For the money, *hombre*. For the money. When does a poor man have enough money to buy a whole hog?"

"But you are known as an honest man; you have a good name. Why don't you buy the pig on credit, sell the meat, and pay the owner the next day?"

Alexandro shook his head. "No," he said. "The people aren't accustomed to doing business that way."

The third thing that the people weren't accustomed to doing involved planting some palm trees in the public plaza. The plaza was a newly cleared piece of dusty ground covered with broken fragments of pre-Incan pottery; in the middle there was a sad little monument to some Negro slaves who, back in 1820, had made a bloody and unsuccessful fight for freedom. A crazy line of posts strung with wire wandered across the square, and a single sixty-watt bulb glowed dimly on the monument on those rare nights when the light plant was operating.

I wanted to get some coconut palms and plant the plaza in a design of walks; maybe later we could even make some benches.

But Alexandro explained that it wouldn't work. Basically his argument was pretty subtle, hinging on the fact that all the land in Río Verde was part of the municipality. You weren't allowed to own your homesite, but you could get a clear and binding title to the palm trees on it. Every palm tree, worth about five dollars, belonged to someone. Now, if you planted coco palms in the public square, who would they belong to? Surely, I could understand that it would be impossible to plant coco on land that could not be used for homesites.

"All I understand," I told him, snorting, "is that's the most ridiculous thing I ever heard of." He laughed, agreeing. "But besides," he said, ending the discussion, "if you plant the coco as seeds the children, those *diablos*, will dig them up and eat them, and if you plant the seedlings the farmers will dig them up and plant them on their own farms."

We had finished dinner by this time, and I was getting ready to go home. Alexandro was holding his youngest daughter on his lap while his wife, having served us, sat in the dark kitchen on the floor eating what was left. "The poor little creature," Alexandro said, looking at his child, weak, pale, skinny, dull. "I think she's coming down with the grippe again."

For two months, I had been explaining about orange juice to Alexandro and his wife; I had read up on the subject in the copy of Dr. Spock in the Peace Corps book locker—how a mother's milk was lacking in vitamin C and how young babies should be fed orange juice. Every two weeks, every time the child was ill, I had explained the whole situation to them in detail—how at first to mix the juice with boiled water and then gradually feed it stronger and stronger; how important it was to balance a diet with vitamins and minerals. By this time, I sort of inwardly boiled every time I saw the child.

"For one thing," I said, "the little creature is suffering from

malnutrition. What about the orange juice? I feel like a real
bobo, bringing it up all the time, but you think I'm a liar about
the orange juice, don't you?"

Alexandro looked at me in shock that I could speak so
impolitely. "But, Don Martín, how could we think you a liar,
you who know so much more than we? It's only," and saying it,
he began to blush, "that we're not accustomed. . . ."

I said two words in English, and Alexandro's son Lucho, to
whom I had been teaching some dirty words in English and who
had been listening to our conversation, understood them and let
out a great horse laugh.

Alexandro worked about ten days a month as a canoe man
for the malaria teams that regularly went as far as the last
house on the river caring for the sick and spraying the houses
with DDT. He was gone on one of those trips when his ten-
month-old daughter got sick. I went over to lunch one day to
find the *señora* distraught, pacing back and forth with the
baby in her arms.

"What's wrong?" I asked.

"Oh, my God, the little creature has *mal aire;* I went into the
cemetery today when they were burying the woman from Pri-
mavera, and I forgot to change my clothes when I got back.
The babies all get *mal aire* when there is a death."

Secretly I had reservations about the child's illness; she was
generally about half sick. But suddenly the child began to
vomit. I went back to my house and got a thermometer. Outside
other women, friends of the *señora*, were walking through the
weeds looking for a particular medicinal plant for cooking into
tea, a sure cure for those ghostly emanations of bad air which
contaminate a town when there is a death. The baby wouldn't
keep the thermometer in her mouth, and I was a little shy about
explaining the other method, so we put the thermometer be-

tween the baby's legs and held them together; she had a temperature of 102.

"You'd better get into Esmeraldas to the doctor," I told the *señora*.

The truck across the river left at three that afternoon, and the *señora* came by the house just before she left to tell me that I would eat my meals with her mother and that she would return as soon as possible. She was surrounded by women as she talked to me, and they followed her out onto the pier, all of them frightened, solicitous, hovering around the child, peering into its face, rearranging the little blanket in which it was wrapped. The trip involved an hour's wait on the other side, a two-hour ride up the beach in a broken-down truck, another hour squatting in a canoe across the Esmeraldas River, then a mile-and-a-half walk out to the hospital. Word came back the next day that the child had *colerín*, that she was out of danger, and that the *señora* needed money. What *colerín* was I didn't know, except that it was a stomach infection and that many babies, untreated, died from it. The *señora*'s mother went over to Alexandro's house, caught all the chickens in the yard, tied their feet together with vines, and sent them back on the truck to be sold. There were about twelve chickens, and they represented all of the family's liquid assets. It was in the last days of the month, and I had been living on credit for a week. I could give them nothing, but sent word that on payday I would be in town.

I had very complicated feelings about this child. My relationship with the family was strained on her account. At mealtime, with the baby sleeping on the floor or eating pieces of bananas or rice off the floor, I would get so mad, and so mad at my anger and my inability to function, that I couldn't speak. We had had many discussions about the child's nutrition, some of them quite intense and sarcastic. Maybe they *did* have good native herbs for treating their sicknesses, but I kept telling them that with decent nutrition the child would grow and maintain a degree of health. (They had treated me once with an evil-tasting brew, promising instant and magical relief, but the cold lasted just as long as all my others, and in addition I got a slight case of diarrhea.)

Somehow the child had gotten in the way of our friendship. I had pushed too hard to get them to feed her decently, and in a terrible way she was in her sickness less a sick child than the illustration of an argument. On her good days she was bounced before me proudly, and Alexandro's face wore a victorious look, as though he were saying, "You see, the little creature is fine; she doesn't need the things you talk about—the orange juice, the milk, the eggs; she's getting stronger every day on rice and yuca." On those days when, too weak to hold her head up or even to cry, she lay on the floor listless and almost unconscious, I couldn't help but feel a cruel stab of triumph and then an awful guilt for the satisfaction that the child's illness gave me. It got so I could not look at the baby or, when Alexandro sat across the table from me at mealtimes with the baby in his arms, even speak.

So I was glad to eat in the house of the *señora's* mother, a house which sat higher on the hill in back of town. Over the tops of the palm trees you could see miles of surf, the mouth of the river, the row of bamboo houses in Palestina across the river, and farther out the beach spreading away endlessly to north and south. At suppertime, sea, sky, and river all blazed and burned with one light—orange or lemon yellow or scarlet.

At three o'clock in the morning Alexandro woke me up; he had been fifty miles up the river when the messsage came to him that the child was dying. I reassured him, but he was too overwrought to sleep and said he would walk the twenty or twenty-five miles along the beach to Esmeraldas. The next day the *señora* and the child came back, and the day after that, having missed them somehow, Alexandro returned. The trip and the doctor bills had cost them everything they owned, plus ten dollars that they had borrowed.

A month later everything was back to normal again. The child had been sick twice more and was steadily losing weight, but an old woman up on the hill was treating her with herbs and powders. "There are women, you know," the *señora* explained, telling me very carefully because I was just a gringo who didn't understand such things, "there are women who have great powers, who can cure the sick or curse the well, women who can change into animals, and who at night can fly through the air."

"Ah, *dios mío*," Alexandro said, shaking his head, "there are such things in the jungle and in the darkness as you have never heard of, and on the beaches what things, what things of horror are washed up in the darkness in the winter storms."

Listening to this talk I felt my own horror as I was allowed to glimpse deep, deep into their minds for just a second, feeling as though I were peering across an immense abyss, realizing that I was not half as close as I had thought.

A new and tender sadness lived in the house then, a feeling of defeat and of waiting; it was as though a gift of time had been given to the family to prepare themselves for the child's death. And sometimes, watching the family as I ate supper, I wondered if we were really struggling for the child or if the whole thing was in my imagination.

□□

Alexandro, like most of the people in Río Verde, had lived there all his life, but he was more sophisticated than many, having traveled as far away as Guayaquil many times. He seemed to have a soft spot in his heart for gringos, a possibility

which worried me a little since people who liked gringos usually
liked them because of some misconception that lived in the
mind, and they would assign a gringo qualities that he didn't
necessarily have. I was sure that one of Alexandro's misconcep-
tions would turn out to be built around the common Latin idea
that all gringos are rich, though this was something he denied
the first week that I knew him. "I'm the only man in town who
knows there's such a thing as a poor gringo," he boasted,
telling me that as a child he had met a gringo staggering down
the beach with his clothes in ribbons and his feet bloody. "I
took him to my mother, and she fed him, and the next morning
when he left my mother gave him a sucre."

Alexandro was about forty-five years old, and he knew the
river and all the families living along its banks—the good ones,
the lazy ones, the thieves, the alcoholics. When we went by
horseback up the beach and inland, he identified every farm-
house for miles along the jungle trials, and he told me something (usually bad) about every family. As a young man he
had acted as a guide for an American paymaster of a geologi-
cal survey team, and this was probably the high point in his
life. How his heart must have leapt when I returned to Río
Verde with my clothes packed in wooden boxes that I had had
made in La Unión. "Just like the wooden boxes that the paymaster had," Alexandro told me. "And all of them packed solid
with one-hundred-sucre bills." I quickly invited him to my
house so that he could watch me unpack my tawdry collection
of dirty clothes and Peace Corps books.

I don't know how Alexandro made his living before the
malaria teams arrived with their DDT and hired him as a
guide, but I realized after only a few days that he was extremely poor. He lived in a three-room bamboo house raised
about five feet above the gound. He had run out of money while

roofing the house, and had finished the section over the kitchen with *ranconcha*, a tremendous leafed plant, like a great philodendron, a leaf that dried and split and disintegrated after a few months. The leaves above the kitchen were dry and torn by then, and they rattled in the wind. When it rained it rained just a little bit more in the kitchen that it did outside, since the whole roof drained into it. If my figures were correct, he needed about $1.50 worth of palm thatch. He seemed worried that he might not be able to save this much before the rainy season started.

From my first day in Río Verde, when I began trying to explain what a Peace Corps Volunteer was, Alexandro was interested in making a garden with the CARE seeds that I had. The morning after he saw them he was out cutting weeds in the vacant lot next to his house—and stealing a little of his neighbor's land for a larger spread. When I told him I was bringing in some chickens—day-old, first-generation layers from Miami—he got really excited. On paper it figured out that we could clear almost fifty cents a month per laying hen; a man with one hundred hens could live like a king.

For a few days it was all he could talk about, but then he began stalling when I pushed him to get the bamboo to make chicken houses. He finally explained that he wanted to raise chickens, he had a real passion to raise chickens, but that bamboo sold for two dollars for a dozen thirty-foot-long pieces and that he couldn't figure out how he was going to raise so much money right away. I was running into this problem with everyone in town; I was asking people to risk more than they had in a project that, if it failed, would complicate their lives.

There was also the problem of the feed. At the time corn was cheap; it was still being harvested. But as the dry season

advanced it would double and triple in price from the low of
thirty sucres a sack. Alexandro didn't want to get started with
chickens in April and then have to buy four-dollar corn in
January. He was like everyone else in town, plunged into a
catatonic depression when I told him that one laying hen would
eat almost a sack of corn a year.

Realizing that he had no funds, I told him that if he would
keep it very secret I would loan him the money to buy a few
sacks of corn while the price was low, and that he could pay me
back later when his chickens began to lay. I explained that this
was a private loan, that I was only making two thousand sucres
a month, that I couldn't afford to finance the whole town, and
that it *had* to be a secret. (*"Only,"* Alexandro said, looking at
me with a new respect.)

This conversation made a couple of complications. Before
our secret talk I think he had dreams of raising about twenty-
five chickens; afterward he was talking about eighty. Somehow
I had to bring him back to earth so that I wouldn't be investing
my whole living allowance in tons of corn. I could see another
bloody-footed gringo staggering naked down the beach if Alexandro had his way. The other thing I didn't particularly like
was the change that took place in our relationship after I
offered to help him. The offer had somehow made a *patrón* out
of me; I had been catalogued and placed. It was a relationship
that almost every poor Latin sought, to be subservient and
protected by a powerful father figure. It was the very thing I
was trying to destroy. I'd damn well not be Alexandro's
daddy.

Yet, to be honest, I have to mention the other side of the
coin. I used Alexandro, too. When I had to buy water, for
instance, I didn't go out and make my own deal with the kids; I
simply told Alexandro, and he scouted around for me. It was
the subtle relationship of master and slave, engendered on his

part by custom and insecurity, and on mine by laziness and insecurity.

Talking about the good old days at the dinner table one night, Alexandro said: "A couple of years ago it was really nice in town; the priests across the river brought in CARE food and sold it very reasonably, five sucres, for example, for a liter of cooking oil, wonderful American oil, and there was flour and sometimes even cans of sardines. We all ate very well in the town, or we could sell what we didn't like to other people. But then the priests got mad at us; they said we were pagans because we didn't send our children to catechism and that they would no longer help us."

This picture of a town on perpetual relief horrified me, but I was more horrified by the complacency with which Alexandro accepted this gift of food. "But giving you food is no solution," I said. "You can buy oil in the stores; you can buy sardines and flour in the stores. Wouldn't you rather be able to buy your own food and tell the priests to go to hell? Do you like having to put your children on the block to get free food?" Alexandro looked at me without answering; he probably understood neither my lousy Spanish nor the ideas I was trying to express.

I began to understand the reasons for Alexandro's poverty; it was a product of his own idea of himself, of how he saw himself in relation to the town. His father was the political lieutenant of the zone, a sort of combined judge, sheriff, prosecuting attorney, and jailer. Alexandro hated his father, but at the same time he felt himself to be one of the aristocratic families, and for this reason there were certain types of work that he could not consider. He would not work with a machete, for instance. "I am not a machete man," he said with dignity

when I asked him why he didn't work with some of the younger
guys as a day laborer. And when I asked him why he didn't
earn a little money ferrying people across the river, he gave me
a scornful look, as though I were impugning his manhood.

□□

During my first weeks in Río Verde, misunderstandings kept
cropping up when I tried to speak Spanish in the village. Let
me explain: my house had two rooms, all plaster, and a tin roof
designed to collect rain water outside the bedroom window in a
large cement barrel. I not only had the best house but the only
sweet water, since the well in the street pumped brine, and most
of the drinking water had to be hauled down the river in
canoes.

At that time the back room of my house was full of corn and
chickens; they were separated by a narrow aisle in which I had
put my bed. I slept there, rather tentatively, with a flashlight
in one hand and several rocks in the other, the object being to
be forever on tippy-toe alert and to scare the hell out of the
rats when they swaggered in to kill the chicks. We had made a
temporary deal, the rats and I; they could eat the corn as long
as they left the chicks alone and as long as they entered nicely,
in sedate twos and threes rather than as an unruly, brawling,
bickering mob.

Río Verde was a seacoast town, and there wasn't a house, of
course, that wasn't cursed with rats. A bamboo wall was no
challenge at all; a good self-respecting rat could walk through
one without slowing down. I had awakened several times, my
flesh crawling, with rats running across my legs or over my
arms, and the kids told me that they must wash their hands
after having eaten fish or the rats would chew on their fingers
while they slept.

For whoever might come to visit me from the outside, I had

borrowed another bed; it sat in my front room ready for instant occupation. I sometimes wished it were used more often, and apparently I was not the only one. I was talking to Jorge Avila after supper one evening out on the dock, where we would go to sit on benches, watch the sunset, and receive the first cool night winds from the ocean. Jorge was about twenty-one, unemployed along with everyone else in town; he made a few sucres carrying passengers across the river in his father's canoe or, at low tide, hauling tins of water to the different houses. Jorge was a nice guy, not funny and flashy like many of the young men, but very quiet, very stolid. He was invisible in a crowd, but when he got you alone he rambled on endlessly and earnestly in an incomprehensible flood of soft words. He spoke a very bad, lazy, coastal Spanish, made more than usually liquid by the absence of two front teeth.

"And isn't it sad for you, sleeping alone in that big house?" he asked me.

"No, it's not so bad," I said. "I sleep very *tranquilo*."

"But those bandits, those rats," he insisted. "It must be very bad being alone in the night when the rats come."

"Well, yes, I don't like the rat part very much."

"You need a companion," Jorge said. "Someone to sleep in the house with you, to keep you company."

"Yes, Jorge," I said, "that's what I need all right."

But it became apparent after about an hour that we were not talking about the same thing, because at eight o'clock, bedtime, as we were walking back down the street, Jorge called his brother over and told him that I was sad and that he was going to sleep in the house with me.

"Good," little brother Ricardo said. "I'll go get Jesús."

"Well, now look," I said. "I'm not *that* sad."

"It's no trouble at all," Jorge said. "It's sad to live alone, and we can be your companions and talk."

"And furthermore," Ricardo said, "I have never slept in a bed and have a great desire to sleep in one."

"You're a savage brute," Jorge said. "I have slept in a bed many times; once at the school in Conocoto I slept in a bed for more than a month."

Now, I can reconstruct this conversation; but at the time much of it was conjectural. I wasn't completely sure that I understood them—or whether they were serious if I *did* understand them. I finally left them talking in the street, went into the house, and got ready for bed. Getting ready for bed involved no more than watering the chicks, putting a kerosene lamp in their sleeping quarters, and pounding on the floor several times with a large stick to let the rats know that the old boy upstairs was still moving around vigorously.

I lay down just about the time there was a knock on the door. When I opened it, Jorge, Jesús, and Ricardo solemnly filed in and matter-of-factly marched across the room and stretched out on the spare bed. They all pretended to be very sleepy, yawning elaborately, but long after I had gone into the back room with the chickens and the rats, I could hear them talking. Mostly they were analyzing the fine quality of the bed and exclaiming over its great comfort—a bed made of wooden slats covered with a petate of woven vines. I woke up once and Jorge was telling them about his month in Conocoto and about the tremendous buildings in Quito—at least, that's what I think he was talking about—Jorge, the traveler to distant parts.

How any of them slept, I'll never know. Two of the kids were fully grown, and Ricardo, sort of a runty type, was fifteen years old; the bed was slightly larger than an army cot. But there they were in the morning, curled up like young fox cubs. I sat drinking the three or four cups of coffee I need to face another day, and one by one they awoke and drifted out of the house.

I thought that was the end of it until that night at bedtime when there was a knock on the door, and Jorge—very shy, very sweet—appeared, with a row of faces dimly visible in the darkness behind him.

"I've got Miguel and Ernesto this time," he said. "And of course, my brother, Ricardo; we've come to keep you company for the sadness of the rats."

"Thank you very much," I told him, beginning to laugh hysterically, "but, truly, there isn't room for four of you, and furthermore I'm not sad any more. I think you scared the rats away last night."

I closed the door on four disappointed, unbelieving faces, and instead of going to bed, I studied Spanish verbs for half an hour.

Some people have a special feeling of accommodation when it comes to learning a foreign tongue; other people will forever blunder and stutter drunkenly, unable to make that first decisive change-over, to begin thinking in the language they are learning. I am one of the slow ones who hears a word a hundred times before it clicks into place.

For instance, Alexandro had a wild four-year-old daughter who was always showing off. "Grosera" the parents kept calling her; I thought it was her name. "Good morning, little Grosera," I'd say, only slightly put off when they called one of the boys "Grosero" from time to time. Then one day, in a brilliant burst of illumination, I realized that the word was sort of like "gross." Sure enough, in the dictionary *"grosera"* turned out to be a lout, a rude, crude, unpolished person.

Another example of my facility with Spanish: in Ecuador an introduction is a rather formal moment. You are presented to an Ecuadorian, who nicely says that he is absolutely enchanted to meet you and that he is at your service—*a sus órdenes*. For months I simply acknowledged these gracious speeches of pleasure by mumbling over and over, "*Mucho gusto, Señor, mucho gusto.*" But later, bloated with a self-confidence that had no basis in reality, I began to reply with a few gracious comments of my own. "*A su servicio,*" I would say, smiling brightly and shaking my new friend's hand. "*A su servicio,*" at your service. Someone drew me aside one day and pointed out very discreetly that if I were saying anything at all, I was only offering a toast, "Here's to your bathroom," and that in many cases, particularly if the man had no bathroom, I might conceivably be treading on sensitive nerve endings.

The best, the only way to learn Spanish, everyone in the Peace Corps agreed, was to live in a village where only Spanish was spoken. Then as a matter of simple survival the words and phrases would live and harden in the mind. Up to a point it was true; in no time at all I could express the fundamentals. "To me it is very friendly and rich this fish them," I would say in impeccable Spanish, receiving a dazed smile of appreciation from my hostess. Or out on a jungle trail I had only to say, "I am almost dead of the drys and have somewhat of a great yearning for a wet thing," and from the nearest palm a coconut appeared, its top cut away to reveal the fresh, sweet milk.

But after I had polished up these fundamentals of survival, a basic frustration of communication still remained. I could only go so far with smiles, titters, slaps on the back, little grunts of amazement and pleasure, happy foot stampings and soft-shoe shuffles. This was fine for those superficial relationships that formed on a bus or in a store, but for the long haul—for the friendships which began to grow in my own village, in the house where I ate my meals, with the kids who swam with me almost every day—this inability to talk easily and deeply about ideas, convictions, prejudices was an infuri-

ating thing. For we were, of course, very curious about one
another, and we wished to probe each other to our own limits.

The limits of curiosity in some cases didn't go very deep.
Most of the housewives in the village were fanatically interested mainly in the number of clothes I sent each week to the
señora's to be washed, and they were scandalized by the number
of cigarettes I smoked, but this was just the usual small-town
stuff. It was slightly flattering to be so closely observed and to
be the object of such intense interest until I realized that I was
set apart, separated from the true life of the town. I had come
to show them my best side, and this was what they wanted to
show me, too. About the time the bad side started showing
through—the hatred between particular families, the jealousies between disenchanted friends, my awareness of the town
alcoholics—my own bad side was also coming to the front. And
when the kids started pounding on my door at five in the morning bumming paint for their tops, it was impossible not to use
my wonderful new word and yell "*Groseros!*" at them through
the still-locked door.

At the same time there would always exist a separation.
After forty-five years Mister Swanson was still a gringo. Everyone knew how many beers he drank each day, how he made
love, what he said the last time his son came to see him. You
were separated by the color of your skin, that sickly paleness
that in this country was so ugly as to be embarrassing. You
were separated by your lousy Spanish, by the typewriter that
sat on your table or the camera you sometimes packed around;
you were separated from many by the simple fact that on the
day you arrived you had the carpenter make you a bed—sleeping on a bed of wooden slats somehow indicated refinement, real
sensibility. Even the fact that you didn't eat those horrible
baked or boiled platanos with every meal set you apart and
made a sort of freak of you.

When Alexandro's wife introduced me to her mother, she said, "This is Don Martín; he won't eat platano or yuca; he drinks two cups of coffee with every meal and smokes innumerable cigarettes." And the older woman, too amazed even to acknowledge the introduction, simply sat there slack-jawed trying to visualize a man who wouldn't eat platano. It was just too unbelievable. All through the meal she squatted in one dark corner of the room watching me drink two cups of coffee, muttering to herself.

Occasionally, more often that it would seem possible, someone—a friend—would begin to appear out of the crowds of people with whom I lived and worked. There came a time when I realized that someone regarded me as just another human being rather than as an exotic curiosity. It was always miraculous when it happened. It was a break-through, a transcending of all the things that made us look at each other strangely or suspiciously.

We had been trained in the Peace Corps to see through, a little way at least, that cultural veneer to the common humanity that binds us together, but no one in Río Verde had had that training. We were trained to give of ourselves, we were trained to overlook or partially understand the eccentricities of an alien culture. I don't remember that anything was ever said about receiving this same understanding.

"I think you're a good man; let's be brothers," Ramón Prado, the young fisherman, said to me as we sat eating oranges and talking by candlelight on a night of profound darkness, and it was said so naturally, so sweetly, that for a second the room actually blazed with light.

"Yes," I said, extremely moved, "let's be brothers."

But I wanted to say more; I felt deprived, almost idiotic, for it was a moment of great seriousness for both of us. "Yes, let's be brothers." For the time being, at any rate, that's all I had to know how to say; it was enough.

◻◻

My first weeks in Río Verde I talked to everyone in town and went up and down the beach blowing off to the tobacco farmers. and the fishermen about chickens. They are the most expensive meat in Ecuador at forty cents a pound. With all the cheap corn and fish and a perfect climate, it seemed that the best way to dazzle the local people with the brilliance of the Peace Corps was to get some successful chicken projects going. There was enthusiasm for the idea of chickens, but the initial cost of bamboo, roof thatching, nails, and lumber represented almost prohibitive investments. I had a hundred chickens living in my bedroom; it would be time soon to distribute them, and so far there wasn't a single chicken coop in town.

I was sitting in my house drinking morning coffee when my new brother, Ramón, stopped by to visit. He was carrying a paddle.

"Where are you going?" I asked him.

"Up the river," he said. "I've been thinking and thinking about what you told us; I'm going up the river to buy bamboo. I've talked the whole thing over with my wife. If you'll draw me the plans for a *gallinero* I've decided to go in the chicken business."

Ramón was my first real live customer, the first guy in town with enough faith in me to take a chance. "Good," I said. "That's great. I'll even help you build it; I'll donate the nails. Now tell me, what kind of chickens do you want, for eggs or for meat?"

He thought that over for a while and then very gravely told me, "About half and half, I think."

"That's a good idea," I said. "We'll have to divide the house down the middle. Then you can see which type makes the most money for you. Now, as I told you, the main thing is that you have enough money for a balanced ration. Without a balanced ration, without protein, this whole new system is worthless."

"Yes, I understand," he said.

"They have to have milled corn, fish meal, and a vitamin supplement."

"Exactly," Ramón said.

"Good. Now how many chickens do you think you can afford to raise? We have to make the *gallinero* big enough, two and one half square feet for each chicken."

"Yes," Ramón said. "I want to do everything just right. I think I can handle six chickens—three for meat and three for eggs."

God, how I loved Ramón in that moment, for his innocence and for his honesty and for the modesty of his ambitions.

Just because I was Ramón's brother didn't, I discovered, make me a member of the family. Orestes, Ramón's oldest brother, started to hang around the house in the evenings. He was darkly silent and brooding around me, suspicious of the projects I talked about, half under the spell, I think, of the *Policía Rural,* who was convinced that I was an FBI spy and who, Ramón told me, was preaching this conviction in the town. "I don't know what is here, but there is something here, some great richness, some great national treasure, for why else would an *Americano* come to live in a town like this?"

Orestes was a *mocho*, someone who has lost part of his body —an arm, a leg, or, in the case of Orestes, his fingers. "Mocho" was one of his nicknames, a name he loathed. He had never become reconciled to the maiming of his right hand, and this loss, perhaps more than anything, had poisoned his whole way of looking at life. Life for Orestes was pretty lousy, and so were all the people in it.

The day after Ramón went up the river for bamboo Orestes came to my house and said he wanted chickens, too. Unlike Ramón, who spoke with charm, Orestes was as blunt and clear as a bulldozer; he didn't know how to ingratiate himself with anyone and probably would have scorned such tactics. I drew up some plans for him, and he listened intently as I explained the spaces between the bamboo, but I was uncomfortable with him still and didn't offer to help him in the construction.

As he was leaving, he turned and showed me a face tight and drawn with some deep feeling of deprivation. "You have to help me build it, too," he said, not looking into my eyes. "You're going to help Ramón; you have to help me too."

"*Encantado*," I said. Enchanted. "Whenever you're ready, tell me."

"And is it true that you are buying the nails for Ramón?"

"Yes," I said. "I told Ramón I'd get the nails."

"Then I want you to buy me nails, too," he said staring bleakly at a spot on the floor.

It was amazing to compare the faces of the two brothers, faces which were almost identical in their features, and find such disparate qualities. Ramón's face was all delight, quickness, light. His humor was constant and a real part of his way of seeing things; life was a great joke in spite of everything. He was like a trick pony, quick on his legs, volatile, a real prancer. Orestes was a work horse. There wasn't a trick in him; he was built for the long pull. His sense of humor, unlike Ramón's, which was a bubbling over of youth and optimism (and many times quite foolish), was black, bitter, and profound. Everyone in town laughed with Ramón, he was so quick and lightly mocking. But no one laughed when Orestes spoke. His humor was much deeper and cutting. A couple of months after we built the chicken coops, when Orestes realized that I thought his jokes were something quite special, he began to like me. It was always hard to tell with Orestes, but it's almost impossible to dislike someone who thinks your jokes are belly-busters.

Finally the first one hundred Heifer–Peace Corps chickens were ready to sell to the farmers. I charged only for the feed and the vaccine that I had used raising them up to six weeks— about twenty-seven cents each. The magnificent squawkers weighed well over a pound, and after living in the same room with me they were extremely lovable creatures, although sort of domineering. I had enjoyed the close relationship, but I was glad to see them go. A few of them had seemed determined to peck my eyes out and had perched on the edge of my bed in the early mornings waiting for me to wake up. Wise to their tricks, I would lie there, eyes tightly shut, and think about Alfred Hitchcock.

Over a period of about three days the farmers arrived with baskets, and we loaded them up, each farmer picking out particular birds that he wanted in his flock. Finally, except for about six hundred pounds of chicken shit in my bedroom, nicely mixed with balsa shavings from the mill upstream, everything turned tranquil and placid around the house. I had kept the bottom chicken in the pecking order, a scrawny bird named Condor, and he continued to live in the house with me. He was the sweetest chicken I ever knew, a true friend who would wail and cry whenever I left him alone, and rush into my arms when called, moaning with ecstasy. Every kid in town wanted Condor, and finally the pressure was too great; I gave him to Miguel, my favorite, who built a special chicken house for him on a high bluff overlooking the ocean.

I had browbeaten Ramón into building a house for twelve
chickens, but he was a little nervous starting out so big. I got a
terrific pleasure out of working with Ramón because he was so
enchanted with the things we built. His chicken house looked
the same as everyone else's, but he never tired of talking about

how beautiful it was, how much prettier than the others. I visited him three days after he had taken the chickens home and found that he had made little balsa-wood shades for the feed and water. He and his wife Ester spent their free time petting the chickens and lifting each one up to exclaim over its great weight.

I visited the other chicken projects, and there seemed to be no problems. This was a relief, because a week before the distribution the local chickens running free and wild in the town had all come down with cholera and most of them were dead. Nobody was worrying about the gringo chickens catching cholera because "they were vaccinated chickens." When I explained that they were vaccinated only against Newcastle and not cholera, there was no reaction. Nothing could happen to those great-footed, magnificent creatures.

Everything was fine for a couple of weeks, and then Ramón rushed into town one morning to tell me that one of his chickens was picking all the tail feathers out of the others. He was very worried. Some of the chickens had bloody rear ends. "You'll have to separate the chicken right away," I told him. He went home and put the outlaw chicken in the house, tied by a piece of vine to the leg of a stool. The next morning he was back; another chicken in the group was madly pecking out tail feathers.

"Don't panic," I said. "You'll have to separate this one too." Within five days he had separated five chickens; they were tied in the kitchen, outside under palm trees, under the steps. Ramón had a harried look, and he came in one day utterly defeated; all the chickens were pecking each other's tail feathers. "Oh, my God," he said, "I don't want my chickens to die."

I read up on debeaking. We went out and used a red-hot wood chisel to cut and burn a piece of beak from the neurotic creatures. All through the operation Ramón was distraught. I was killing his chickens; I was cutting off too much; I was making them suffer. They looked sort of stupid with their beaks cut off, and I made the mistake of laughing at their appearance. Ramón was furious with me. "You're really enjoying yourself, aren't you?" he would ask me after each hen had gone through her ordeal, giving me the cold glance of total rejection. When we had debeaked ten of the twelve he told me that that was all, meaning, I found out later, that that was all he could stand for one day.

Before that Ramón used to come by the house almost every evening, along with other of my friends, and visit for a few minutes, but he didn't show up for several days. He sat in the doorway of his *salón* across the street, tilted against the wall, staring at the palm trees. On some days he probably didn't sell more than half a dozen cigarettes and a *Siete Oop*—which means Seven Up, just in case your Castilian is a little rusty. I would stop by to ask him about the chickens, but he was in a depression, a sort of shock, and he would begin his sentences with expressions like, "If it is God's will." The chickens weren't eating, he told me. How could they, poor creatures? "And you're right, they are sort of ugly."

"But almost every chicken in the United States is debeaked," I said. "Just keep more feed in the bamboo."

"All they eat is the corn, the poor little ones; they can't eat the concentrate, it's too fine."

"You'll have to grind the corn finer, is all."

"Yes, I'll grind it finer; perhaps, God willing, they will learn to eat."

The next day Ramón arrived at the house very early in the morning to tell me that the chickens were very nervous and that some of them were going, "Squawk, squawk," and turning around in circles. We went out and watched the chickens. They seemed perfectly normal, but some of them were very thin.

"I think it's your imagination," I told him. "In a few days they'll learn how to eat better."

"If God wishes," Ramón said, sadly.

That afternoon the first of the chickens died, and the next day two more died. We had a long conference at the chicken house; we doubled the Terramycin, changed the waterers, ground up new corn with new concentrate. I pointed out a crack in the roof to be fixed. "They have to sleep dry," I told him sternly. "I think they have cholera."

"Vaccinated chickens with cholera," Ramón said. "No, my poor babies are starving to death."

The next night, after all the farmers had left the house, Ramón came to talk; the fourth chicken had just died. "Before you came," he said, "well, you know how poor I was; I had nothing. But I was happy; I lived without worries. But now. My God, I am half crazy with worry." His voice broke and great tears swam in his eyes. "Oh, my poor chickens," he said. "Oh, I don't want them to die."

I had talked to him before about how little by little he could increase his flock; I had told him that I hoped one day he would have one hundred chickens. Now, he said, this plan was terrifying. "I think it is God's will that I not have chickens," he told me. "It may even be God's will that I always live poorly, but now I think I will just raise the pair of pigs that you have promised to bring me and not have chickens."

"You can't let four lousy chickens wreck your life," I told him. "I don't think God is involved in this business; you have to consider this experience as a valuable lesson and keep trying."

"No one else has sick chickens," Ramón said. "Only this ignorant, brute *zambo* has sick chickens."

I had to go to Quito for seeds and chicken concentrate, and I talked to my boss, Eduardo Sotomayor, about the problem. Eduardo decided to take me back to Río Verde and look things over. As we walked up the beach with Ramón to look at the chickens, I asked Eduardo to give a good inspirational talk in Spanish about "if at first you don't succeed," etc. Eduardo was magnificent, and Ramón listened intently, impaled on eloquence.

"Did I cut off too much beak?" I asked Eduardo at the chicken house.

"You could have cut off even more," Eduardo said.

"Tell Ramón in Spanish," I said. "He doesn't believe me; he thinks I ruined his chickens."

"But it's not the beaks that's wrong; the birds had cholera."

"Tell Ramón in Spanish," I said. "Tell him in your beautiful, clear Spanish so that he understands perfectly."

Eduardo took the last of the sick chickens back to Quito and sent me the results of the lab report—cholera. Passing Ramón's house a few days later I stopped a minute to talk to Ester. Ramón's seven chickens were eating and dancing around. "Ramón just left," she told me. "He was cutting off the beaks of a couple of chickens that you missed before."

That night Ramón came by the house and apologized for the long doubts he had had about me. "I want to get started right away on the new chicken house," he said. "I'd like to buy forty-three of the new chickens to make an even fifty, and then after the corn is planted, build another chicken house. By June, God willing, I will have one hundred chickens. You know what I'm going to buy when I am rich?" he said, beginning to laugh with delight at the idea. "A pair of shoes. Oh, my God. My God."

□□

For months I fought the urge to write about my personal war with the food in Río Verde, an urge which gradually took an obsessional turn. I didn't write about it at first because, well, at first, I couldn't believe it; and then later I became too intensely involved with my stomach and was afraid that I might say some things that would sound self-pitying. Not that I hadn't had my self-pitying moments.

When you sit down to the table and are given three soda biscuits and a cup of instant coffee for supper, you at first want to break down and cry like a baby and later, if you are strong enough, begin stamping your little feet on the floor in baby rage. What stops you is the knowledge that not only in your village but in villages all over the world there are families who are eating less than you, if they are eating at all.

Peace Corps Volunteers enter their new country so well briefed by their doctors on the hazards of the local foods that their first meals are terror-stricken experiences, gastronomic tightrope performances balanced between starvation and revulsion. This is probably an unfair generalization, but at any rate it describes my own personal difficulties. On my first day in Río Verde I made arrangements to eat lunch and supper with Alexandro; what we had was invariably the same at lunch—fish soup cooked in coconut juice and a pile of rice with a pile of fish on top. For supper we had a pile of fish with a pile of rice on top, or sometimes a scrambled egg cooked with pieces of crab meat. I was paying twenty-five cents a meal.

Then one day, if I am to believe Alexandro, the fish in the Pacific Ocean stopped biting, and they hadn't appeared on the table in any quantity for about four months. Instead of fish and rice, we were tucking away *aba* soup, and rice with *abas*, *abas* being a large, fat, tasteless bean about 200 per cent blander than a lima bean. The evening meal became more and more spiritual. A dozen or so times I staggered over to Alexandro's house, ravenous with hunger and anticipation, to find that supper was one well-centered and naked fried egg cowering on the plate. What made even this more or less tasteless was my knowledge that it was the only egg in the house and that the rest of the family was supping on cups of hot water and brown sugar and platano, an enormous, banana-like monstrosity, about 99 per cent starch, which was as tasteless as paper. Eating the only egg in the house while the youngest child slowly wasted away from malnutrition didn't help things either.

And yet, at the same time I did feel put upon. I was paying my twenty five cents for a fried egg that in the store was worth four cents, and I felt as I picked my way back home, where I surreptitiously boiled three or four eggs and consumed a half-dozen oranges, that Alexandro was a pretty poor manager. What was happening, of course, was that the fifty cents a day I paid for my meals was feeding the whole family, and probably even paying off a few old bills.

Alexandro's job taking the malaria teams up the river had ended two months earlier. The teams had begun to use a flat-bottomed boat with an outboard motor instead of the canoe, and they covered the same territory in one-third the time. And so, after working with them for five or six years, Alexandro was superfluous. He had no income except three or four dollars a month that I paid his wife for having my clothes systematically beaten to death on rocks—plus the twenty-five cents a day that I paid him for lunch. Out of desperation, I had planted a garden, blatantly stealing a package of CARE seeds, and started cooking my own supper. Two facts besides the shortage of fish in the Pacific helped force me to this change of plan— the orange season ended abruptly, and a cholera epidemic killed almost every chicken in town.

I would eat little gourmet snacks by candlelight, alternating between fried rice made almost palatable with onion, green peppers, and a smidgen of McCormick's best curry powder one night and chard, squash, radishes, and fried eggs the next night, both meals washed down with a quart of beer. On the fried-rice nights, Ricardo would stand outside my door whistling Ecuadorian love songs to let me know that he was there in case I had fried more rice than I could handle. On the vegetable nights he was nowhere to be found, having decided that chard and squash were food fit only for rabbits and that radishes were not even fit for animals.

Well, I had made a sort of separate peace by then, and many of those stomach-churning things that I had stared at on my plate had come to seem pretty good. I couldn't understand how five months earlier I had had to force myself to drink coconut milk, a drink much more satisfying than the Pepsi I had been putting away before. But on my first horseback trips into the farming country I was given food and drink so strange, so unfamiliar, that I simply couldn't hack it. I would be really hungry or thirsty, and I would stand staring at this offered cup of stuff, perhaps a cup filled with a green, pulpy, seedy mixture, completely new, and I would talk to myself as everyone watched me. "Now look, big boy, you are going to drink that cup of whatever it is, and you are going to drink it to the dregs, and you are going to smile doing it." And, absolutely determined, I would lift the cup to my lips. My mouth would simply refuse to cooperate; I would tilt the cup and the stuff would run and dribble down my face, the throat muscles in a sort of paralysis and the mouth in complete revolt. The same thing had happened at Bozeman, Montana, with an Ecuadorian agronomist who had come up to help us in our Peace Corps training. American food simply revolted him; his throat muscles became permanently paralyzed, and he ended up in the hospital being fed intravenously.

Along the river I had seen poor bloodied sloths, tied to the bamboo houses, waiting to be eaten; and farther back the people talked about monkey meat, parrots, *noopa* (a great fat snake), iguana, and other inappropriate foods. For three days I ate at lunch the meat of an animal called the *juanta,* all of the time insanely questioning Alexandro trying to find out what the hell it was. Bill Deane, a Volunteer from Santo Domingo, finally told me that it was something like an enormous rat, "but really fine meat," and another gringo said it was more like a cross between a rabbit and a hedgehog.

You draw your lines and you say, "I will go this far," but it ends up that you are always drawing new ones. God knows, perhaps in another year I would have smacked my lips over barbecued snake or toasted monkey on a stick. But I doubt it; my lines were pretty well extended. And the truth is that I felt relatively sophisticated. We used to discuss in training how to be nice and gracious while refusing a drink that we knew had been prepared with unboiled river water and was probably swarming with wriggly gringo-killers. But it never occurred to us to wonder what to do when, after several hours on the trail, you get so thirsty that you don't give a damn what kind of a wriggly animal you are swallowing as long as it is a wet one.

□□

From the beginning the garden I planted next to my house to keep from starving to death was an area of fascination for the people in the town. While planting it I had visualized the garden as a quiet oasis, a secret haven where I would escape to work alone and where at night I would sit alone on a little hand-carved stool, or with perhaps no more than two friends, to drink coffee, relax, and watch the sunset after a day's work in the town; but it immediately became a public institution. I think anyone who has not lived the wholly public life of a foreigner in a small town, where every scratch and belch is noted with fascinated curiosity, cannot realize how essential it is to have a place of refuge where you can hide from time to time and reform yourself.

I hauled reject chunks of balsa wood up from the river beaches and built a fence about eight feet tall, not only chicken-tight but boy-tight, cleverly arranging the pieces so that any small boys climbing over the fence would either be impaled on sharp points or left dangling above ground, caught by the seats of their pants. The really small boys who didn't wear pants or anything else I simply gave up on; they apparently could seep through the cracks in the walls.

One reason I planted the garden was because no one else would plant one. "No one plants anything in the dry season," everyone told me. But what a dry season. About twice a week there were downpours of rain in the night that drummed on the tin roof of the house and gurgled in the water barrel. If this was the dry season I hated to think what the rainy season would be like. As soon as I started spading the ground I realized that the whole idea of gardens was on trial. The balsa chunks would slowly move apart on the street side, and pairs of eyes would appear in the open spaces, sometimes a half-dozen pairs at a time. They had a cynical look to them. On one side of the garden was the empty framework of a house in the process of construction. After school whole bands of children would lie on the beams or swing from the rafters like Christmas tree ornaments, watching me work or asking questions or telling me that it was the dry season and that nobody planted things in the dry season. I would point to the mud puddles in the street and make little superior jokes about how easy it would be to drown here in the dry season, and the children would laugh politely.

I spaded and raked and threw out rocks and weeds. I used string to measure out precise paths between the seedbeds. I made the prettiest garden you ever saw, everything by the book, everything absolutely perfect. And the day after it was planted the clouds moved away from coastal Ecuador, the sun came out with complete seriousness, and it didn't rain a drop for over a month.

It was an embarrassing situation, made doubly embarrassing because at the same time that I was planting the garden I was raising the first bunch of one hundred chickens in my bedroom and many of the people were openly skeptical about the possibility of raising gringo chickens in Ecuador. There was something preposterous about the idea of shipping day-old chickens in cardboard boxes all the way from the United States and expecting them to live more than a day or two. The political chief of the town had appeared in my house one day, openly hostile, and had bluntly told me that chicks raised without mothers to teach them how to scratch would grow up weak and stupid and that they would soon die. "But just in case they do live," he said, "I want two of the roosters to put in with my flock."

I explained that I couldn't sell him any chickens if he didn't first build a raised chicken house to keep them in, that my primary business wasn't selling chickens but trying to teach new and better ways to raise them. "Do you seriously believe," Segundo asked me, "that as a complete stranger to this country you can come walking in here where we have been raising chickens all our lives and tell us how to do it better?"

"Yes, exactly," I said, "that's the whole idea."

"Ay, *caramba*," he said, shaking his head and marching out the door. The great political chief to the very end.

A couple of hours later his son, a friend of mine, came to the house. He had obviously been sent. "I hope in the interest of peace that you can see your way clear to sell my father a pair of roosters," he said.

"Quite a few people want chickens," I explained, "but

hardly anyone is building chicken houses. If I sell your father chickens without a house to put them in everyone is going to say that only the poor people have to build chicken houses."

He thought that over for a moment and nodded his head. But a week later the town was divided between those who had a blind, heart-breaking faith that the chickens would make money for them and those who, along with Segundo, said that chickens raised without mothers would die. The chickens were available for everyone to see night and day, and it didn't seem to matter that they were growing like mad, doubling their weight every few days, cackling and flying around the house like a bunch of condors, taking over all the furniture and completely dominating the scene with their brute health.

Meanwhile back at the ranch I was watching the ground in the garden dry up with a growing dismay. Certainly I had rushed ahead, trying to prove how easy it was to grow vegetables when I should have been listening. But a couple of nice inspirational things happened. On the third day after planting and in what appeared to be completely dry earth my two rows of radishes exploded out of the ground. The other thing: whenever I washed or brushed my teeth I very carefully poured the old water over the dry rows, and wherever I had sprinkled a few drops, the seeds began to appear, first the squash, cucumbers, and sunflowers.

So, when no one was looking, I began to go up and down the rows with a bucket of water, and in a short time all the seeds had sprouted—all except the lettuce. The lettuce appeared very tentatively, took one horrified look at the Ecuadorian sun blazing in the sky, and promptly died from shock. I had one lettuce plant growing in the shade of the fence, a real seedy-looking character. On very still nights, when all the dogs and radios had been turned off, I imagined I could hear the poor thing moaning outside my window. "Salinas, Salinas," it said.

The water in my barrel lasted about four days, and then I had to buy it in five-gallon cans from Ricardo, who hauled it from the river at low tide or from the community tank. Cost, about a penny a gallon. The needs of the garden steadily increased, but I was committed to the damned thing and had to keep it growing. There were some farmers who were peeking between the spaces in the fence a half-dozen times a day. I watered the rows in late evening with a flashlight so that not everyone would know that I was being bankrupted. Finally, one night, percussion by Varèse on the roof, a beautiful sound; I went out and stood in the rain and watched the squash grow.

To my disappointment there was no rush to plant gardens after mine turned out to be so beautiful. The sad fact is that hardly anyone liked radishes, chard, or squash. As for the okra, well, I agreed with the town—okra was inedible. They waited to see how the tomatoes and green peppers would turn out.

I had made two trips into Chungillo to talk to the schoolteacher, Oswaldo Estupiñan, about a school garden. Oswaldo was the most enthusiastic of the local teachers, and the only one who wanted to plant a garden in the middle of the dry season. On my last trip I had left a few seeds and several pages of instructions on seed spacing written in my own unique and baffling Spanish. A couple of weeks later, when Oswaldo was passing through Río Verde, I gave him a CARE school-garden kit that had been entrusted to me by the CARE office in Quito —a shovel, a hoe, a rake, a fork, and three smaller scratching tools.

A short time later wild rumors of a fantastic school garden began to drift out of the jungle. The Chungillo kids who were in Río Verde to buy rice or kerosene would come by the house to learn another English word or to look at my chickens, and they would tell me about the enormous tomatoes, eggplants, beets, chard, and radishes that they were turning out. "The tomatoes are this big," they would say in awed tones, their eyes as big as tomatoes and the form made by their hands the size of a cantaloupe.

Actually, I was somewhat griped by the phenomenal success of this garden, since I had done so little to bring it about. I felt guilty about having neglected the place, but I had been busy around Río Verde building bamboo chicken houses and working with a school on a river to the north. Another more honest reason: I hated the trip to Chungillo and always found an excuse for putting it off. It was only three hours by horseback, but for an hour you rode through high pasture grass swarming with ticks, *garrapatas*. After every trip my ankles would be solid, bloody, itching sores. If you saw someone on the street in Río Verde roll up his pants legs and begin to examine himself minutely, you could be pretty sure that the fellow had just arrived from Chungillo.

At any rate, I finally ran out of excuses, and one day when Oswaldo was in Río Verde he promised to send me a horse and I promised to come galloping back to his school. I arrived, scratching, one Wednesday afternoon. Oswaldo moved his things out of his room and gave me the bed, and while I rested his mother stirred up a tremendous salad of beets, onions, tomatoes, and carrots—all out of the garden—along with the usual company chicken and rice. It was the best meal I had seen for weeks, and I was ravenous for vegetables. I overlooked the menace of the unpeeled tomatoes and ate so much that I completely captured the heart of the good *señora*, who after that first meeting was unable to talk with me without holding my arm tightly and softly pinching me all over, testing the state of my health.

I never could figure out why Chungillo existed. There was a

school with about sixty students, and two or three small houses. A little creek, the Río Mate, in this dry season ran brown and sluggish at the bottom of a ravine behind the school, and across the creek a hill of about ten acres swelled up out of the country-side, covered with enormous trees, each one, I think, a different variety. We sat on the school veranda one afternoon as a cloudburst moved down the hill. For sheer emotional impact, the sound of the raindrops striking the leaves of the trees like drums and moving slowly closer to a shattering climax of sound beat hollow all the works of Beethoven; it was the voice of God —and He wasn't exceedingly pleased.

It was true about the garden; it was a fine one, a little past its prime but still producing well. The problem was that most of the vegetables were strange to the people. The radishes, for instance, were the size of tennis balls. "Just about ready to harvest, I think," Oswaldo told me proudly. The eggplants were enormous, but no one knew what they were for. I took some up to the kitchen and fried them, but they had an ominous look like the spooky parts of strange animals, and everyone nibbled at them apprehensively. The summer squash, too, had reached its peak a month before and was now quite inedible. The string beans were dead and drying on the vines. I argued with Oswaldo for five minutes about the necessity of harvesting the beans when they were young and tender, but when he realized that the whole bean was supposed to be eaten he simply refused to listen to me. "This is a civilized country," he told me. "Here we eat only the good part, the heart of the fruit."

Thursday and Friday we worked in the garden, and the usual problem arose. The CARE tools are fine tools, but they are designed for kids who wear shoes. A barefoot boy cannot spade ground, it is impossible. I asked Oswaldo to send me one boy at a time for thirty minutes, and each kid put on one of my boots while I worked with the other. This was a big deal for some of them who had never worn shoes, and they strutted and stumbled in the clods or stood immobilized staring at their shod foot, speechless—whether with admiration or terror I could not tell, although a size ten boot on a size five foot does contain certain aspects of terror, even for me.

In the afternoons the whole school turned out to work in the garden, preparing seedbeds and hauling water up from the river. It was an amazing performance, and I got wonderful insights into the construction of the pyramids. The boys lined up on each side of the seedbeds we had prepared, squatted on their haunches, and crumbled the clods of dirt into a mulch with their hands; and the girls, with gourds that held about a quart of water, trooped up and down from the river in an endless line.

I had told the kids that I was anxious to buy the pre-Incan figures that were always turning up in the river or being discovered on the farmland, and Friday morning school had to be delayed for an hour while I dickered with each kid who had brought in something—a little frog, a pipe made into a face, a whistle in the shape of a very pregnant woman, or the fragments of statues. I gave a final English lesson to one boy who was worried that when he reached the United States he would die of hunger unless he learned how to order a meal. "Give me chicken soup" was what I had taught him to say when we were working alone in the garden, and as I rode off the whole school gathered on the playground to say good-by. "Give me chicken soup," they all yelled as I disappeared into pasture grass eight feet tall and began to itch and scratch.

▣▣

By any standard the town of Río Verde could only be described as depressed. I don't think life had ever been very easy there, though during the war years a balsa sawmill operated at the mouth of the river, the price of bananas was high, and the wild rubber trees back in the hills brought in a supply of cash. Everyone worked for the foreign companies. There was pork on the table and the gringo bosses bought up all the chickens in the country, paying the unheard of price of two dollars apiece. There were fine fiestas; Saturday nights were something to write home about. A few exceptional people saved their money and bought farms, but even the most thoughtless were earning around seventy-five cents a day, and they were wild with this flood of cash; there was simply no way to spend it.

They told the story of the old baker who sold bread in those flush times and who left rich. He was the guy whose house I rented. He made most of his profit, they said, by being unable to make change. If he were handed a five-sucre bill for four sucres' worth of bread, he never had change, but it didn't matter; the people were rich and mad for bread.

By 1965 there was nothing; no sawmill, no bananas, no rubber. The banana planting had been turned into pastures, and the acres that once employed a hundred workers now employed perhaps six or seven. The economic mechanics of exist ence was something that I simply could not figure out. Just exactly from where did X get the sucres to buy rice and sugar, or Y, the town alcoholic, the sucres to sit forlornly on the little porch of the *salón* by the pier, drinking *aguardiente* day after day?

Saturday nights were still frequently something to write home about. How these celebrations were financed I guess I will never know, though I got a hint one Sunday morning when I met Duco wandering up and down the street trying to sell the shirt off his back for a few more hours of illusion. At first I was bitter about Saturday nights, not only because of the tireless insistence of the *salón*'s phonograph playing its dozen or so raucous *Colombianos* over and over until six in the morning,

but because of the shock of knowing that Jorge, who on Friday
night had asked me for a piece of bread for his dinner, on Saturday night was very happily sipping *puro* and dreamily
dancing boleros all by himself. There was something immoral
about it; I couldn't believe that the music was really gay, or
that the laughter in the street was really happy, or that the
people could so easily forget their poverty or invest their
sucres in a few hours of forgetfulness, knowing that on Sunday
there would be nothing to eat.

"What in the hell have they got to be so happy about?" I
would think, stuffing the pillow over my ears. "Boy, if I were a
Río Verdenian I would be in perpetual mourning, I would dress
in pure black like the Cañaris for the poverty of this place."

It took me some months of plain living to understand the
necessity for a Saturday night, and to realize that drinking
beer or *aguardiente* in a sad little *salón*, talking and arguing,
four or five friends around a candle, was a real peak of excitement and release in a week of suffocating and crushing monot-
ony. I didn't realize that I had realized this truth until one
night when, after about five quarts of beer, I found myself
enthusiastically dancing the bolero with a bunch of my friends,
farmers and fishermen. Or rather they were trying to teach me
how to dance some Ecuadorian steps which closely resembled in
my befuddled mind a flock of chickens madly scratching for
corn.

I came to Río Verde with the beer-drinking habit, not an
overpowering one but strong enough so that I really looked
forward to a beer with supper, one of the great joys of life.
Ecuadorian beer was very good and cheap; a quart cost about
twenty-five cents, so that even a Peace Corps Volunteer could
afford a bottle every day. But in Río Verde beer was not drunk
moderately or regularly, or with meals. You saved up for a
fiesta or a Saturday night, and then you gave her all you had,

everyone at the table drinking from one bottle out of little
Coke glasses, drinking together in unison, the buyer of the
particular bottle setting the pace.

As a newcomer to the town I decided that drinking beer
every day, simply for the taste, would be ostentatious, and I
gave it up, breaking my pledge at first only two or three times
in moments of depression when I would sneak a quart of the
lukewarm stuff into my house and sit in a dark corner living
a private life. I also avoided the Saturday night blow-outs,
mainly because they didn't look like very much fun, containing
such a burden of desperation and frustration as I had never
known. I was also just a little afraid of the *Policía Rural,* one
of the town's more enthusiastic drinkers, who after a few beers
would walk up and down the street shooting off his revolver
and when he had reached some critical point would be obsessed
with the necessity of throwing someone in jail.

On Saturday nights I was a caricature of a Peace Corps
Volunteer, giving English lessons to the smaller kids while
outside life swirled and pulsed in the streets. The children
would stand it as long as they could and then dash off to join
the fun. Well, anyway, I thought, I must be making a good
impression in the town.

One day I overheard Alexandro apologizing for me to one of
the fishermen. "It's his religion," he was saying. "It is forbidden by his religion."

"What's forbidden?" I asked him later.

"Well, you don't drink," Alexandro said. "You lead a very
sad life, a very unnatural one. You have refused to take a
woman in to cook for you and tend to your needs. Some of the
people think you must be very sad here. I tell them it's your
religion."

The night that I got back from Chungillo, Ramón came over
to my house.

"To celebrate your return we have to have a beer together," he said.

"Good."

"Shall I bring it over here?"

"Sure, if you want to."

"Or perhaps, just possibly, you would like to drink in my *salón?*"

"Yes," I said, "I think I would prefer that."

Ramón went back across the street to his cubbyhole *salón*, and a second later one of the fishermen dashed out, running toward Alvaro's store.

"What's wrong?" someone yelled.

"Nothing. I'm going to buy beer; we're going to drink beer with the *gringito*."

There were four of us drinking beer that night, but outside the ring of light from our candle Ernesto, Orestes, the other Ramón, Miguel, Pancho, and a couple of others stood around watching. Ramón played his records, very loud; the batteries were growing weak, and the music quavered and faltered. We yelled back and forth at each other over the sound of the music, and very steadily we put away the beer. We did it sociably, with the grace and formality of the Ecuadorian manner but with a certain mechanical insistence, the point being, of course, to get the gringo drunk. I came back into the *salón* at one time to find that they had spiked my beer with about half a pint of *aguardiente;* they were amazed and incredulous when I pointed it out.

What saved me was the fact that two of the farmers had a head start on me, and in the general gaiety their plan to test my drinking qualities was all but forgotten. Also, toward the end I had some help from Herman, the schoolteacher, who dropped in about midnight to buy a cigarette and who lingered just outside the candlelight behind me, listening to our talk.

When no one was looking I would hand him my beers, and he would eagerly kill them for me. He did not join our table until much later in the evening when the free beers had completely destroyed his prudence. Herman was from Quito and by far the best educated and most sophisticated man in town, but it seemed to me that he got drunker quicker than anyone else—and philosophic.

"It's a jail, you know, this little town, and what else is there to do at night? You can't read without light. And how many nights can you walk back and forth on the dock? In Esmeraldas there are women to visit or maybe you've got a nice girl you can take to the show. And afterward have an ice cream on the sidewalk and watch the people walking. Here it's just pure darkness, pure jail."

About 1:00 A.M. the dancing lessons started, and about 1:30 I slipped across the street to my house. The next morning, after just a little practice, I discovered that I had mastered another useful Ecuadorian expression—*Estoy con chuchaqui*, I've got a hangover.

◻◻

One night the rainy season arrived with thunder and flourishes of lightning about four feet from the house and with catastrophic cloudbursts of rain. The fifty-gallon rain barrel outside my window filled up in about twenty seconds, the gutters overflowed, pouring water down through the ceiling in a straight line along one end of the kitchen and bedroom, and muddy torrents cut three-foot gullies down the middle of the street. I awoke with slightly fractured eardrums, staggered outside, hauled the rabbits out of their cages, and turned them loose in the house where they hopped around all night terrifying the rats. They made much more noise than the rats ever did, acting completely without restraint, turning over benches, breaking plates, and knocking empty beer bottles off the shelves, but the noise was almost drowned out in the thundering of rain on the tin roof.

The next morning was gray and tranquil, with bunches of fat clouds hanging in the valleys behind the town. But the river was at flood, a deep dirty orange, and loaded down with the trunks of enormous trees that rushed past the town and disappeared out to sea, majestic, half-completed sculptures by Henry Moore. Banana trees, clots of vines, islands of water hyacinth, a couple of canoes without drivers, a dead hog—all floated past at about fifteen miles an hour.

Upstream, there was the constant sound of earth banks crashing into the river. Trees, their roots cut away by the rush of water, leaned and fell into the torrent. On the ocean beaches to the north and south of town the sand was covered with six inches of mud, branches, and dead leaves, and farther to the south, toward Esmeraldas, so much clay from the bluffs was washed onto the beach that the truck was stuck tight for two days.

This first big rain coincided with the three-day high tide that threatened Río Verde every two weeks. And this time it really went to work, tearing out an acre of palm trees, destroying Señor Castro's pineapple garden, and devouring another fifty feet of shore line. The sand barrier at the edge of the beach washed away, and a river of sea water poured down the main street. Watching all this was like watching complete chaos; everything seemed to be getting out of control, the whole shape of the world was changing before my eyes. But when I tried to talk about it, I felt like that sharp-nosed man in the *New Yorker* advertisements who screams disaster while everyone else is reading his copy of the *Philadelphia Bulletin*. No one seemed in the least impressed. "This is nothing," they told me. "Wait until it starts to rain."

But I knew they were kidding because it was obvious that

many days of such rains would wash all of coastal Ecuador into the open sea. After a few days the sun came out, the river slowed down in its gutting operations, and the tides confined themselves to the ocean. Once more you could walk around without feeling that you were watching the creation of the earth, or without half expecting to see a dinosaur sticking his nose out of the steaming jungle growth at the edge of town, or a volcano rising up out of the middle of the plaza to throw hot mud in all directions.

With the ground well soaked, I began to remind the farmers that before no one had wanted a garden because it was too dry. One or two of them pointed out that it was now too wet, but a half dozen or so said they were ready to try anything once. For about ten days I showed the farmers or the farmers' kids how to build raised beds with deep ditches between the rows so the rain water, if it ever rained as hard again, would run off rather than stand in the beds. Some of the gardens inland from the ocean were hacked out of jungle on fairly steep hillside. There, a quarter of a mile or so from the house, where the danger of the chickens eating the seed out of the ground was not a problem, we planted squash, melons, and cucumbers in the sunny spaces by the banana trees; the smaller vegetables like cabbages or carrots we planted in rows.

About a week after everything was planted in a military manner, it *really* began to rain, the kind of a rain that doubled in volume about every two minutes. It reached the point where you would say, "Well, it can't rain any harder than this," and the rain would say, "Oh, yeah?" and double up again. It made that first rain three weeks before seem like a ten-year drought.

It rained for a couple of days, four hours on, four hours off. In the spaces between the rains everyone in town would wade through the streams of water in the main street or in the plaza, where water was pouring off the hill in back of town, looking for pre-Incan gold earrings or nosepieces that washed out of the earth from time to time. The beach was a mess as little dry gullies suddenly began discharging Sacramento Rivers and cutting such high banks across the beach that it was impossible to walk into town at high tide.

The day before this second rain, Ramón and Ester had transplanted a dozen tomato plants in a garden plot that we had spent a day spading. The garden was at the edge of a sleepy little salt lagoon that looked like it had been there forever. When I waded up the beach, dodging breakers, to tell them that they'd better cover the tomato plants with palm leaves, I discovered that the sleepy lagoon was a raging river, and that all the tomatoes, along with two rows of peanuts, had washed away, and that the rest of the garden was about to follow after. Ramón and I stood on the bank, from time to time taking a step backward as the cucumbers and radishes crashed into the river, and Ramón made little philosophical remarks about the bad luck of the poor and questioning the ultimate aims of the Creator.

Going back to town, I joined up with Orestes. "How's your garden?" I asked him.

"What garden?" Orestes snorted. "It all washed away last night, first the seed and then all the dirt."

We stopped at Wai's house and watched him making a shrimp net. "And your garden, Wai? Do you still have one?"

"There's still a couple of melons, I think," Wai said, "but everything else washed away."

And so on.

Gumercindo lost his garden; Teobaldo lost half his garden; Don Julio, who never had much to start with, ended up with three rows of cabbages and one eggplant. Alexandro salvaged one row of twenty-pound radishes, which is about all he had anyway.

And so we bid a fond farewell to the gardens of Río Verde; another Peace Corps project brought to a successful conclusion, teaching the people how to eat better. Once I had showed them how to make gardens, I decided to concentrate on how to grow corn. And the basic problem still remains: if it is too dry in the dry season and too wet in the wet season, just how and when does one make a garden?

▫▫

Don Julio was the aristocrat of Río Verde; he lived across the street from me in a large, plaster-fronted house which looked out over the palm trees to the ocean and from the doors of which poured an inexhaustible stream of tiny grandchildren. Don Julio was about sixty-five, a handsome old boy with curly gray hair and a quiet smile which seemed to suggest that he had put aside the lusts and passions of manhood and was pursuing more satisfying, philosophical goals. He wanted desperately to have serious conversations with me about the agricultural and political problems of Ecuador, but he very politely hid his frustration when I answered him with the blank, stupid stare of incomprehension.

About once a month Don Julio—dressed in black rubber boots, white linen pants, and a tremendous Panama slave-trader's hat—rode off into the jungle for a week or so. He had three farms, one for each of his married sons, and he took turns visiting the farms and keeping things under control. I think, actually, he didn't much care about the farms any more; what he liked was those swarms of grandchildren circling about him.

I had shied away from the sons because they were relatively well off and because they knew more about farming in Ecuador than I did. Two of the sons—Fernando and Julio Junior— looked exactly alike; they had farms up the river about twenty miles, and for several months they had been putting increasing pressure on me to visit them and to give them animals, a situation which became more and more confused because I never knew which son I was talking to and because I wasn't too hot about getting involved with the *"ricos."*

One day Don Julio told me that he was taking the motor canoe up the river to visit one of the farms, that the trip would take about two hours, that the canoe was returning the next morning, and that his son had especially invited me to come along, to see his animals, his corrals, and his chicken facilities. Fine.

The next morning I stuffed some CARE seeds in one pocket and a copy of Carl Sandburg's *Abraham Lincoln, the Prairie*

Years in the other and went down to the wharf. Gradually over
a period of about an hour the boat filled up with sacks of feed,
saddles, and boxes of supplies; Don Julio and his wife; Alfonso, the oldest son; a whole slew of grandchildren; two
women who were going halfway, to Sanduval; Pedro, the manager of the outboard; and two teenaged kids to stand in the
front and look out for snags and shallow water.

Most of the town was gathered on the dock to wave good-by,
and at nine o'clock we cast off. But the motor was slow in
starting, and we rapidly drifted out toward the breakers in the
open sea. About 9:30 we roared past the dock; everyone waved
madly. Around the first bend the motor conked out, and we
drifted out to sea again, past the dock which was still swarming
with waving people. I began to read the life of Lincoln.

Another half hour of tinkering, and the motor came to life
again—but sadly. We pooped and coughed and snorted past
the dock, waving good-by, up around the bend by the old
gringo's deserted sawmill, past the mangrove swamp and the
dead trees where the frigate birds roost. About a mile from
town the motor died, and we anchored in the shade of the river
bank. The boy Lincoln shot a deer and said he would never
again kill anything but birds. He farmed, split rails, took a
raft of farm produce down the Mississippi to New Orleans.

A woman drifted downstream in a canoe with kettles of a
coarse corn custard for sale. But to whom on this stretch of
deserted river? Don Julio bought most of it, and we had lunch.
Custard for the main course, and custard mixed with river water to drink. Lincoln moved to Illinois, wandered the woods,
worked at odd jobs. His friends were backwoods people, hard
drinkers, farmers clearing the forests of hardwood.

At noon we broke down again about five miles from Río
Verde and poled and paddled another half mile to Nelson
Estupiñan's balsa sawmill. We ate bananas and visited with the

workmen in the mill until—wonder of wonders—a banana boat
about twice the size of the *African Queen* appeared. It rammed
into the bank and began to take on reject balsa planks for a
hacendado upstream. We all jumped aboard and went another
five miles to Sanduval—two balsa rafts with stores on them, a
boxing shed for bananas, a school, a scattering of bamboo
houses, and completely dominating everything a large plaster
house—very tall, square, and white, but impressive so far
away.

We had crackers and coffee with the schoolteacher, a sister-
in-law of Don Julio; I planned a school garden with her and
promised CARE tools. We all sat on a long bench above the
stores and waited, for what I had no idea. A large dark canoe
with a coffin in it floated past; eight or nine people stood in the
canoe, a bottle of *aguardiente* sat on top of the coffin.

The country of Lincoln, that hard, coarse, brutal America of
the 1830's, began to mix in my mind with this river settlement,
the floating rafts, the badly fed people in ragged clothing who
were bringing in canoe loads of bananas and staggering up the
muddy banks to the packing shed. A mechanic off the banana
boat, a very drunk albino, sat at a rickety table on one of the
rafts drinking beer and shouting at everyone. Saddled horses
stood motionless in the shade of mango trees; pigs grunted
lazily in mud wallows in the doorways of the houses; chickens
wandered in and out of kitchens pecking at scraps.

Late in the afternoon Pedro and the two kids triumphantly
steamed into port in the motor canoe. We all climbed aboard
and got at least a mile farther up the river before the motor
finally and irrevocably died; it died with such a horrible gasping finality that no one even tried to fix it. We started to
paddle and pole.

We had picked up a banana buyer and *hacendado*, a friend
of Don Julio's who sat in front drinking *aguardiente*. At each

farm along the river he yelled that the boat would be back in Sanduval on Friday, and that he was sorry but he wouldn't be able to pay for the last heads until the next week.

The river twisted between small hills; clumps of fifty-foot bamboo hung over the banks, and we tunneled through. Wild cane and bananas grew thick on the narrow strip of level land along the river; in the hills it was mostly second-growth scrub, but a few isolated and enormous trees grew on the sky line *matapalos,* kapok, trees whose names I would never know dripping with lianas, the trees so out of proportion with the hills that everything seemed unstable.

At darkness the banana buyer, impatient with our slow progress and made generous by the *aguardiente,* hired two kids who were sitting on the bank to help us pole. It started to rain lightly. The feeling of living in the 1830's grew. We were poling our way through the outpost country, a country of lonely, isolated farms, of messages that never arrive or arrive too late, of sudden sickness and inexplicable fevers and death, of snakes and bugs and downpours of rain, of loneliness, of women living and working alone all day in hacked out jungle clearings, hauling water in gourds, pounding clothes on rocks, caring for sickly children, worrying. It was a country of distances, separations, longing, of deferred dreams, of small rewards; of muddy trails, stumbling horses, plants that grow two feet a day and choke the crops, armies of ants, blood-sucking lice on the bodies and in the eyes of the livestock. It is heroic country, too.

But when you ask yourself why anyone would live here, completely cut off from the world of comfort and security, there is no easy answer. Perhaps it is man's deepest wish to struggle against great odds, or perhaps the answer lies in that little band of grandchildren swarming around Don Julio. Maybe it is all for them.

🔲🔲

One day at lunch Alexandro was complaining about the power of the police in the Ecuadorian villages and how they often abused that power. I was in one of my more snippy moods and immediately used his confidence to give him a lecture on freedom. "You're always using the word *'humilde'* as a good quality in a man," I told him, crossly. "Nona is *humilde*, Wai is *humilde*, you tell me, as though this were the reason that you respect them. But I think you guys carry humility too far; you've got a lot of problems here because you never fight back. If you want justice and freedom you have to fight for it; it's never a present."

"Ay *caramba*," Alexandro said, smiling at the memory, "we did fight for it once. We made history one time here in Río Verde.

"It happened about thirty or thirty-five years ago. I was just a child, Don Julio was a young man, and your friend —— who is now a great politician, was just entering politics. He had a hacienda up the beach to the north.

"I don't remember the year, but the government fell and for some time we were without authority. You can't imagine how it was in those days, the power that the politicians had. The president of the country appointed his friends to govern the different sections, and these men were absolute masters in their areas. They were above the police, and they did what they wanted; they were very corrupt, evil, and grasping men.

"Well, the government fell. The news finally reached Río Verde, and we were talking about it in the town. It was a time when we felt very free and powerful, and we decided after several days that what we wanted to do more than anything was to kill the *Policía Rural* because of his many excesses and because of his cruelty to us; he was a completely evil man without pity or any redeeming qualities. We were in a crowd, almost the whole town, sitting on the beach out by the point, and——came riding down the beach. He was one of the young leaders of the Socialist party then, and we had a certain respect for him. 'What shall we do about the *Policía Rural?*' we asked him. 'What do you want to do?' he asked. 'We want to kill him,' we said. 'Then kill him,' he said, and spurred his horse and left us.

"We walked across the point to the river beach where the *Policía Rural* was standing, and we surrounded him, the whole town, no one saying a word. It was a community effort, you see, something we all had to be involved in, and when we were all around him, with him in the center not saying anything but slowly turning to watch us, one of us shot him in the back. We loathed that man, my God, but we loathed that man, and we shot him in the back like a dog. We killed him and left him there in the sand.

" 'Now, let's kill the President of the council,' someone said. We were feeling heady. We walked over to the President's house and pushed open the door and crowded upstairs. We went into his bedroom, and he was there in his underwear under the bed. He had crawled under the bed and was lying there trembling, his arms and legs jerking uncontrollably.

" 'Now, *Señor*,' someone said, 'if you will be so kind as to come outside; we have a little business with you.'

"At this moment Don Julio arrived from across the river. He was, as I said, still a young man but already a great landowner, and in spite of his power a man very much respected by us all. He walked into the bedroom calmly, and he said something to the leaders, something, I don't know what he said. And then he turned to the President of the council who was still under the bed and said very calmly, very softly, '*Buenos días*, Don Pablo, why don't you dress and come over to the house? My *señora* is preparing a little lunch.'

"We stood there without doing anything and watched the President of the council slowly dress, falling over with terror as he tried to step into his pants, trembling violently as he tried to dress himself. Don Julio, smoking a cigarette now, and with a fixed smile, watched him too, but like a great man, a really brave and noble man. They left together, walking very slowly, and we parted in front of the door and let them pass.

"Later, when the wife of the *Policía Rural* began to scream, we gathered again on the beach, but no one, not one of us, would help her wrap the body.

"Several weeks later a group of investigators arrived to probe the death of the *Rural*. No one knew anything; no one said a word. I suppose it was the only time in the history of the town when we were united. But it was God's will, you know. It was the will of God that those two men die. It wasn't ten days later that the President of the council went out through the breakers in his canoe, and it turned over. He was swimming toward the canoe, and the propeller blade from the outboard motor cut his throat from ear to ear. His death like that so soon after we had shot the *Rural* was like an exoneration, though I think none of us in the town felt guilt for his murder. But we were glad then that we had not killed the President of the council but let God do it for us. And in a sense, you know, it was as though He had blessed us with a sign, as though you could actually see the hand of God, the palm upraised in judgment and justice above the town."

□□

At five months and two days of age Alexandro's chickens began to lay Peace Corps eggs, first one a day, then two a day, until soon with his twenty-two hens he harvested nineteen eggs. Secretly, I was delighted because the chickens were laying about a month ahead of schedule. There was one trouble at first; the eggs were very small, and nothing I could say would convince anyone that the situation was temporary.

Pancho came in every day from his farm up the beach, and when he saw me would moan, "Oh, my God, *estamos jodido*," which softly translated means, "We're all screwed up"—a reaction which I found slightly ridiculous, since his chickens hadn't laid an egg yet, nor were they supposed to. Instead of being happy with the egg situation then, everyone with chickens was brooding and worrying and making fatalistic remarks. I began to feel that the world was about ready to come to an end, and the whole thing was getting on my nerves.

I went around explaining that Alexandro's hens were laying because he had fed them well and that bananas would not make eggs. "Just wait, have patience, I swear the eggs will get bigger; all you have to do is feed your babies well." Remarks like this did not sit well with Ramón, who with his fifty chickens was feeding almost twelve pounds of corn a day and going into debt at the rate of about forty cents a day. He was under a new and crushing pressure to think ahead and to have corn on hand; the situation was driving him in the direction of a nervous collapse.

Ramón spent two days of every week in his canoe buying corn along the coast or up the river. Returning home with a sack of ear corn in his canoe, exhausted but grinning, he would dance around me; five days later he would be in the depths of depression. His corn was running out again. Ramón's search for corn was a difficult one because the new corn was mostly in the roasting-ear stage and the old corn was very expensive. Also, his two Heifer–Peace Corps pigs were uttering piercing chow calls at thirty-minute intervals. It seemed that when he

wasn't beating the jungle for corn he was hauling in bundles of
sugar cane or bunches of bananas for the hogs, and in the early
mornings he was out on the sea trying to net shrimp. He had
resurrected an old canoe that had been abandoned, a canoe in
which he could net shrimp about 40 per cent of the time; the
rest of the time he was bailing like mad to keep from sinking
into the deep. On lucky days he brought in little gourds full of
shrimp which drove the pigs slavering mad with ecstasy, and on
really lucky days there was even enough for Ramón and Ester.

But it was a new, a very trying and seemingly endless and
thankless, way of living, this terrible tightrope-walk out of
poverty. The old life—that existence when only his and Ester's
stomachs had to be quieted, a life without a future but without
responsibilities and worries—lived nostalgically in his memory.
The idea of borrowing money from me month after month and
pouring it into the insatiable open mouths of his animals filled
him with a growing horror. He owed me over a thousand sucres,
more than fifty dollars; he had never made that much money in
a year.

"And now the people are talking against me," Ramón told
me. "They say that I am pretending to be your friend for the
money I am getting out of you; they say you have given me
fifteen thousand sucres, and they are trying to borrow money
from me because I am so rich in animals. You know, Ester can't
even come to town any more because she has no shoes, and her
dress is all torn. You know what Ester and I had to eat
yesterday? *Nada. Absolutemente nada,* and the town is talking
about my richness."

His own clothes were wearing out too, but the wagging
tongues in the village kept him from wearing a pair of pants
and a shirt that I had given him. Ramón's clothes consisted of a
pair of white duck pants and a white shirt that he came to town

in, and an old pair of pants cut off above the knees and
endlessly patched for working. One afternoon, as we were coming out of the brush with bundles of *ranconcha*, both his hat
and his tennis shoes simply disintegrated in one twenty-minute
period, and he left them in the trail, a sort of tattered and

pathetic spoor that I followed as I came in behind him with my
burden of leaves. He was waiting for me on the beach—his
shoes and hat gone, his work pants split down the middle,
almost naked, covered with sweat and insect bites—and he
looked at me and said, "Ah, my poor little gringo; you're too
delicate for this kind of work." I thought to myself, "Yes, I
sure as hell am, but so are you." I had pressured him into
wanting a hundred chickens and a pair of hogs. He had come to
me one night and said, "I want six chickens; I can take care of
six chickens properly." And I had pressured him and pressured
him and enflamed his mind. He was a natural dreamer, anyway.

When I had first known Ramón he was basically a happy man; he liked to laugh and dance and prance around making jokes. His life was one big fantasy. He was always going to give me presents, impossible, beautiful presents so that I would understand how important our friendship was. He used to invite me to his little shack of a house up the beach—the leaningest, leakingest house in the whole area—and for a couple of days beforehand he would describe the meal in detail. For lunch we would have chicken and an egg *torta*, and he would buy a bottle of catsup and have it on the table; afterward I would lie in his hammock and drink beer. He was even going to buy coffee because he knew that I drank coffee all the time. We would eat just like gringos. "Ayee, *dios mío*," he would say, doing a little dance step, completely carried away with the sheer beauty of the lunch party. I would arrive for lunch, and we would have shrimp soup and a little dish of rice, but everyone was apologetic, depressed, dream and reality too far apart.

When my boss, Eduardo, had come out to inspect the chickens, Ramón had taken a great liking to him. A few days after Eduardo left, Ramón said he wanted me to design him a new house, one that would hold two hammocks. And every day with the new plans he would dream out loud about the party he was going to have when Eduardo came back. He would serve Eduardo's favorite dishes—lobster, oysters, and shrimp—and there would be a bottle of catsup on the table, and afterward both Eduardo and I would lie in hammocks and drink beer and rest in the soft ocean winds.

"What you need a new house for is so you can live dry," I would tell him, trying to bring him back to earth, "so that everything you own doesn't get soaked every time it rains."

Well, yes, this was a reason too, but the real reason was that lunch party with Eduardo.

For months I had been talking to Don Julio, trying to convince him to sell some of the land around town, but the idea held no attraction for him. Then after Ramón and I had started building a new house on his father's land, Ramón made a deal with Don Julio to rent ten acres for five years (rent: $2.50 a year). He decided that it would be better to move the house, the chicken coops, and the pigpens onto his new land. I had been pressuring him to plant coconuts against the future, and now he wanted to plant corn for the chickens, and coconuts as an expression of faith in the Peace Corps. To Ramón, planting a tree that wouldn't bear fruit for five years was way past madness. It was blasphemy, as though he were challenging God, as though he were announcing to God the certainty of his being alive in five years.

We cleared about two acres of jungle, weeds, and vines only a year old, and planted corn and fourteen coconuts. We used pieces of bamboo split in half to fence off a large, grassy pen for the pigs, and we began to build a tremendous chicken house that would hold fifty chickens. It involved about two months of solid work, everything squeezed in between those incessant forays into the jungle looking for corn and hog rations, and there were probably a dozen days in that period when neither Ramón nor Ester ate anything but a length of sugar cane. At night they would take turns coming into town and opening up the *salón*, waiting for someone to wander in and order a glass of *puro*. They bought food with the profits, and then finally they ate the capital and closed the *salón* when the last cigarette was sold. After that, with nothing to sell, Ramón would sometimes come in and sit tilted back against the wall in front of the *salón*, staring at the stars, with his radio playing ear-shattering Ecuadorian fandangos. Either he was wildly elated at the way the hybrid corn was growing or at the sweet and clever way his gilt, Rikel, would come bounding through the grass when called, or he was down in the dumps, all his work halted because he didn't have a hammer or a pound of nails or a nickel's worth of vine to tie the fences with. It was still months before his second group of chickens would begin laying eggs and bringing in income.

About this time everything became increasingly complicated for me. Alexandro's chickens were laying pea-sized eggs. Ramón's six chickens in this same age group simply lolled around guzzling corn; laying eggs was the farthest thing from their minds. Ramón had confiscated the poles from his half-completed house on his father's land to build the new chicken coop, and had moved onto his new land, where he and Ester were living in a deserted and worthless house that belonged to his godfather. But the godfather, Mageen, had returned to Río Verde, and Ramón was muttering *"Jodido; jodido,"* every time I met him.

Ramón's canoe had split down the middle one morning while he was riding in on the breakers, and he was desperate for a new *bongo*, a short, wide-bottomed canoe that he could use in the ocean for netting shrimp. The time of the shrimp harvest was approaching, and on good days he could bring in perhaps fifty pounds of shrimp and clear more than a dollar. If he could earn a dollar a day, Ramón would dream out loud, dreaming impossible dreams, if he could only earn a dollar a day until his hens started to lay. . . .

A *bongo* cost about six dollars, about a million dollars more than Ramón had. It was the middle of the month, and I didn't have six dollars to lend him. He was running out of corn again, and I had promised to lend him the corn money until the moment of the first egg, and the truth is, I didn't know where the corn money was coming from, let alone the *bongo* money. And then what seemed like a very wonderful thing happened. I got a letter from a woman in Hillsborough, California, who sent me twenty-five dollars and asked me to give part of it to

Alexandro for his sick baby and use the rest to help Ramón with his chickens. I told Alexandro that I had fifteen dollars for medicine for his child from a friend in California, and he made a terrible gasping sound and tears swam in his eyes. I told Ramón I had ten dollars for him, and he began to dance and yell. He danced on the beach, pounding the sand with his feet and waving his arms and yelling. Now he would buy his *bongo* and four dollars' worth of corn all in one moment so that he wouldn't have to search for over a week.

That night wild rumors swept the town about the millionaire in California who had sent a gift of fifteen thousand sucres to Ramón, and the next morning Mageen told Ramón that he wanted ten dollars for the three lemon trees and the dozen pineapples he had planted and abandoned, and for the house. I advised Ramón to go ahead and buy the canoe and to tell the former owner to go to hell. Ramón said he couldn't because the man was his godfather and he must treat him with special respect. But he finally agreed that the canoe was more important and that with luck he could sell shrimp and pay off his godfather later.

Late that afternoon we talked again; he had spent the ten dollars a hundred different ways in his imagination trying to make it work. He thought that perhaps he should rent a canoe to fish with, buy *two* dollars worth of corn, a pair of shoes for Ester and a pair of pants for himself, and use the rest of the money to stock his store with cigarettes and *aguardiente;* that way he could make ten or fifteen cents a day profit to buy food. And he was worried about his godfather, he had a feeling his godfather was going to make trouble. He had to start thinking seriously about building a new house, and this would cost at least ten dollars. We had a long, unpleasant discussion in which I drew philosophical diagrams on a piece of paper, playing at being God again but with a growing insecurity. "Look, you are here at X and here is Y, your destination when your corn is ready to harvest and your chickens are laying eggs, and this straight line is the road to where you want to go; you must drive in a straight line and not go wandering off down uncertain paths."

But all of these problems, and the problems of Pancho and Alexandro, were putting me in a foul mood. When Pancho ran out of corn, for instance, instead of looking for corn like Miguel and Ramón, he would go into shock for a couple of days, muttering "*jodido*," and sit on a bench in front of the store shaking his head. He was sick, perhaps with malaria, perhaps with some uncertain jungle fever, but I didn't really believe him then. All I knew was that everything was falling apart for him, and when he asked me to bring him medicine I thought he was just covering up what looked like monumental irresponsibility.

Alexandro, who had always been *humilde*, began to act sadder and sadder, as though the size of his eggs were crushing him. He never looked at me when we talked any more, and I could feel little waves of accusation directed toward me for having involved him in this crazy chicken business where giant hens laid pygmy eggs. Now he decided that the eggs had a bad color; the yolks were too pale. I had repeated over and over that he should give the hens more grass to change the color of the yolks, but it had never registered. How could it? I had only told him fifty times.

About three o'clock one morning Ramón and Orestes left for Esmeraldas by canoe to buy a *bongo*. That afternoon I went up to Ramón's new land, and I was burning brush when Mageen appeared and began to tear off the bamboo walls and to dismantle the house. He was drunk. Ester was terribly embarrassed that I should see this and pretended that nothing out of the way was happening. She was cooking up a pot of platano

for the pigs, and this drunk bastard was tearing the walls off
her house. It made me furious because Ramón wasn't there to
defend himself, and I walked down the hill and stood close to
Mageen, not saying a word, but watching him intently and
scowling an ugly gringo smile. He got embarrassed and staggered off into the underbrush.

I was very worried about Ramón and Ester. At dark I
passed Orestes and Ramón on the beach going home; they had
paddled about fifty miles that day, to Esmeraldas and back,
and were walking in the curious disembodied way of men aware
of nothing but the weight of their limbs. Ramón had been
unable to find a *bongo* in Esmeraldas but had left 180 sucres
with another godfather to buy one. He carried a bundle under
his arm that looked suspiciously like bottles of *puro*, and I
didn't know whether he was lying or not.

"You have bad luck with your godfathers," I told him sarcastically. "There's one tearing your house down now, and the
other one is probably halfway to Guayaquil by this time with
your money."

"I'll come back into town later, and we'll talk about it,"
Ramón said. "Is Mageen really tearing the house down? *Jodido, jodido.*"

I went home and cooked dinner and waited for Ramón.
About ten o'clock I looked out the front door and saw him
sitting in front of his deserted *salón* staring at the stars; there
were three full bottles of *puro* sitting on the shelf behind him. I
slammed the door and went to bed. Early the next morning I
woke up and looked out the window; I was still mad. A motor
canoe across the river was getting ready to make the ocean trip
into Esmeraldas. I was boiling water for coffee, and suddenly,
without thinking about it rationally, I was throwing socks and
shirts into a suitcase. Some part of me insisted that I get away
for a couple of days. To hell with Río Verde and all its sordid,

tangled problems—the little eggs, the collapsing walls, Pancho's banana-fed chickens, Ramón's empty corn box and pro-
jected nervous collapse. There was a big fiesta coming up, too,
and for three days no one would work but simply weave around
in the street. I rushed out onto the dock and yelled for the
canoe across the river, and a few minutes later Río Verde was
fading in the distance, a sad little town drowning in palm trees.
But even before it was out of sight I began to feel guilty, as
though I were copping out, as though I were deserting everything that was important to me. I kept muttering over and over
to myself, "Oh, to hell with you; to hell with you, you crummy
little dump, you *jodido* little dump."

I left on the sixth, expecting to be gone for no more than
three or four days, believing that six or eight T-bone steaks
and an endless supply of chocolate sundaes would once more
put me in a decent frame of mind. But upon arriving in Quito I
discovered that on the fourteenth I was scheduled to talk like a
hog expert to a group of new Volunteers.

It ended up, then, that I was away from Río Verde for
almost two weeks, a time of growing depression, guilt, and
restlessness. I had gone away without telling anyone I was
leaving. The farmers, I knew, were absolutely without money to
buy corn for the chickens; Orestes needed twenty cents to buy
nails for a chicken house he was building, and his work would
have come to a halt. I was especially worried about Ramón and
his drunken godfather; besides I had special feelings of friendship for him. I had been responsible for getting Ramón to
break away from the domination of his father and to start
farming on his own, and this move to new land was terribly
hard for him to manage.

I got back late one afternoon, more dead than alive after the bus trip. I had brought a bunch of guilt offerings with me to try to patch things up—a second-hand flit gun for Alexandro, some second-hand fishhooks for Miguel, five pounds of rice and a pair of second-hand pants for Ramón. As a climax Eduardo Sotomayor had loaned me a Peace Corps incubator to pass around to the different farmers with chickens.

A little crowd met me at the dock and helped me pack all the stuff up to the house, but everyone seemed quiet and abashed, as though that two-week desertion had made strangers of us. Alexandro's face was longer and sadder than ever. Ramón, who usually did a dance for me when I had been gone, didn't even come over to say hello but sat on a bench on the dock with a tragic face. I went over to say hello to him, and when he got up to shake hands he began to tremble violently.

In the house the usual crowd milled around delicately peering into bags and checking out my boxes. The incubator—a simple wooden box without brass whistles, fantastic gears, or anything sensational about it—seemed to depress everyone. Ramón stood silently in one corner of the room; when I looked for him after a couple of minutes he was gone. Alexandro was sitting at the table, his face down, staring at cracks.

"What's wrong?" I asked finally. "Are your crazy chickens still laying small eggs?"

"Oh, no, Don Martín," Alexandro said. "In fact some of the eggs are getting so big that I am suffering for the poor hens; it gives me much pain the size of those gringo eggs."

"Well, then, why the sad face?" I looked around the house. "Is my pet chicken, Guardian, dead?"

"No, Don Martín, she's out making a *paseo* in the garden. It's worse than that. Two of the three rabbits died, and I might as well tell you everything. Someone came in and stole one of the sea shells from your collection."

It was standard operating procedure that when a Volunteer left his town for any length of time his rabbits died. No one seemed to know why. The guy who was responsible for the animals always swore that he practically lived in the cage with them prechewing their rations.

"Is that all?"

"Yes, if you took your camera to Quito with you."

I told him that I had, and he shook his head with relief. "After the shell was stolen I couldn't find your camera, and I haven't slept for a week worrying."

It got dark and the crowd gradually faded away. I was left alone with Alexandro, who spent ten minutes apologizing for the rabbits and telling me what excellent care they had had. The theft of the sea shell simply threw him; no one, absolutely no one outside his family had entered my house, he told me, which cleared things up, since I had observed that his five-year-old son Demetrio seemed to suffer frequent seizures of kleptomania. That kid could clean out a fair-sized room of everything but the furniture too large to handle in about thirty seconds flat. Finally Alexandro left to see if supper was being prepared for me.

I went across the street to Ramón's *salón* and sat outside with him in the darkness. He was waiting for me, terribly agitated, having prepared a statement which he now proceeded to deliver in a voice that broke with emotion after the first few words.

"Listen, Martín, I'm leaving," he said. "I've been waiting for eight days for you to come back, because I couldn't leave without saying good-by, just pack up and leave without a word."

He was, of course, referring to my sudden departure two weeks before. And I knew immediately, also, that he had no intention of leaving; he was too much in love with his Peace Corps hogs.

"But why are you leaving? Where are you going? Who's going to take care of your animals?"

"I have to get a job," he said. "Maybe I can find work in Santo Domingo for a few weeks. Ester can take care of the animals. Listen, I haven't had any corn for five days; the chickens are all outside; I had to turn them out. As for the pigs, I don't have the money to buy *picigua* to fix the fences, and the pigs won't stay in the pen. Oh, my God, Martín, they are eating all the young cocos, and they are in the house, the pigs stepping on Ester's feet and the chickens pecking her toes all day, the poor creature without shoes, crying, and the pigs walking around crying for corn.

"I tell you I can't stand the suffering of my animals. I've got to earn some money, and I think I want to get away from here for a few days because I am absolutely bored with the whole situation. Of course, it goes without saying, we have absolutely nothing to buy food with."

Before I left, Ramón had been living in a wreck of a house, but the floor of rotting planks was raised three feet above the ground. "Tell me," I said, "how are the pigs getting up the ladder into your house?"

"Listen, the day after you left, Mageen came to the house and said if I didn't pay him 180 sucres he wanted the house for himself."

"But the house is on your land."

"But he has babies; he has to have a house, and he is my godfather. We gave him the house and moved out in the weeds. I used the plans you made me for a little storage shed and built a *bodega*, and we moved in there, but with all the rain it is just pure mud.

"As for Mageen, I told him that I no longer care if he is my godfather; the house is on my land and he must move it. We have been fighting all week, and he has threatened to kill me. He has all those children, and they are destroying the crops, walking on the peanuts, tormenting the animals, stealing the cucumbers. And Mageen, as everyone knows, is a thief, and one of us has to stay near the chickens all day so that he doesn't rob us.

"Listen, Martín, I want to tell you the worst thing. I had to sell the six big chickens to buy corn for the others. I spent all day looking for a buyer, someone who would use them for layers instead of killing them, because I couldn't stand to have them killed. And listen, Martín, it is not all my fault; it is your fault, too. I've got to say this, it is your fault, too, because I always had it in my mind that I could dominate about six chickens, and at the most a dozen—but seventy-three? My God.

"Before you came, you know, we were living in blindness, yes, in blindness, and now we can see, but the change is very hard, and the one thing I am learning is that perhaps the pain and suffering of not being poor are worse than that blind poverty we lived in before."

He was silent. I could hear the light plant starting up, an amazing development, since we hadn't had lights in the town for almost five months. There was a long silence and then Ramón said, "How could you leave like you did, without a word, without telling us when you would be back? How could you do a thing like that?" Then the thirteen lights in the main street of the town flashed on and the light in the *salón* went on and lit up our faces, and Ramón said, "Oh *Jesu Cristo*, it's not your fault; I didn't mean that it was your fault." We looked at each other and began to laugh because the tears were streaming down our faces.

I hated to get involved with the *Policía Rural* because justice in Río Verde was often simply a question of who you were and had little to do with the realities of the situation. But at supper I talked over Ramón's problem with Alexandro, who told me that Mageen was tormenting Ramón to get money out of him. It was Mageen's idea that the Peace Corps gringo would not stand by and let Ramón be tormented, but would pay well for peace. We decided that if Ramón would agree, the police should be used as a weapon of terror against Mageen. Ramón agreed; he was passive, at the point where he welcomed someone else making decisions for him. "But I don't want to put him in jail," he said. "I just want him to move that house off my land." The three of us went across the river and found the *Policía Rural;* we gave him ten sucres, and he came back with us. Mageen was drinking *puro* in front of Alvaro's store. I don't know what the *Policía Rural* said to him, but it was very effective. By eight o'clock the next morning Mageen had moved out of the house and was staying with friends in town.

The word got around that Mageen was going after Ramón's chickens with rat poison, and for the next few days Ramón never came into town without his machete. He told me that a year before Mageen had gotten into a fight with a neighbor over a hog and finally he had said, "Well, since we can't decide who it belongs to it's better if no one has it," and had killed the animal, slashing it twice in the back with a machete and severing its spinal column. If King Solomon had had to judge that conflict, I decided, he would have come out looking pretty idiotic.

I loaned Ramón two hundred sucres to buy corn. He gave part of it to Mageen, used some of it for groceries, and then began wandering up the coast again looking for cheap corn. He returned one evening loaded down with ear corn, about a three-day supply, and he did his dance of delight for me, but it was an abstracted and stylized performance, only a formality. He had lost about ten pounds, his ribs were beginning to stick out, and there was a harried, tormented look on his face.

The stolen sea shell, Alexandro and I had decided, would turn up after a week or so, because the only reason anyone would steal it would be to sell it back to me. Sure enough, the first morning after I got back, Wai's nine-year-old son, Clever, approached me with the shell. I was sure it was mine; it was the only one like it we had found on the whole stretch of beach. But Clever carried it off like a teeny-bopper Jimmy Valentine. After a couple of days of interrogation, during which he gazed into my suspicious face with the clear, unblinking eyes of an angel, I finally bought the shell back for a nickel; there was just that one chance in a thousand that the little hood was telling the truth.

□□

I heard about Wai a couple of months before I met him. He lived up the beach from town and was almost always out on the sea trying to catch enough fish for his seven or eight children, his widowed mother, and his constantly pregnant wife. The town was boasting about him after one of the local fiestas. In a way he was the town's proudest possession, for he did things that stirred the people in the depths of their unconscious. He had been getting quietly drunk in Pablo's *salón*, and five or maybe eight men from across the river had taunted him, secure in their collective strength. Wai had taken them all on at once, tossing them out through doors and windows, along with all the tables and chairs and finally Pablo himself, and then had stood alone in the *salón*, made dark now by the overturned and broken lamp, bawling to all his friends who stayed discreetly alert in the corners of the empty room, "Just don't touch me, just please, don't anybody touch me." So I liked Wai before I ever saw him. I knew just how he felt; he stirred things in my own unconscious.

I met Wai on my first Christmas Eve in Río Verde in Ramón's depressing *salón* where I had gone to drink beer. Wai was sitting at a table with three other fishermen, all of them wearing tattered clothes and no shoes, all of them with the patient but slightly distraught faces of alcoholics without a penny between them for a drink but secure in the possibility of a miracle.

Wai dominated the table; no, he dominated the whole room. He wasn't a giant exactly, but in this country of small, delicate people, his six feet and 190 pounds gave him all the qualities of a monument. He was thirty-four years old, and the amazing thing about his face was that there was nothing written on it, absolutely nothing. It was as pure and open, as free from vice, passion, sadness, or terror—in short, from life itself—as the carved alabaster mask of an Egyptian god. In one light his face was almost pure Negro, in another light, pure Indian. He held his great hands peacefully open and unmoving upon his knees. Looking at him you knew that his rags, made doubly conspicuous in the midst of all the Christmas finery, were only a disguise. He had arrived on earth to test mankind.

"Is that guy over there the one who beat up on all the Palestina tramps?" I asked Ramón, already knowing.

"Yes," Ramón said, proudly. "That's my friend, Wai." He rushed over and, like a small puppy attacking a tiger, began feinting and pummeling at Wai, who sat there as placidly as an idol accepting Ramón's homage.

An hour later the four fishermen were still sitting at the table waiting, with those quiet, patient, peaceful expressions on their faces, as the Christmas celebration swirled around them. I couldn't stand it and asked Ramón to send a bottle of *aguar-*

diente over to their table. Half an hour later Wai bought a bottle of beer, came over to our table, introduced himself, and presented me with the beer. He was a man of propriety.

He was as shy as a girl with me, and I with him. I was in a presence. For the first time in my life I had come up against a natural man, a man without a façade, without a mask. He was as simple, as placid, as uncomplicated as Adam—before the episode with the apple. It shook me to my foundations.

That first year I could never work with Wai. He was wildly independent and not a little in love with his own poverty. He was probably the poorest man in town aside from a couple of hopeless drunkards and my neighbor, Carlos Torres, who was so shiftless that he and his family would have died of hunger if his mother didn't somehow feed them. (He was also unafraid of the night snakes, apparently, and made expeditions out through the country robbing his neighbors—Don Julio's coconuts, Vicenta's beans, Wilfrido's watermelons.) Wai's poverty gave him a certain status. Everyone loved him because he nourished no envy in anyone, and he was poor for good, acceptable reasons—his enormous family, which drove him to drink.

Wai could never understand what the Peace Corps was all about. It went against everything he had learned about life; there was something preposterous, something dangerous, about a rich white man living in his town and talking about working with him, helping him make more money—for nothing. He knew that there were strings attached, that he would end up compromised, his integrity flawed. No, no, no. No thanks.

Trying to sneak in the back door, I planted a small garden with four or five of his children. On planting day we were followed up to the garden site by Wai's mother's pet pig, and as we planted he harvested. What the pig hadn't rooted up, the first heavy winter rains washed away a couple of weeks later.

A year passed. One day I overheard Ramón talking with

someone. "Ay, that poor man, Wai. The fish aren't biting and his kids haven't eaten for a couple of days." Wai, fifty cents in debt to Alvaro, the storekeeper, had no more credit, but my credit was still good. I bought ten pounds of rice and some beans and took them up to Wai's house. Wai was out fishing; I left the packages with Gloria, his wife. About two weeks later gourds full of shrimp and oysters began arriving at my house every afternoon, five and six pounds at a time. Wai, it turned out, was splitting his catch with me. I went up to his house on Sunday, thanked him, and explained that since I had no plans for opening a seafood restaurant, I was giving away 90 per cent of what he brought me.

Later in that same month Wai came to my house on a Saturday night. He had been drinking a little, which was about the only way he could ever talk to me easily. He began to thank me for the rice, but he choked up, stopped talking, and suddenly burst into tears. When he could speak again, he told me that I was the only one in town who had helped him and that I was his friend forever. For a dollar's worth of rice and beans, I figured it was the biggest bargain of my life. He told me that he had talked everything over with his wife and his mother, and they had decided that there would be no danger in working with me. "The truth is," Wai said, "you were like a god out of heaven to us." Since I was already secretly convinced that Wai was some primitive deity, it turned into a real confrontation of the gods.

Well, we began to work together in various little projects, but none of them was very successful. He couldn't figure out the relationship that I wanted to develop, one that would teach him independence and a reliance on his own abilities. I wanted him to get into something that would sustain him after I was gone. But he couldn't see it that way. He gave me his friendship and *mates* of shrimp, and I was his *patrón;* he came to me when he was in trouble. About once a month he would show up when he knew that I was going into Esmeraldas. He needed half a pound of fishline or a mill for grinding corn or a bottle of worm medicine for one of his children. He never questioned whether I would bring him the things he needed.

His beautiful old mother, the Señora Pancha, stopped me on the beach one day. She needed a sewing machine, one with a pedal. Would I please bring it to her the next time I went to Quito? "No," I told her. "I don't have that much money; it's impossible."

"When it comes," she said, "I'll patch your clothes; the way you walk around is scandalous."

Every day she combed the beach after the high tide, looking for Indian gold. "How much gold have you got?" I asked her. "Give me your gold and I'll sell it; if there's enough I'll bring you the machine."

"I want to leave the gold to my children," she explained. "It's not good for a mother to die and have nothing to leave her children." She produced a small glass bottle from some hidden pocket in some hidden skirt and poured the gold into my hand, little flakes of gold that she had found through the months, an Indian nose ring, a twisted object like a spoon.

"Sell your gold," I said. "You can make much more money sewing clothes, and leave your children real money instead."

"Take it," she said, with perfect trust.

In Quito a jeweler appraised the gold at around twelve dollars; I told Sue McCartney, one of the Peace Corps secretaries, about the problem, and she wrote to her father, who sent me another fifteen dollars. I went back and made an elaborate deal with Señora Pancha; she was to repair my worn-out pants for the rest of my life. About a month later I brought her a new sewing machine. It was something she had dreamed about owning for twenty-five years, at least, but she accepted it as naturally as a glass of water. Didn't the family have a *patrón* now, Don Martín, who took care of all their needs? A few days later I was working up on the farm with brand new clothes made out of old feed bags, and you could tell that she regarded me as someone as big and monumental as her son, for everything was double size. Hoeing weeds I looked like a ship under full sail.

Wai's projects? I brought him a simple and beautiful little stool carved out of a single block of wood by the Jivaro Indians in the Amazon Basin. He copied it with his machete and a tool that he used for making canoes, and in a few months he was turning out one or two a week. But I was soon glutted with stools. I sold about fifteen to other Volunteers but could find no store in Quito that would pay the two dollars that we figured we had to get.

We tried weaving swinging basket-like chairs out of a jungle vine called *picigua*. Wai made nice baskets, but those chairs were something else. They were like traps; once you sat in one you were immediately entangled in grasping pieces of vine, and it took at least three of his kids to pull you out. I put Wai's mother to work sewing flaming roosters on gunny sacks with bright-colored yarns. But they were terrible. The yarn alone cost three dollars, which was the highest price I was ever offered in the tourist market.

Wai was afraid of the chicken business. It took two years of watching Ramón and Orestes cleaning up on their eggs before he was willing to try it. Finally he started clearing jungle behind his house for corn, and one day he asked me to bring him some chickens. He built a drunken chicken coop, so leaning and erratic, so oblivious to all the laws of gravity, that when he showed it to me, we both broke down into hoots of laughter. It was unbelievable. "Oh, well," I told him, "I guess the chickens won't know the difference."

This project was a total flop. He had the corn but lacked the money for protein supplement. He felt that supplying his thirty chickens with protein was my job, but I didn't have the money either. And actually he never really believed that chickens needed a supplement. Giving them pure corn and keeping them locked up was so revolutionary that the mind boggled; he couldn't go any further.

Most of the chickens grew up finally, but they never went into paying production, and Wai's son Clever kept stealing the eggs to buy candy. After a few months, feeling the necessity for a good drunk, Wai sold a few of his hens for a party; after that he had a party every week until the hens were gone. Under the circumstances it was the best course.

Ramón stopped by the house one morning and asked if I would help him make a big box to store corn in. I had been working out volumes and sizes for just such an eventuality and had even invented a corn box made out of driftwood balsa off the beach that would cost only a few cents to make and would eliminate almost entirely the need to buy hardwood from the sawmill. Ramón knew this, and he also knew that when I built something for the first time, something which could be regarded as experimental, I would send a bill to the Peace Corps office for the cost of the material—in this case about sixty cents. Ramón was getting smart; by asking first he could get himself a free corn box. I wanted everyone in town who raised corn or chickens to have the chance to see how with a very little effort they could protect their grain against the rats.

We took a saw and a wood chisel and walked up the beach. When we came to Wai's house, I asked Ramón if he would go up and get the hand ax from Wai, who had borrowed it to make stools. (I was avoiding Wai because I had sold three of his stools and owed him almost a hundred sucres, but I didn't want to give him the money yet. The night before he had been drinking in town; I was afraid that he still might have a fire in his stomach to put out with *puro*.)

"Please, Don Martín," Ramón said, "don't ask me to go up there. I am not friends with the mother of Wai and never go to the house."

"It's not the mother of Wai who has the ax; just go up and yell in the window for Wai; you don't have to talk to the mother."

He went, but reluctantly. Wai's mother, like Wai, was sort of spectacular. She had great square teeth, strong and yellow, and her smile was like some aristocratic but fading French countess right out of Proust. She was in her sixties, but her hair was still dark and tied in two teenaged pigtails; they stuck out wildly from beneath a limp and incredibly well-used straw hat, the top of which was broken and hinged. When you talked to her on the beach and a breeze was blowing, the top of the hat kept opening and shutting mysteriously, as though it were trying to send you a secret message without Wai's mother seeing. She was a good woman, a hard-working woman, and one of the few who had passed on to her children the art of weaving baskets and fish nets.

As well as I knew her, I had noticed only one small eccentricity; she refused to live in the house with the family, saying that one night the sea would wash away the house with everyone in it. Instead she lived in a three-walled lean-to back from the beach a hundred yards at the very edge of the jungle, a mysterious, cave-like lean-to set so neatly into the line of trees that it seemed to have been carved out of the jungle itself. Looking at it, the imagination reeled, for her proudest possession—completely filling the room, a legacy probably from her dead husband—was a tremendous double bed with springs and mattress, the best, no doubt the only, bed on the whole stretch of beach.

It sat in that open-air pergola like the royal divan of a Persian empress, made almost holy by your knowledge of the tremendous number of children who had been brought forth through the years upon its sagging but proud bulk. And perhaps she was not so cracked after all, because in an eight-month period all of the palm trees in front of Wai's house had been torn away by the high tides, and by then only a fringe of balsa drift separated the house from the advancing sea.

Ramón came back with the ax, and as we continued up the beach I asked him why he was not friends with the mother of Wai. It was puzzling because I knew that he, along with everyone else in town, almost venerated Wai.

"Well," Ramón said, "I told you before how when my mother was living with my father, she was carrying on with another man. The other man was Wai's brother, and it was all the fault of his mother. The truth is that Wai's mother is a *bruja*, a witch, and she was obsessed that her son get whatever he wanted. Well, he wanted my mother, and this witch cast spells, cooked brews of secret leaves, and did the things that witches do. Within a month my mother was completely mad, completely out of her head for the man. It was all quite open and shameless, and then she ran away with him to Colombia, where he deserted her."

I snorted my disbelief in this black witchcraft, and he looked at me, smiling coldly and snorting back.

"Oh yes," he said. "I know very well that gringos don't believe in this or in the herbs we use to cure our sicknesses or in the saints that watch over us in heaven, but perhaps gringos don't know everything. And I can't help but wonder if everything wouldn't have been different for us, for the children, if my mother had not run away with the brother of Wai. Because you know, it almost killed my father. For a year he was a completely different man, chasing after women, drinking, and disappearing on trips for a week at a time when he would spend up to twenty dollars in one moment, drinking and whoring, or drinking at home, howling down on the beach all alone like a dog howling at the moon.

"And he had seven children; there were seven of us, very young, then, waiting in that house, sitting in that house waiting for my father to come back, wondering where our mother was, with nothing to eat except what the neighbors gave us, while he squandered the cattle and the crops with his wild and tormented living.

"No, I will not speak to the mother of Wai, nor will I ever. And my father will not even look into her face nor acknowledge her existence, for perhaps it is because of her that we live as we do, hopelessly poor."

As I came back along the beach alone, I looked out at the ocean. A large canoe filled with men, all of them working furiously, swept by me, one man poling in front, three men paddling, one man bailing, a couple of youngsters sitting tensely in the stern. This sudden, violent, and angry picture, flashing on a vacant mind, filled me for a moment with stark, delighted terror. I stepped behind a palm tree trying to hide myself, but they had seen me, and they waved. So they were friends. I recognized none of them. They passed quickly, naked and sweating, working very close to the shore, moving through that inshore area where the breakers churned up just before washing the beach.

What had so delighted and terrified me was that in those first few seconds the canoe and those paddling men had looked exactly like the N. C. Wyeth picture of the naked, man-eating cannibals in his illustrations for *Robinson Crusoe*. It wasn't just the men, but the whole color and texture of the moment— the hot, washed-out dazzle of that tranquil, baking sea and the thunderheads in the background, clouds and sky all violets, soft grays, and gray-blues. And that wonderful terror was a full-scale reproduction of a ten-year-old kid's terror as he is about to be captured and eaten in that lovely, hidden attic bedroom at Grandmother's house a million years ago.

□□

March was the poorest time of year in Río Verde, the time before the shrimp harvest began, and there was probably not five dollars in cash in the whole town. Many nights the street was deserted by 7:30, the radios dead and the people sleeping. Perhaps one or two young men filled with feisty and lustful thoughts wandered the street, dreaming of a beckoning hand at a candlelit window, but by nine they too had given up.

The light plant had been broken down for four months, and at night the bamboo houses showed black and deserted looking against the stars or glowed coldly silver in moonlight. It was deathly quiet except for the occasional crying of a baby; overhead in moonlight the sea birds circled the town catching the updraft from the shore winds as they struck the hill. All night long the birds floated above the town; *tijeras* they are called because of their long scissor-like tails.

When I go to bed at eight I feel like hitting the deck by four, and many times I was the first man awake in town. After a cup of coffee I used to walk out on the dock and watch the sky begin to brighten over the hills. The river caught the first light and seemed to hold more than the sky, and then out past the sand bar the sea began to glow palely.

The town came awake with the roosters announcing the day. The sound of the roosters used to be raucous and disturbing, but when there were Peace Corps roosters in that brassy overture, it was like music to me. ("Ah *dios mío*," Alexandro said, "how I love to lie in bed in the morning darkness and listen to my roosters sing.") They challenged each other in town and in

Palestina across the river, philosophizing, proclaiming their existence like a celebration.

The first fishermen walked barefoot down the street, in their tattered work clothes and big straw hats, carrying paddles, furled sails, and a ball of string or a shrimp net. The pump in town began its bleak squawking as the kids appeared with gourds to collect brine water for washing. Don Julio in an undershirt, the head of the town council, washed in the pump and walked the length of the town like a watchdog checking things out and then hoed weeds in the street. The weeds were knee-high, and Don Julio was a realist. He went inside and stood a long time in the window gazing out over the ocean.

Alvaro opened his store; smoke drifted out of the kitchens and hung over the houses in the still air. The children shopped for breakfast, perhaps trading an egg for a half pound of rice or a chunk of brown sugar mixed with coconut. The farmers left for the cornfields or the banana plantings. The sun came up and the vultures clustered in the tops of palm trees or on the beach with their wings spread open, drying themselves out like badly washed laundry. The birds cried in the salt grass, harsh, rasping Ecuadorian bird cries. One outside the back door called to me every day; according to Lucho, it was the bird who announces a death. Go away, bird!

Lastly, the teenagers appeared in the streets wandering up and down like lost souls. The day had begun, an unchanging day full of very small surprises hardly worth finding out about.

And this rhythm of life was closely tied to the past; we were living on an enormous garbage dump of pre-Incan clay fragments. The plaza, bulldozed out of the hill by a highway Cat, was almost pure fragments—broken pieces of pots, children's tops, ceremonial whistles, heads, torsos, and feet of human and animal figures. Farther up the hill Alexandro could hardly plant his corn for the fragments in his field, and in the gardens almost every shovelful of dirt held some reminder of the town's ancient life. The cemetery appeared to have been in continual use for over two thousand years; the remains of a *tola*, a grave mound, still lay just over the fence.

When school let out three months earlier, the town's more ambitious or desperate kids gradually disappeared—Wilson, Jorge, Pancho, Ricardo, Ernesto, a couple of others—the country kids with no work who were finally driven away. I used to see them wandering in the streets of Esmeraldas with that same vacant, dreaming look, in a gentle shock.

"How are you doing, Ernesto?"

"Oh, fine, I have a job when the banana boats are in."

"Well, that's great."

"Yes, it's good to have a job. . . . Listen, Don Martín can you loan me a nickel; I haven't eaten yet today. . . . Tell Mother I'll be back in the time of carnival."

But most of them never did come back, and in time dreamed of an idyllic childhood, remembering running the bulls, riding the breakers, or the sound of the sea and the dry sound of the wind in the palm trees, or some odd but vivid sunset that lived in the memory—forgetting the hunger and the sameness of the days.

◻◻

During one six-week period when I was playing out my role of Big Daddy, the Peace Corps Volunteer with the answers, the whole experience turned into a rout. Toward the end, instead of running all over comforting and advising people I was moping around the house finding deep and personal meanings in Hamlet's famous soliloquy. I was hoping that someone would pick me up and gently rock me back and forth for a few hours.

What happened? It all began quietly—a time of vague depression, dissatisfaction, sadness, a neurotic apprehension. For one thing, I guess, I was beginning to get inside the town, becoming very emotionally involved with everything. For another, and mainly, I wasn't eating very well. I was eating better than anyone in town, with imported tomatoes and bread from Esmeraldas; I had the money to buy a can of tuna fish every evening—that party food which was reserved for days of fiesta —and I was buying eggs, too. I was probably the only person in town who was eating eggs, since everyone with laying hens was establishing a market in Esmeraldas. I knew what the trouble was, but I was unable to rationalize my way out of the situation, and life darkened day by day.

In the black, still nights with the light plant broken down again, the evenings assumed a crushing sameness—three or four, sometimes six or seven, farmers sitting in the house around the candle, all of them staying about half an hour longer than I could keep my eyes open and all of them talking about chickens. Don Alfonso would describe every character trait of every chicken in his pen. (He had about thirty.) Alexandro would one-up him with an ample biography of every chicken that he had or had had, with vivid descriptions of the more dramatic eggs that each one had laid. Then it was someone else's turn. My God, I was getting tired of talking about chickens. I could never think of anything very sensational to add to the general discussion, and Ramón would sit there, nervously watching me, and later, as everyone was finally leaving he would try to get me alone for a second to say, "You're bored with the town, aren't you? You're thinking about leaving us, aren't you? You're not happy here."

I had always been aware of the jealousies in the town, but now I began to see that I had underestimated their power to order the lives of the people. It began to get through to me. Ramón Arcos, drunk, buttonholed me on the street. He wanted ten sucres to get drunker and when I said "No," he said I was a

bad man who helped only the rich like Ramón Prado and
Alexandro. "Rich?" I cried. "They're the poorest people in
town." But, of course, it wasn't true any more. Ramón was
about to get his hundredth chicken, and Alexandro was up to
seventy. A year ago they had been among the poorest people;
now they were about to be the richest. There was real dissatisfaction in Río Verde about the job I was doing, and every day
I heard reports of my favoritism. Rumors reached me that a
couple of old wise guys who knew all about the Peace Corps
were telling everyone that I was making money off the people,
that the chickens I sold should be gifts, and that the loans I was
making did not have to be repaid. It was part of my job to give
people money, they said.

It was a curious, back-biting time. Everyone was angry, and
jealous of Ramón and Alexandro, who were each selling about
forty eggs a day. I was putting Miguel on my chicken list
for the new chickens, but I hadn't put Milton's name down.
I was spending all my time working on Ramón's farm. I was
helping Wai make stools to sell but had rebuffed Lucho when
he wanted to make stools, too. Orestes had said, "To hell with
the gringo, I don't have to pay back any of the money for the
chickens if I don't want to." Pancho had said, "I am bored with
these damned chickens and would like to get rid of them." Miguel had said, "————." I tried to ignore all of these small-
town, whispered stories, but in the back of my mind I was
growing suspicious and uncertain. I tried to balance, for instance, this secret report of what Orestes had said with his own
words to my face, sweet words in which he had told me that he
had more regard for me than for his own father. Which was
true? Hell, I couldn't tell, but I felt sad when Orestes came to
visit me and I held back and couldn't talk easily, half afraid
that I was being conned.

I moved the sacks of chicken concentrate out of my house

and into a store that Alexandro had rented for $1.50 a month
and where he sold handfuls of scraped ice to the kids or iced
drinks of *naranjilla*. I asked him to take over the handling of
the concentrate, anticipating the day when there would be no
Volunteer in the town. This distressed the farmers because Alexandro, and therefore everyone, would know who was paying
cash for his concentrate and who was buying on credit. Young
Miguel, proudly independent and secretive about his forty
chickens, stopped buying concentrate altogether, and his hens
almost stopped laying until I heard about it and gave him a
repeat performance of Chicken Lecture Number Five, on
chicken nutrition—for the umpteenth time—both of us terribly bored. Orestes arrived in town one night about eight to find
Alexandro's store closed. He began yelling at Lucho about not
keeping the store open and about how everyone who was abus-
ing his credit was robbing the poor gringo of his chicken
concentrate. They almost came to blows when the argument
disintegrated into passionate observations on how their respective mothers made their livings.

Late one afternoon, a murdered Negro—his stomach slashed
open with a machete, his eyes and hair gone, and his swollen
arms raised as though he were addressing a multitude—bobbed
lightly in the wavelets at the river's edge in front of town,
riding very high in the water. In the crowd of people who stood
quietly transfixed with handkerchiefs over their noses, perhaps
waiting for him to speak, I studied him. For many days I
couldn't forget his face. He had a message for me, not entirely
unpleasant, about the mortality of man, but I couldn't quite
get it; it was out there just past my fingertips, a personal
message—profound and deeper than reassurance.

At unexpected times I would find his unaccusing, disintegrating face superimposed over the faces of my friends, those
delicate and vulnerable people, tottering on the edge of sudden

fevers and malnutrition. Their laughter, their savage will to
endure, the grace and simplicity of their movements, all those
qualities that stood opposed to death struck me as miraculous.
But everyone seemed so vulnerable; death was so close even to
the youngest.

I broke one terrible night when Rufo, Ramón's young
brother, arrived at the house begging me to bring medicine for
Ramón and Ester, who were suddenly burning up with fever.
Carrying aspirin and a thermometer, I walked up the beach
through the waves at high tide, under a billion blazing southern stars, the most furiously beautiful night of my life. But the
contrast of that night with the utter squalor of Ramón's house,
the sweating bodies, the babbling delirium, their childlike faith
that now that I had come everything would be all right, the
pathetic collection of objects they had piled in bed around
them—a plaster of Paris dog with half the paint peeled off, a
rusty flit gun, a jar of watermelon seed, a pail of ground corn
for the chickens, a pair of worn-out gringo shoes, all their
treasures—so knocked me out that walking back along the
beach I began to cry as I hadn't cried since I was six years old.
What finally made it funny was that I couldn't stop and had to
stay on the beach for almost an hour, embarrassed to go wailing through the sleeping streets of Río Verde, announcing the
fact that I was cracking up.

Ramón and Ester both had fevers of 105, the whites of their
eyes had turned dark brown, and they were urinating blood.
They were too weak to leave the house, but Ramón somehow fed
the chickens and got Rufo to haul water and grass for the hogs.
And it was true when the people said I had favorites; they were
Ramón and Ester, and the possibility that they were dying
filled me with terror. I wrote a letter, put some money in it, and
gave it to Ramón. "Go to Esmeraldas immediately and give
this to Tom Brigham, my friend, the great walrus-bearded

Volunteer; he will take you to a doctor and see that you get medicine and a place to stay."

For three days Ramón refused to leave. He had never been to a doctor in his life; he had heard rumors that a doctor examined *all* your body, and this was too shocking to contemplate. He was afraid to leave Ester; he was afraid that Rufo would leave the chickens unguarded and that someone would steal them. We argued bitterly, but nothing I said reached him. Then on the third day he staggered out of the house to where I was hoeing a patch of corn and collapsed on the ground by me. He was trembling with terror. It was not just that he had suddenly grasped the fact that he was dying, but that he had seen, he had *seen* the grinning face of death peering in at him through the mosquito netting.

"Look, Martín, for the love of God, tell me what to do," he wept. "Whatever you tell me to do, I'll do."

I got him across the river onto the bus with the letter to Tom, and he was back from Esmeraldas late the next day, weak but cured. He had medicine for Ester and himself. The doctor had told him that he was two weeks away from death, that the malaria had been working in his liver and kidneys.

▢▢

Along with everyone else I had been under the spell of Washington Peace Corps propaganda, which reports on the experiences of Volunteers in their different jobs. They are all reports of success—how Volunteer W comes to the high, arid town of A and leaves it two years later with running water, a chlorination system, and communal showers; how Volunteer X with a couple of shovels and a hoe doubles the income of village B by establishing a tomato-marketing co-op; how rambling Volunteer Y leaves behind him an endless string of latrines stretching from here to the far horizon, none of them ever used, if the truth were known, except for storing corn, but proudly exhibited by their owners as glistening symbols of status and the open mind.

As a Volunteer, you are oriented toward this kind of success; you want it desperately, unashamedly. When you make a mess of a project, as I did one day, it shakes you to your roots. It makes you feel, in fact, like the highly unpublicized case of Volunteer Z working in the mountain village of C. All his projects had gone to hell, and his girl had written him that she was getting married that week to friend Q; Volunteer Z lay on his bed without moving for three days and, when the old Indian selling ice cream stuck his head through the window and yelled "*Helados*," suddenly jumped out of bed, ran outside, and bit the overeager salesman. Of course, the truth is that some days running outside and biting someone is probably the only rational move left to the Volunteer—especially if a Good Humor man is conveniently available.

Anyway, to get down to the case of Volunteer T in the seacoast town of RV. I had been working with Pancho Arcos, a twenty-eight-year-old farmer who lived up the beach. He was a man of dry, cynical wit, pleasantly realistic, a little sarcastic, as though he didn't expect much good to come of anything. He lived apart from his wife. He had problems, and he kept looking into that bottle of Cayapa for the solution. But when he worked, he worked hard, and when he drank he usually didn't get crazy but only giggly philosophical; he also got very sick.

I thought I had him figured out and that we could work together. We planted a garden on a hillside in back of the farm (which washed away in the first heavy rains), I showed him how to fertilize corn the way the Mexicans do, and how to spray weeds with 2-4-D. We talked about clearing a big piece of jungle and planting as much as five acres of corn in the next crop year, both of us carried away with this great dream. He

built a chicken house, and at first his chickens did very well.
When he told me that he wanted a pair of Heifer pigs and that
he would feed them the way we wanted them fed, I told him to

build his pen, get everything ready, and I would get him the
pigs.

From the day they arrived about a month later everything
went wrong. The pig shelter on the ranch was only half roofed,
and Pancho kept the pigs in town, belly deep in mud, in a small
pen made out of balsa chunks. After three days of waiting, I
got mad and tore the pen down. The pigs, smiling, wandered
off into the bushes. I left word with Pancho's mother that I
would tear the pen down every time he put the pigs back in it.

Pancho moved the pigs up to the ranch the next day, with
the shelter still half roofed, and the arguments began. I
couldn't get it into his head that pigs needed protein—some-

thing that he had understood beautifully before the pigs arrived. Sugar cane and bananas were what the local pigs ate, and
they were ready to market in eighteen months; it was unreason-
able of the gringo to keep mentioning fish and corn and the
fact, no doubt a lie, that a well-fed pig would be ready for
market in five months. There was no water near the ranch. It
all had to be hauled there in gourds that held less than a gallon
—either from the river at low low tide or from a contaminated
mudhole a half mile out in the bushes. I don't think I ever saw
those pigs when they wouldn't have welcomed a drink of water.

Two months before the new corn harvest, everyone ran out of
corn, and all the chicken projects began to falter—especially
Pancho's. What teed me off was that I was loaning Pancho the
money to buy corn; all he had to do was find it, and he couldn't
manage even that. I would arrive at the ranch to find his
chickens roaming through the brush looking for bugs instead
of living in the chicken house where they belonged. Before long
they came down with colds and diarrhea, and had funny sores
on their faces. The time arrived when they should have begun
to lay. Not an egg.

Pancho was a nice guy, but he had no resistance against
disaster. When things started to go wrong he unraveled. One
time he borrowed one hundred sucres to buy corn, the last one
hundred sucres that I had to live on that month, and then he
found that he couldn't quite make the effort. He spent three
days sadly smiling and nodding on Segundo's store porch,
delicately sipping *aguardiente* and talking about fate. That
was one time, come to think of it, when I felt like running down
the street biting people, and especially Pancho.

The corn crisis passed, and finally Pancho's chickens began
to produce; he was selling all his eggs to a Spaniard from
Esmeraldas who bought them to incubate. Things looked

pretty good. Then I discovered another thing that Pancho couldn't handle—success. One Sunday I found Pancho's chickens up on the bluff unfed and unwatered; rows of piled-up eggs lay in the sun just outside the nests. The pigs—poor, runty, suffering creatures—cried for water in the pen. Back in town I saw Pancho drowsing on the steps of Pablo's *salón*. I didn't say anything to him, I was too mad to talk, but I left word with his mother that if he had no interest in the pigs it would be better to give them to someone else. I wasn't too serious, because he loved his pigs, and I knew what a disaster, what a humiliation, it would be to have them taken away. I only wanted to scare the hell out of him.

A week later Pancho went up the river to work for three days for some gringo gold miners, and his brother, Nona, who was taking care of the animals, said that Pancho was bored with the chickens and would like to sell them. He had forty chickens, and the rumor had it that he was getting about three eggs a day. I asked Ramón and Alexandro if they would like to buy Pancho's chickens; they both said "Yes," but that it was a delicate situation. They would buy only if Pancho offered to sell them. I told Nona to tell Pancho that Ramón and Alexandro would buy the chickens if he wanted to sell them. I was in a delicate situation myself, for everyone was watching those first chicken projects, and I was desperately anxious that they be successful. I could feel a groundswell of interest in the idea of chickens in the whole town, but the people were still holding off, waiting.

Pancho returned from up the river but didn't come to the house. Nona said that Pancho wanted to work for the gold miners and get rid of his animals. I told Nona that it was a good idea, that having forty chickens who laid only three eggs was real madness and that Pancho could never pay his debts with that kind of production. Late that afternoon Pancho showed up at the house; he had been drinking a little and had worked himself up into a state.

"Everything," he said, "everything is for Ramón and Alexandro; now you want to give them my pigs and my chickens. Well, do it, then. I no longer want the pigs; I no longer want to work with the Peace Corps in any way. You know what you can do with the Peace Corps chickens?" He told me what I could do. "I'm a free man," he went on. "I don't want to be a slave to a couple of pigs, and I don't want to be criticized because I am a man. It is a man's right to have a few drinks when he feels like it. You have no business talking about me in the town that I will not pay my debt."

He was angry, but worse, he was defeated, his will to keep the animals destroyed. We stood there looking at each other, both of us appalled, all the plans we had made shattering around us so violently that you could almost hear the breaking sound. I bought two beers and asked Pancho to come in the house and get everything straight. We sat at the table for two hours while I explained over and over and over what I had actually said. Nothing registered. He was through with the pigs. He wanted to sell the chickens. He wanted to show me that he was honest and would pay his debt. It was God's will that he not be a farmer, and he would look for another way to live. I argued and tried to reason; it did no good. The last half hour, we simply sat silent in the darkening house staring at the floor, exhausted. It was a moment of defeat for both of us.

The next day (Pancho drunk and adamant) I made arrangements with Alfonso Estupiñan to pick up the two pigs. The three of us sat in the house, all of us sad and speaking delicately. I noticed that Pancho did not mention selling the chickens; perhaps he was beginning to realize the magnitude of the disaster he had created and was backing away from that insane pleasure in destroying himself. I hoped he would calm down and keep the chickens, because I honestly could not see much of a future for him with the gold miners, who were simply irresponsible adventurers. Besides, I knew that they would not relish wild trips down the river with a giggling philosopher managing the outboard motor; I knew how that job would end.

Three weeks later Pancho still had the chickens. I never mentioned them, but I heard rumors that they were laying well. Pancho made feeble efforts to sell them, but only to people with no money. We became friends again, in a formal and self-conscious way; those easy days when we kidded and insulted each other were gone.

□□

Ecuador is cut into two parts by the equator; and since the sun, within narrow variations, always slices directly through the middle of things, the days and nights are equal, there are no seasons, and the spectacular sunsets are short and violent. The first few times watching the sun rush screaming into the ocean, about 50 per cent faster than it does in, say, Seattle, Washington, you are totally amazed. You have the crazy feeling that the celestial watch has broken down and that your life is passing at double speed.

This impression was reinforced when the Peace Corps office in Quito invited me to take part in the termination proceedings of my group. I would be practically a guest, since I had been sick and I still had five months or so to make up. But in a rather untypical example of mindless Peace Corps bureaucracy, I was told to go through the motions of terminating, just as though I weren't going back to Río Verde.

My God, was it almost over? This was one of the few things we had in common, a feeling of amazement that the contract was almost fulfilled and that it was time to go home. It seemed

only yesterday that we arrived in Ecuador secretly convinced
that we were going to change everything and solve all problems. Well, Ecuador was still pretty much the same—but some
of the members of my group were scarcely recognizable. The
baby fat was gone for one thing, and for another, though it
sounds sentimental and corny to say it, there was a raw and
vulnerable look in many of the eyes; they were visibly marked
by the suffering they had seen. They were all anxious to get
home, but it was confused by the sadness of leaving their villages and by a queer, sad dissatisfaction with a lot of uncompleted projects. We tended to overemphasize our failures,
thinking more of what we hadn't done or what we had done
badly than of our successful projects.

Our clothes were worn out, too, and we had a battered,
tattered, well-used look. One morning the maid brought a big
pile of clean socks for Dave Hofmeister, a Volunteer from Salt
Lake City. Since Dave was leaving for home in a couple of
days, he asked if I could use the socks—about the nicest potential gift I ever got, since I was practically barefoot. But when I
went to pack them I discovered that they had no toes, heels, or
bottoms; they were like the phony cuffs that people pin inside
their coat sleeves—all bravado. Thanks, Dave.

As for the termination ceremony, it was simple, sad, and
pretty basically scatological. Part of the medical procedure
involved delivering stool samples to one of the local clinics each
morning; objective, three consecutive worm-free samples. Most
of us were wormy and had to make considerably more than
three trips. By eight o'clock in the morning, then, we would all
be on buses scattering to our respective labs—a little Peace
Corps army armed with little paper cups discreetly encased in
little paper bags. Some of the worms that came out of us—
great six-inch long Ascaris—had us giggling hysterically or

pale with disbelief that such monsters could live in us unde-
tected. Toward the end, with all of us obsessively concerned
with our bowel movements, the pension was, I would imagine,
like an old folks' home, with everyone talking about nothing
else, and the number of worms you had became a status symbol.
Ron Dudley, for example, was taking twenty pills with every
meal for three different kinds. He was our leader until Bill
Deane showed up with thirty pills, four kinds of worms, and
two kinds of amoebas. Ron didn't like it a bit, playing second
fiddle to Bill.

We had a farewell party at Eduardo Sotomayor's house,
where unbelievable quantities of beer were consumed and where
officials of the Ecuadorian Department of Agriculture presented us with certificates of achievement and thanked us for
our work in speeches made sweetly sad by the beer and by our
awareness of the end of an adventure. I found to my horror
that even after having heard a hundred Spanish speeches I still
wasn't sure just exactly what was being said. I put this down to
the beer, which had put a vague gold aura, like sweet memory,
over everything. We played volleyball and poker and some
Ecuadorian card game where everyone slapped his card on the
table furiously, and we stood around Eduardo's pet llama waiting for him to spit on us.

Two Washington Peace Corps people showed up, and we
had three days of conferences with them. They listened to
everything we had to say, trying to make some generalizations
from thirty unique and disparate experiences, and to put it all
down statistically in five or six pages. This was probably the
most amazing thing that happened all week—listening to the
other Volunteers talk about Ecuador and discovering that we
had each been living in a different country. About the only
thing we all agreed on was that we had not lost too many

illusions about the Peace Corps, that it was more important than ever to us, and that knowing what we now knew we would all do it again.

What had we liked most about Ecuador? There was no agreement, only a vague common thread woven through the fabric of our experience. The people, other Volunteers, the great sweeping land itself, the chance to see another, stranger world, the chance to be, however ephemerally, a real part of history, engaged.

What had we liked least? Again no agreement. The food, an educational system based on memorization, the transportation system and the Peace Corps tendencies to ignore our transportation problems (Big Daddies in the Quito office: I really *do* need that outboard motor), certain Washington policies which ended up overtaxing the Peace Corps Representatives who were there to help the Volunteer in his work, and a vague feeling that the Quito office should have been a little more closely involved with what each of us was doing and that the chain of command should contain less buck-passing.

Were we getting enough money? I was sure, judging from my own problems, with over half my wages invested in corn and chickens, that everyone would say "No," but only about a third of the group thought that our hundred-dollars-a-month salary was inadequate.

Had we been, judging ourselves individually, outstanding, average, or less than average as Volunteers? Twenty-two out of thirty said we had been about average, and this dismayed the Washington people, who thought we should have displayed stronger egos. But each of us was judging his work on the basis of what would remain of his projects a year or two after he had left. And we were all uncertain and depressed by the possibility that the little businesses, the cooperative ventures, this whole new cooperative philosophy which was so foreign to the Latin

temperament, would gradually poop out in jealousies and sus-
picions. Two years was such a short time to find out and train
the potential leaders in a village.

"Oh God," Loren Finnell said, "the worst thing about Ecuador is the day you have to leave your town, with everybody
hugging you and crying and their faces all screwed up and
streaming with tears. I could never go through that again."

"Yes," another more realistic Volunteer said, "in my town
they were crying and wailing, and five minutes later I caught
one of my best friends stealing a pair of scissors." He shook his
head, half laughing and half crying as he said it, not quite sure
after two years in which world he was living—that familiar
Yankee world, where your best friend does not steal your scissors, or the more pragmatic Latin one, where a friend can be
equally as heartbroken that you are leaving as that your
scissors are leaving.

The jets took off each day about noon; finally everyone was
gone except for Hank Tiarks, who wanted to stay another five
months to finish up some cattle projects, Walt Burke, who was
marrying an Ecuadorian girl, and Ron Dudley, who signed up
for an extra year to finish his projects more completely. It was
strangely comfortable to be a part of the group who were
remaining. It was so comforting that I sneaked into the Heifer
office one morning and typed out a letter requesting an extension of one year in Río Verde. I typed it all out, signed it, and
tore it up; and then I went back to Río Verde and thought real
hard for another month and typed the letter out again. There
wouldn't be anyone crying and weeping when I left *my* town—
except maybe with joy to see me go.

Living in Río Verde was in a very real sense like living in
another world. The "real" world of change—of riots, revolu-
tions, politics, and business—only began to begin in Esmeral-

das at the end of that twenty-five miles of beach and ocean that separated the two places. It was, for me at any rate, in many ways a profound experience to be isolated from that world that we had been taught to believe was the real one and to be absorbed into a world every bit as complicated but whose main realities were the tides, the planting seasons, the winter storms, the betrayals of neighbors, and the fight to stay alive. It was like switching from the nervous, frenetic music of Bernstein or Copland to the soaring, tragic music of Roy Harris, who speaks of more elemental things.

The Ecuadorian government, a military junta, fell one day with riots, shooting, and mobs of determined students marching in the streets of the main towns. (The government fell because of these student demonstrations, and the students were furious because they weren't allowed to run things.) That day I was helping Ramón and Ester split strips of bamboo for a new chicken house about a hundred feet from the ocean in the shade of a large ebony tree. Ramón had his radio outside, and we listened to the birth pangs of the new regime—the patriotic speeches and screeches, and the sound of martial music.

But after a while he turned it off. It didn't seem to have much do with Río Verde. "Well," Ramón said, "the old gang made its millions; now a new gang wants to rob us. You know, it will be the same for us whoever wins. We are completely forgotten here in Río Verde."

Río Verde had a public monument in its plaza, a ten-foot cement column standing in the middle of a field of pigweed, thinly painted in pink and blue; over it hung a fifty-watt electric light bulb that danced wildly in the ocean winds. The monument commemorated the first cry of independence in Ecuador, and the day it celebrated was a great day in both Río

Verde and the province of Esmeraldas, much like our own July fourth.

A young Communist I met in Esmeraldas told me that the Esmeraldian cry for independence involved about five drunk Negro slaves who whacked off a few land-owning white heads in 1820. But I hesitated to accept this cynical version, especially since this same guy insisted on believing, even after I had explained at least three times, that the people in the United States are so rich that they never wash their clothes but simply throw them away when they are dirty—a conception no doubt based on the enormous quantities of old clothes sent by Catholic relief agencies and sold to the poor by the local priests.

A few days before Río Verde's big independence celebration I had to go to Guayaquil on business, but the idea that I might miss the fiesta so distressed my friends that I promised to come back for it. "It is the most beautiful fiesta you ever saw," they told me, "and your presence would do us a great honor."

About 7:30 the evening of the fiesta, soaking wet and more dead than alive after fifteen hours of riding the bus, I arrived in Río Verde in pitch darkness over a wildly rolling sea in an outboard motor canoe. There were two little light plants in operation (both of them owned by storekeepers up the river who had come down with their electrical equipment, ten or fifteen phonograph records, and several dozen cases of beer and *aguardiente*), and after five months of darkness the town had a festive appearance. Three or four lights were twinkling in the school building, which had been turned into a dance hall, and on the other side of town three or four lights shone above a cement slab, which had been roofed over with palm leaves that threw great languorous shadows on the wall of the *Teniente Político*'s office and reminded me of the simple, primitive elegance of Acapulco in the 1930's.

The provincial authorities had sent a mechanic to fix the light plant, I learned later. He had spent two days repairing everything, and Pancho, the new manager of the plant, had been so elated at the prospect of lights once more in Río Verde that he had started drinking *aguardiente*. About twenty minutes before dark he had passed out cold—along with the mechanic—but after so many months without light the people were only slightly outraged. The darkness in the town emphasized the brilliance of the two *salones*.

I had taken four of Wai's hand-carved stools and sold them in Esmeraldas for forty sucres each, and he met me on the dock as I disembarked, overcome with relief that I had brought the money. I gave him half of it, the other half to be put away for a more sober day. As we walked toward my house I invited about seven of my friends to come in and have a drink of whiskey, for to celebrate the big day I had invested 20 per cent of my monthly salary in a bottle of scotch. Except for Santo, who said that at fifteen he had worked as a bus boy in a Guayaquil hotel and had drained the whiskey bottles that hotel guests left on the table, no one had ever tasted whiskey before, and it was almost a sacred moment for them. Actually, it was almost a sacred moment for me, too, since except for one night in Esmeraldas with a couple of American soldiers I hadn't tasted good scotch for over a year.

I was entertaining the beach Negroes, the more vital and turbulent element in the town, the guys who always yelled the loudest listening to the football games on the radio, who fished the farthest out in the sea, who danced the craziest, who lived freest and wildest—the poorest, the happiest, the most recklessly delighted with life. I had only seen them in work clothes, half naked, or modestly dressed up for Sunday; now they were wearing heavily starched white ducks with fourteen-inch cuffs and new white shirts, the creases ironed to razor sharpness, a

magnificent bunch of men, all of them very quiet and overwhelmed with each other's new clothes.

We sat around in a circle and passed the bottle and a glass
around and around, each of us solemnly taking a slug, shuddering, smiling gravely, and then sitting in a sort of trance
with the eyes softly going glazed. We didn't stop until the
bottle was empty; it took about thirty minutes. We went outside and sat at a table under the electric lights, directly under
the loudspeaker. Wai had asked for the empty whiskey bottle,
which he put in the middle of the table so that everyone in town
could see it, and then he ordered seven beers, blowing in one
glorious moment almost half the money he had for the whole
fiesta—two days' work carving a wooden stool out of a solid
block of *cedro*.

We drank beer and listened to the music, music so loud that
it was painful, so loud that no one could speak. Ramón appeared. He had been talking for weeks about the fiesta and the
new clothes he was going to buy, but he was very conserva-
tively, almost poorly, dressed in brown cotton drill and a white
shirt, barefooted. I yelled in his ear congratulations for not
spending his egg money on fancy clothes and strutting about
like a fanfaron, but he only smiled a little cardsharp smile and
said nothing.

He joined us at the table, and Orestes bought eight beers. A
few people were dancing, but mostly it was girls dancing with
girls, and when they weren't dancing they sat apart waiting for
the proper time to take part in the party. The teenagers stood
off in the shadows watching everything, learning how to be
men. I went over and talked to fourteen-year-old Rufo and
asked him why he didn't dance; he had been staring steadily at
one of the out-of-town girls ever since we had arrived. He said
he didn't know how to dance. Alvarez came to the table and
very formally presented me with a bottle of beer. About twenty

minutes later, obeying the rules, I bought a formal bottle of beer for Alvarez.

About midnight, dazed with noise, we moved the table away from underneath the loudspeaker, but the music was still unbelievably loud. I think we had all by this time undergone permanent personality damage, the blood vessels in the brain irrevocably burst. Crucelio bought eight beers. The men were dancing now, and the married women, dressed in their finest, began to appear. Ramón bought eight beers. Alvaro very formally brought a beer to the table and presented it to me. About one o'clock, surrounded by a rapidly growing enthusiasm and at least six full bottles of beer which I couldn't seem to dominate, I mentioned to someone that the fiesta was indeed beautiful. "Oh, this isn't the fiesta," he said. "The fiesta doesn't start until tomorrow." When no one was looking I slipped away and went to bed—but not to sleep.

At eight o'clock the next morning the music was still playing. Don Pablo and Mujujo across the street both had their loudspeakers aimed at my house. Up on the cement slab a half-dozen couples still danced, their faces grave and abstracted, dancing as partners but completely ignoring one another.

I began to drink strong coffee. Wai, his clothes soiled and his tongue thick, came by the house and got the other half of his money. Alvarez, Antonio, Orestes, and Ramón each very secretly borrowed fifty sucres. About 10:00 A.M. the school children with flags, the firemen with their red shirts and red eyes, the town officials, and the honored guests collected at the dock and marched down the street. In front of the cement column they sang the national anthem, but it could scarcely be heard above the phonographs playing Ecuadorian and Colombian dance music. In the afternoon the *futbolistas* crossed the river and played a game against Palestina, but only a few of the school children watched.

By seven o'clock that night 40 per cent of the people in the town had been more or less drunk for twenty-four hours. I stood on the porch with Alexandro and Orestes and watched Carlos Torres trying to pick the pockets of the Esmeraldas mechanic, who had fixed the light plant and who had been waving hundred-sucre bills around; he was sleeping in the street. Carlos was too far gone to realize that at least six people were watching him. Alexandro finally went over and took the money out of the mechanic's pocket for safekeeping. It grew dark. Pancho had passed out again. Another night of darkness.

The firemen had been sent a gift of 240 sucres by the provincial government and had invested it in a private party; I think I was the only outsider invited. I went up to the warehouse where they had the hoses stored and drank a Seven Up and watched the firemen dividing up the *aguardiente;* they were very serious and didn't seem to be having much fun. I told them that I had been praying all day that a fire wouldn't start, because if it did the whole town would go. One of them pointed out that even when they were all cold sober it took about an hour to string up the hoses, so it didn't make much difference. "The town burns down about every fifteen years," he said. "Being a fireman is an honorary thing; we're not really supposed to fight fires."

Carlos Torres, overcome with a crying jag, came over to talk to me. He was a guy I had never liked much, mainly because he was lazy and dishonest. Now he started to tell me all his problems. His wife and children were sick in Esmeraldas; he was broke and the firemen had refused to give him any of the money they had received; he had lost his job with the gold miners; he had lost his house because he couldn't pay the $1.50 rent. I watched him as he talked, noting with scientific amazement how as he mentioned each problem the whites of his eyes would suddenly turn bright red as the blood vessels swelled and a moment later the tears would gush. I tried to fight the growing pity I felt for him and pretty much succeeded—the gringo moralist unable to reconcile Carlos' children sick in Esmeraldas with his own ability to buy *aguardiente* and stagger around in the street.

Wai came by again. He had a stool almost ready to sell, and he wanted to borrow twenty sucres to buy a bottle of *puro*. His face was gray, and there was clotted blood on his hand where he had cut himself showing off with a machete.

About nine o'clock Ramón appeared at the house where I had retreated to wait out the fiesta. He was wearing new clothes— black oxfords, a patent leather belt, a hat, everything new. He was radiant and trying to hide his joy. His pants had a sort of blue and gold and violet rainbow effect, changing color in the light. He looked like a young executive from the American embassy, with a very formal, pin-striped shirt. He walked into the house, trying to be calm, as though nothing were out of the ordinary.

"My God," I said.

He tried to talk about the fiesta, but after a minute he couldn't stand it, and he got up and pulled a little piece of his underwear up above the waist of his pants to show me.

"Everything is new," he said, "everything. Even the shorts." And then, because I didn't seem to enjoy his splendor sufficiently, his face clouded over. "You don't like my clothes," he said.

"Sure, I do," I told him, "but in a sense you are mocking the whole town and making everyone else look shoddy by comparison."

"Of course, I'm mocking the town," Ramón said. "I've got a

hundred Peace Corps chickens now, twice as many as anyone. I took all the first risks, I worked twice as hard, I suffered twice as much. I went many days without food so that my chickens would live well. And now. Now the town must know that I am no longer just a poor beach *zambo*. Ha! I am a man of negotiations, and Martín, in a way it is for you and for the Peace Corps that I want to dress well. Fine clothes, that is something a poor man understands."

"Maybe you're right," I said, "but it worries me when you spend money on clothes before you buy the corn for the dry months ahead."

"Don't worry. I am buying the pants for seventy-five cents a month; that's only about a dozen eggs; in four months, little by little, the pants will be paid for."

Ramón wanted to visit with me, but more he wanted to walk in the street in his fine new clothes and soon he left. "I am going to walk around a little," he said, "and then I am going to drink no more than two beers, at the very most two beers, and then I am going to walk around a little more and go home." He told me that Rufo finally had started to dance the night before, that he had fallen madly in love with the teenager from Montalvo and that suddenly he started to dance; he had danced all night and he was sick with love.

Outside the music played. Across the street next to the cement slab three or four women stood by the crack in the jail wall handing bananas and bread into the cell, where their husbands were recuperating from the glorious hand-to-hand combat in the street. In the half-built house next to my garden six out-of-town visitors slept; from time to time one of them would rise, pick his way over the sleeping bodies, and be sick on my eggplants.

The third day of the fiesta things slowed down a little. Almost everyone was sick or broke or heavily in debt. The lines of credit had dried up. Heads ached, hands trembled. Walking up the beach to go fishing in the ocean, Ramón and I passed Wai's house; Wai sat in the window looking out over the sea. I asked him why he wasn't fishing. He didn't answer me, but simply put his hands to his head. Three hours later Wai met me as I passed his house again. He wanted me to come up and see the stool that was almost made and tell him if I would consider loaning him another twenty sucres to feed the kids; they hadn't eaten much in the last couple of days, he said. What had I thought of the Río Verde fiesta?

"Absolutely fantastic," I told him.

"Yes," he said, not quite understanding my meaning. "It's a truly beautiful fiesta, but listen, Don Martín, there is a fiesta on the thirtieth in Rocafuerte that is even more beautiful, and you must be sure and honor it with your presence."

Part Three: 1967

*T*HERE is a village called Africa about twenty miles up the coast from Río Verde, a village of six grass houses and five hundred coconut palms. As you sail past the town and think of its name, the village takes on an added freight of exoticness, it is so tranquil, isolated, and lost, submerged in a distant, unchanging, and forgotten world. It is a misplaced village, and it is completely outside history.

But the story has circulated all over Ecuador that this town was founded in the 1820's when a slave ship went aground, and its cargo, after killing the crew, escaped. This foundation of new racial blood, according to the story, influenced the quality and character of the coastal people from Colombia to Peru. While it is true that the coastal people are basically Negro, it can't possibly be true that it all started with one boatload of escaped slaves, no matter how pretty and dramatic the conception. The Negroes of the Chota Valley, for instance, are the descendants of the slaves who worked the haciendas owned by the Church around Pimampiro, and the history of the country, like all the South American countries, has a dark slave chapter. It is a chapter particularly brutal in Ecuador and Peru, where the first slaves were Indians who died by the hundreds of thousands in the Spanish mines.

At any rate this mixture of African blood with the blood of the Indians and the Spanish has created a new race, a people torn by the contradictions of their racial heritage: the surging vitality of the Negro fighting with the humble subservience, the patient endurance, of the Indian and the haughty pride of the Spanish. It is a tormented race, still without an identity, still searching for the qualities which will describe its soul.

In Río Verde the faces of the women are hostile and guarded; they are hard and knowing faces, strongly Negro. Their eyes say, "We have been fooled too many times." Their dark looks burn you. There is a fed-up quality deep in the eyes, a shattering honesty; they are not coquettes. They walk aggressively, the feet coming down hard and firmly as though they were making a dare; their walk contains elements of positive ownership, of domination over this sad land. But their bearing is profoundly sexual, their bodies straight, proud, and full, and their disdain is a vague but perpetually troubling challenge.

When they walk on the beach they are always carrying something—a child slung on the back or hanging from one hip, a wooden *batea* full of clothes balanced on the head, or baskets of food. They walk with disdain, like royalty condemned to servitude. I don't know of anyone in the rest of the world—with the possible exception of Audrey Hepburn—who in bare feet and rags, loaded down like a pack animal, could give an impression so regal and dignified.

The women are the serious ones; their job is to hold together the family and, since the society is based on the family unit, society itself. They do it with their character and by sheer force of will. The society is matriarchal by default, and secretly. No man would ever admit it, and the women are too wise. They have no protection under the law, for 90 per cent of the marriages are common law, but the women, with a fierce but hidden dedication which must spring from a feeling for order and from the maternal impulse to protect their children, somehow keep the society from falling apart.

This is all women's work: to cook, clean the house, and haul water; to wash clothes and care for the children, to feed the chickens, to plant, hoe, and harvest the family garden; to pull weeds in the yard, to find oysters and lobsters in the low-tide waters, and to dig clams on the beach; to make clothes for the family, to sew pants and shirts, and then to patch and patch and patch.

And this is women's work: to stand before God at church on Sunday, representing the family, and to beg for mercy.

The faces of the men are fragile and delicate, vulnerable as the blooms of maimed flowers; they have that same quality of mysterious beauty that is found in the hybrid Polynesian women or the women of Shanghai with Chinese mothers and Russian fathers. No one race predominates in their features. The faces combine the straight patrician Spanish nose, the melting liquid eyes, the soaring delicate eyebrows, and the high cheekbones of the Indian, and the Negro's strong jaw and full sensuous lips. The faces of the men, unlike the full fleshy faces of the women, are lean, pared down, and the fine bone structure shows through. The color of their skin—not Spanish, Indian, or Negro—is rich and glowing, as pure, flawless, and unreal as the tight, unrevealing skin of a movie star. They are in a sense not working models but something decorative; they weren't put here to toil and suffer but to beautify the beach, to hang indolently from the windows of houses, and to brighten up the shady places. They are irresistible; every woman wants one in her house to adorn and beautify it, to cherish and care for.

How delicately and humbly they walk in their bare feet, a silent, effortless walking way beyond grace in its naturalness; they seem to float above the earth they walk on it so easily, making no claims, claiming no domination. Their arms do not swing but hang loosely at their sides when they walk.

The talk of the men is filled with wild and funny sexual allusions. They have taken over a part of the Sierran concept of machoism (a sort of humanized roosterism, but with profoundly Latin overtones), a concept which involves not only sexual inexhaustibility but all the "masculine" traits: personal courage, contempt for death, a sensitivity to insult, a strong feeling for their own personal uniqueness as human beings, dignity. But sometimes this Latin code sounds foreign and incongruous coming from their languorous and tranquil faces. And their sexual preoccupations are more wishes and dreams than realities. Great lovers are nourished on roast beef and mashed potatoes, cream sauces and souffles—not rice and platano. And yet, inexplicably, this is contradicted by the large size of their families and the number of women a man will have, either in turn or simultaneously. A man with only two or three children is looked upon with a certain degree of suspicion, his manhood vaguely suspect.

Like flowers, their splendor fades quickly; before they are thirty their faces are transformed. They have been defeated, and the eyes are as guarded and cynical as the women's. They have a foxy look; they have learned that you have to be sharp to stay alive and that you really can't trust anyone, and the sharpness shows through. They have been corrupted by life, by searing cane alcohol, protein starvation, fevers, worms, and amoebas, and by the sufferings and deaths of their children. At forty they are old.

The sixty- and seventy-year-old men have the bodies of teen-

agers, slim, spare, and reedlike. It is a celebration to watch the
old men tottering down the hill in back of town at dusk, their
steps faltering but still light, woven baskets full of platano, ear
corn, or tobacco strapped to their backs, their faces wide in
toothless grins, their clothes in rags, and their square splayed
feet horny, broken, and scabbed. The joy in their faces is
triumphal; it proclaims that they have lasted through another
day.

(For a long time I had an almost mystical respect for old
Helacio, for his age and for that joy that I saw in his face when
he passed my house each night. Then Wai's mother told me how
Helacio had jumped on her from behind a coco palm as she was
walking up the beach one evening, chortling "Now I've got
you," and how only the intercession of the Holy Virgin had
saved her from a fate worse than death. Helacio is in his late
seventies, and my mystical respect changed to one more
earthy.)

When the sun is clouded over the men work in a patch of
corn, tobacco, or platano hacked out of the hillside jungle, or
they fish in the early morning a mile or so out in the sea,
standing upright, almost stiffly, completely a part of their
small canoe as it rolls and heaves in the ocean swells. But this
work seems almost incidental to the main purpose of their life.
They work only to eat today. There is no refrigeration, no way
to store or save against that tomorrow that never comes. They
try to make a few sucres for a few clothes and a bash with the
boys on Saturday night; they plan ahead for the big fiesta, for
it is shameful to walk in the street looking less fine than one's
neighbor.

If a man is newly married he thinks about a gold-plated
trinket for his wife; when he has children they must be clothed
by the time they reach school age. He thinks also of the notebook and the pencil, and of the white uniforms that his children

will wear in the fiesta parade. Or, if he cannot dominate this problem, it is really not too big a thing. He keeps his children at home. What difference does it make, really? They will come out of the sixth grade able to read but with nothing to read in the town and prepared only to fish in the sea like their fathers, or hack out weeds on a jungle hillside, or tote bundles from the dock to the store for a few centavos.

One dreams. One dreams of a little store; that's where the money is, and the work is not hard and has a certain dignity. In a store, which is the pivot point of the community with a kerosene lamp and perhaps even a radio, one hears everything and meets everyone. One is at the very center of life.

And then there are the children.

I had signed up to extend my time in Río Verde another two years, and one day the enormity of the obligation hit me. For the first time I felt frightened; it seemed that in the first two years I had accomplished nothing, that is had all been *por gusto*. I thought of sad Río Verde, lost and forgotten on this forgotten stretch of beach. It was just as screwed up now as it had been a year and a half earlier when I arrived. I woke up early one morning and lay there wide awake, impaled on those terrible 3:00 A.M. horrors, sinking deeper and deeper into depression.

Ramón came by the house in the morning to discover me drinking coffee, but speechless with feelings of self-pity and futility. He began to study me nervously.

"What's wrong, Martín?" he asked me. "Are you sick?"

"No, I'm not sick, just sad. Boy, I'm really sad."

"But why? What's wrong?"

I told him that it was a sadness without reason, and he gave me a puzzled look of incomprehension. We drank coffee, and

Ramón kept studying me. He was seeing something new in me that frightened him. He tried to make jokes; he turned up the radio and danced lewd dances for me. Nothing worked.

In the afternoon, still feeling completely withdrawn, I walked up the beach with Ramón. We sat down finally on a balsa log, and he began to talk about sadness. He told me about a three-month period in his life when he was twenty years old and living in Guayaquil.

"I was in love with Ester, but she lived in Machala. On week ends I used to take the night boat down to see her. About two weeks before we got married I went down to Machala one Friday night. Well, you know the boat and how you sleep in hammocks on the deck. I woke up in Machala and my wallet was gone—all my money, about fifteen dollars, and all my papers. I had just quit my job with the electrical company because they hadn't paid me in two months. I figured on finding a job in Machala near Ester, but I couldn't without my papers.

" 'I've lost everything,' I told Ester, and without a word she gave me ten dollars. That was when I decided to marry her, because of the nice way she loaned me the money. Monday we went back to Guayaquil, and that same week the company paid me my back wages, almost a hundred dollars. I decided to go into business and invest my money; I had this friend with a motor canoe and we went down the coast to Peru, as *contrabandistas*, and bought matches, but the sea was very rough. I got back with ninety dollars' worth of wet matches, everything competely ruined. This was the week after I was married and I didn't have the money to feed my wife. I had bought some dresses and gifts for Ester in Peru, and we sold them to eat.

" 'I've got to go to Quevedo and get a job in the bananas,' I told her. In Ecuador that is what you do as a final act of desperation when you can't find work in the city; you take up a machete and go back and clean the weeds in the banana plantings. Oh, how she cried. She wanted to come with me, but I said no.

"There was no work in Quevedo, or in Daule. I joined up with a gang of men all looking for work. We heard about a hacienda back near Machala where they paid thirty sucres a day, a dollar and a half a day, for clearing trees to plant pasture. This was very good wages, almost unbelievable, and we went down in a group to work on this new hacienda. It was all a lie. The owner didn't pay by the day but by the number of tree trunks you could hack out of the ground with an iron bar. He paid thirty sucres for seventy trees, and if you really worked hard in a day you could maybe hack out seven. He gave us each a pound of rice a day, platano, and a package of brown sugar. We lived out under the trees like animals. After the first day my hands were so bloody that I had to sleep with my hands wrapped in banana skins. By the sixth day I couldn't hold the bar; the skin had split here between my thumb and first finger, my hands were getting infected, and the wrists had swollen up to twice their size.

"I was sitting on the ground one morning with my hands over my eyes. My God, I was twenty years old, young, strong, anxious to work, and look where I was ending up. I was crying, and the tears were running down my hands and into my wounds; it really burned. I was thinking of my destiny, of Ester waiting for me in Guayaquil without money.

"The owner of the hacienda rode up on a great white horse and stopped before me. 'What's wrong, countryman?' he asked me.

"I put my hands out and showed him the blood; I showed him my wrists. I got up; my clothes were in rags, torn and filthy from working in that damned jungle. 'I'm thinking of my destiny,' I told him. 'I'm thinking of my life and of how it's going to be. The truth is I can't hold the bar any more; my fingers won't close on the bar any more.' I looked into his face and he had turned pale; his lips were trembling. 'Look at my friends, look at those poor men, cooking underneath a tree. Wouldn't we all be better off dead?'

"I talked without looking at him, and then I looked at him again and he was staring at my hands, and the tears were pouring down his cheeks.

" 'I swear before the Holy Virgin,' he cried, 'I haven't got any money nor will I have any before Saturday. I am doing all this with the bank.' He was crying like a child. He gave me ten sucres, that's what I earned that week, and he rode away weeping, and I didn't even say good-by but began to walk toward Guayaquil. My clothes were in rags, the shoes rotting off my feet. It took me six days, I walked six days and begged food along the road to stay alive.

"I was twenty years old, married less than a month, and I was dying. I knew that I was dying. I can't remember those days very well now, just a blackness in my mind with every-thing running together like a great madness, a delirium of fear and hopelessness.

"Now I was walking in the street in Guayaquil, and I met my aunt. This was before I went home to Ester. I think I did not plan to go home to Ester. My aunt saw me walking in the street and she began to scream and weep. 'Oh, my God, my God, what's happened to you?' She took me by the hand and led me to her house and fed me, and I slept. She was also very poor, but she bought me clothes and took me to another aunt who wept when she saw me and bought me shoes.

"I went back and stayed some days with Ester. I looked again for work in Guayaquil and then hopped on a banana truck and went north again. I had some luck; I met a man near Daule who had a savanna of mangoes. 'Look,' he said. 'I can't find anyone to pick my mangoes. I haven't any money, but if you want to pick mangoes I'll give you half the money and also the trucking into Guayaquil.'

"I picked mangoes for ten days in his savanna, first fifty boxes for him and then forty-seven boxes for me. He was an honest man, and he paid the trucking. I sold my share for fifteen hundred sucres in Guayaquil. Ay, but I was a king. I took the money home to Ester and piled it in front of her on the bed, a mountain of money. 'Look,' I said, 'over fifty dollars; our troubles are over.'

" 'Ramón,' Ester said, 'my grandmother is dying; my parents can't afford to take care of her any more, and I want her to come and stay with us.'

" 'Yes,' I said. 'This is something that you must do.'

"We hired a taxi and brought the grandmother to our room. She stayed with us for six weeks. Every day we paid five sucres for a taxi to take her to the clinic and another five sucres to bring her back. And we bought all the medicine that the doctor wrote down on a piece of paper. One of us was with her always; we cooked very special things for her. We even bought meat.

"And you know, that old dying woman never liked me. She kept telling Ester that she had married badly, that she had married beneath her. But I think what is important is how you feel about someone, not how they feel about you, don't you think that's true? I had a great deal of respect for that old woman; she died with a great deal of dignity.

"Finally, when the money was almost gone we took the grandmother back to Río Verde to die in the country where she had lived; that's how I came back to Río Verde by accident, but I'm not sorry, because when I walked in the streets of Guayaquil, I walked in a sort of terror of life. Well, that's the story of my sadness. I've never told you before, but I think now that I want you to know everything, even the worst things that have happened to me. And I want to understand your sadness too. But it is a great problem to understand this sadness that arrives in the night without a reason."

🔲🔳

Living poor is like being sentenced to exist in a stormy sea in a battered canoe, requiring all your strength simply to keep afloat; there is never any question of reaching a destination. True poverty is a state of perpetual crisis, and one wave just a little bigger or coming from an unexpected direction can and usually does wreck things. Some benevolent ignorance denies a poor man the ability to see the squalid sequence of his life, except very rarely; he views it rather as a disconnected string of unfortunate sadnesses. Never having paddled on a calm sea, he is unable to imagine one. I think if he could connect the chronic hunger, the sickness, the death of his children, the almost unrelieved physical and emotional tension into the pattern that his life inevitably takes he would kill himself.

In South America the poor man is an ignorant man, unaware of the forces that shape his destiny. The shattering truth —that he is kept poor and ignorant as the principal and unspoken component of national policy—escapes him. He cries for land reform, a system of farm loans that will carry him along between crops, unaware that the national economy in almost every country sustained by a one-crop export commodity depends for its success on an unlimited supply of cheap labor. Ecuador needs poor men to compete in the world banana market; Brazil needs poverty to sell its coffee; Chile, its tin; Colombia, its cacao and coffee, and so on. The way United States pressures shape the policies of the South American governments can make a Peace Corps Volunteer who is involved and saddened by the poverty in his village tremble to his very roots.

Death, of course, is the great release. I lay in my house one

night trying to sleep, while up the hill a fiesta went on until
dawn—drums in an endless and monotonous rhythm connect-
ing a series of increasingly complicated songs, some chanted by
women, some by men, some by mixed voices. It gradually became beautiful and moving, but I was puzzled because the
celebration was just a week before the great *Semana Santa*,
Holy Easter, a fiesta that everyone saves up for and that leaves
everyone broke and exhausted.

"Why were they *bombiendo* all night on the hill?" I asked
someone.

"They were celebrating the death of Crispín's first-born," I
was told. "He was born dead, an *angelito*." There wasn't a bit
of sadness in the town; it was a real celebration. Crispín's son
had struck it lucky; he was one of God's angels without all of
that intervening crap.

The incapacity of the poor to see the pattern of their lives is
occasionally breached. I took a color photograph of Wai and
his family standing in front of their house, and when the people
of the town saw it, it had the curious power to make them weep.
It was just a picture of a man, like any other in the town, with
his eight children formally lined up in ascending order, his
pregnant wife, and his mother. But there was something awful
in Wai's rags, in the tilt of his head, in the foolish pride that
showed in his mother's face for the voracious horde of naked
kids. The picture summed up his whole life, a symbolic render-
ing of his past and future. The people would look at it and
gasp. "Oh, my God, poor Wai." Perhaps for just a moment
they saw themselves. Wai, of course, was the poorest, but not
by much. You could measure degrees of poverty in Río Verde
with one pot or one woven mat or a dollar's worth of fishhooks.

One week, which seemed to contain a few extra big waves, I
tried to keep track of some of the things that happened in my

town, the unexpected riptides, the sudden squalls that threatened the people.

There was nineteen-year-old Lucho. I had met him on the street in Esmeraldas one night where he had borrowed twenty-five cents from me to buy, he said, groceries to take back to Río Verde—a head of cabbage and some beets. What he brought back instead was a case of gonorrhea from a two-bit whore. He sat on the dock for three days, sinking into a deep depression, lacking the twenty sucres that he needed for penicillin and afraid to tell his father what was wrong. I broke his confidence and told Alexandro, who instead of being angry was rather proud, a reaction I had half-anticipated, knowing something about his lusty old man. He immediately sold one of the ten chickens that he had been raising for his wife's approaching confinement, the only time when, to rebuild a woman's strength for the next assault, chicken is eaten in great quantities. He bought penicillin; a happy ending for Lucho. (Poverty makes a thief of a man who doesn't have monumental character. I found out months later that part of Lucho's depression had been simple fury. Just before his sickness Lucho had stolen the schoolteacher's ring. But in Esmeraldas no one would buy the ring, it was so obviously stolen. There he sat with eight hundred sucres of nonnegotiable assets in his pocket, his manhood polluted, too poor to cure himself.)

I met Alvaro staggering down the beach late one afternoon that week, his jaw swollen and his lips flecked with blood. He had been suddenly overwhelmed by the most violent toothache; too poor to go to an Esmeraldas dentist, he had walked up to Rocafuerte, the next town to the north, where one of the storekeepers did emergency work with a pair of pliers. He told me about it; it was almost a joke by then. "Oh, that *pendejo*. He looked in my mouth and everything was swollen and he didn't know which tooth to pull. 'Oh, Christ, man,' I said, 'pull them both, then; pull them both.' "

One of Orestes' two children came down with typhoid fever. He loaded up half the chickens that he had been pampering until they laid and sent them into Esmeraldas with his wife and child. In one day he lost the work of months.

That week, the week of the spring flood tides, the waves swept high up on the beach and carried away half of Pablo's coconut plantation. For three days as I walked back and forth along the beach I saw Pablo, a deaf old man who walked with a cane, wandering dazedly around in the remains of his *cocal*, the ground littered with piles of balsa chunks, debris from the flooded river, and fallen palm trees. Pablo had other assets, a *salón* by the dock, but this plantation had in his youth been the foundation of his relative affluence, bringing him in perhaps a hundred dollars a year, and it came as a great blow to lose it in one night.

A little farther up the beach the waves broke through the sand barrier and cut away the foundations of Wai's house, fulfilling his mother's prophecy. The sea washed away the steps and the balsa fence that confined his two ducks, three chickens, and a Peace Corps turkey whose feet had been badly gnawed away by rats. The day after the first high tide I found the whole family tearing the sides off the house and getting ready to move it farther back from the beach on the other side of the salt grass.

"You'll need some help with the big timbers," I said. The four corner posts of the house were of guayacan, the hardest, heaviest wood known to man.

"Yes, and with the roof sections," Wai said. "I've got to use the same roof. But I haven't got the money to buy new palm thatch, nor money for the *aguardiente* for a *minga*." (It was dishonorable to organize a *minga* without serving cane alcohol and food to the participants.) I waited a week and nothing happened. I couldn't bear to see Wai and his family sleeping on the beach without a roof, so I bought a bottle of *aguardiente*. Wai killed one of his ducks and invited his friends to help him dismantle his house, and one morning we all gathered at Wai's.

As the *aguardiente* began to take effect, the pace of the work gradually accelerated and the style disintegrated. The roof sections, which Wai desperately wanted to save, turned to powder as they crashed to the ground, released too suddenly on ropes held by drunken hands. The roof was made of ascending strips of bamboo to which had been laced palm leaves, but the bamboo was dry and rotten and the leaves were as brittle as eggshells.

By noon the house-wrecking had turned into a hilarious farce, marred but somehow made funnier by the fact that a four-by-four mahogany roof beam had crashed down and broken Santo's nose. We were all caught up in the joy of destruction, walking warily through the pools of Santo's blood. At one o'clock we gathered together for duck soup in the shattered remains of Wai's house, of which nothing remained standing but the four main corner posts, deeply sunk into the sand. Around us was absolute chaos.

"*Jodido pero feliz*," Wai said, surrounded by friends and family and tipping up the last of the Cayapa. Screwed but happy.

For several months Wai and his family lived in the open under a section of the old roof that they propped up against a dying mango tree. The children played in the tangle of grass and vines around the house, and one of the youngest girls was bitten by a *podridora*, a snake, according to the people, like one out of Greek mythology whose bite, although not fatal, never heals and continually grows and suppurates. For many days she sat under the mango tree in a tormented and dazed immobility, holding her well-greased, rag-covered, swollen hand in her lap. Finally it became infected, and Wai borrowed twenty sucres and took his daughter to a man up the river who understood snake bites, who in fact could call snakes into his house, and who used them instead of watch dogs to guard his house when he was gone. The child's hand slowly healed.

She was a child who stood out in my mind, not only because of her beauty and the size of her eyes but because she was one of the few kids in my whole experience who abhorred my white skin and who howled with terror every time I approached the house. I found out later that she had been brainwashed by Wai's mother. The old woman gleefully told me how when I had first arrived she had told the child that if she weren't good the gringo would come and eat her. Most kids aren't racist until they're about six; Wai's made it before her third birthday.

In almost the same week that Wai's house was destroyed, another house, that of Don Julio, was shaken to its foundations by a more subtle, more devastating event. Don Julio's eight-month-old granddaughter fell from a hammock one afternoon and struck her head on the cement floor. A blue growth appeared on the baby's left cheekbone, and in a short time it grew to the size of an egg, distorting the child's face and forcing one eye almost out of its socket.

Don Julio and his three sons were the landowners of the Río Verde area; they owned thousands of acres of jungle land, and through the years they had laboriously cleared and planted a small percentage of it to pasture, corn, and tropical crops. They were a good family, highly respected, and the sons were hard working, sober, and honest. Two of them resented me, not, unfortunately, because they regarded me as a threat to the local status quo, but simply because I wouldn't give them farm animals from Heifer. But they had certain tenuous lines of

communication with the Esmeraldas banks; they didn't need
the Peace Corps, and I always laughed away their increasingly
insistent demands for help.

Over a twenty-year period, Don Julio, a victim of the Ecuadorian banking system, which required that a man obtaining a
loan must have the loan guaranteed by an outside party, had
gradually lost his money guaranteeing the loans of his friends.
He had been pretty much destroyed by his sense of honor, and
now there was nothing left but the land. One heard rumors that
the family was heavily in debt.

When I talked to my boss in Quito, Tomás Guerrero, about
my job, he at first kept suggesting that I switch my emphasis
from chickens and gardens to crops of a more permanent na-
ture, like coconuts or oranges, trees which would eventually
bring in steady income. My problem was that all the land
around Río Verde was owned and rented out by Don Julio, and
the farmers had little interest in planting permanent crops on
land that they could not own. I had spoken many times with
Don Julio and with his son, Alfonso, about forming a production cooperative of the farmers in Río Verde. They could buy a
couple of hundred acres of land behind the town and learn to
work together as a power in the village. But the family did not
want to sell the land, so I forgot about the coconuts and kept
working with chickens and corn.

It was apparent that we couldn't make a farmers' co-op
without land. But I was convinced that I must somehow reach
the people of the town with the concept of cooperation, show
them that if they would unite and become a force they could
begin to dominate their poverty and to exist as a consideration
in the minds of the outside men who governed them. Until they
felt that they existed outside themselves, until they shed the
conviction that they were a forgotten and abandoned people,
sentenced to the endless cycle of poverty, they would be noth-

ing. Later they would have to learn the harder lesson: that the outside powers had never abandoned them because they had never had the slightest interest in them, that these powers really couldn't help them much, and that their progress lay in their own hands.

After many months of harassment, the Peace Corps finally agreed to give me an outboard motor. Ramón, Miguel, and I took a three-day bus, canoe, and hiking trip seventy miles or so up the beach to receive the motor, and on that same trip we bought an eighteen-foot canoe which had been hollowed out of a great log by the Cayapas Indians. Everyone's chickens were laying eggs by then—we had hundreds to sell each week—and it seemed like a good time to give them a violent push and try to get the idea of community effort etched into their wildly individualistic minds. The idea of owning and operating a motorized canoe was breathtaking to the people with chickens, and they all agreed in principle that it was more sensible for one person to market one thousand eggs than for half the town to make the trip to Esmeraldas each week with his basketful. The main problem with this idea (aside from the impossibility of finding someone besides myself who could be trusted to sell their eggs) was the fact that for the first time many people had the money to make the trip, and they hated to be deprived of the excitements of the large town. It was slightly irrelevant that they spent most of their profits going back and forth; they were getting out into the world, seeing movies at night, walking in those nighttime streets that throbbed with life and music.

We were just beginning to organize a little marketing co-op when Olympia's child, Don Julio's granddaughter, fell. For a month no one in town knew anything about it; the growth was so distorting that they hid the child away. One morning when I was talking to Olympia's mother on the steps of their house she told me what had happened and asked if I could help. I asked to see the child and after a moment's hesitation she called her daughter, who must have been waiting behind a door, since she immediately appeared, holding the stricken baby in her arms.

It was not the child's face that I would remember, but the face of the mother; she was a woman distraught, on the very edge of madness, and she gave me a piercing look which was pleading, hopeless, and disoriented. There was nothing I could do but urge them to see a doctor immediately, that very day if possible. I told them I would talk to Nancy Bartus, a Volunteer from Santo Domingo, who had visited Río Verde many times and who was a friend of all the women, and that I was sure she could arrange hospitalization.

This all happened a few weeks before I was scheduled to take a thirty-day vacation in the United States, a Peace Corps reward for signing up for another two years. Shortly before I was to leave, Don Julio's son, Alfonso, asked me if the farmers of Río Verde were still interested in forming a farming co-op and buying a piece of the jungle land in back of town. "We need the money desperately for the doctor bills," Alfonso told me. Of course, we were interested, and for the next ten days I divided my time between riding around on a horse with Alfonso, hopelessly lost in a chaos of jungle growth and spiny second-growth scrub, and talking with the farmers in town about the possibilities of the area and the price they were willing to pay. The farmers finally agreed that the land was worth seven dollars an acre; Alfonso wanted ten.

The transaction took a couple of weeks, and I slowly grew to realize just how delicate and sensitive this business was, this assault on the family property. It was like a terrible, unhealable breach, an unmistakable indication that the future would be hard and the family solidarity threatened. But we finally agreed on a price (a price which, because my Spanish was still unsure and faltering and because the sounds of the words "sixty" and "seventy," *sesenta* and *setenta,* were to me identical, gave us problems later). I promised to loan the farmers a 50 per cent down payment on the land, about five hundred dollars, if I could raise it in California.

I came back to Río Verde with the promise of money to follow, and I came back to a town in a kind of shock. Olympia had had a nervous breakdown just a few days before I returned. They had taken the child to a doctor in Guayaquil, who had diagnosed cancer. He had said that the child's eye would have to be cut out; Olympia, on hearing this news, had lost her mind.

"That sweet, quiet girl," one of my friends told me sadly. "Really, the nicest girl in town. A terrible, terrible thing. She started coming out into the street and telling people the truth about themselves."

"For example?"

"She told Duco that he was a dirty alcoholic bum and that he needed a bath."

"You can't deny that. What else?"

"She told the storekeeper that he was the biggest thief in town, that his pound only weighed twelve ounces."

"We all knew that. What did she tell you?"

"Well, not everything was true," my friend said. "She said many wild things, too."

"What did she say about you?" I asked again.

"It was just *pendejadas,* just inconsequential wildness," he said.

Later another friend told me what she had said. "She said he was the laziest man in town, a deadbeat who hung around the *salón* waiting for a free drink but who never reciprocated, and she told him that his unfaithfulness to his wife while she was pregnant was shameful enough but doubly so since he went around boasting about it."

"A very fair analysis," I said. "But I'm glad I wasn't here when all this took place."

"Yes," my friend said. "She would have divined your most vulnerable qualities and impaled you with her truth. But, you know, you wouldn't have believed it. Olympia only spoke the truth about others, not about oneself."

Olympia was taken to a sanitarium in Guayaquil; the child stayed in Río Verde. Whatever the final diagnosis, she was too young to be operated on. And so, out of all that suffering, we had the land. All we had to do was clear it, make it produce, and pay for it.

For many days different farmers walked with me through the dry stream beds that cut down to the beach. We would hack our way through the wild growth, trying to figure out what we had bought and how to divide it. But it remained an enigma. There was no single spot in all those 160 acres where you could see more than 50 feet before you. You could walk for hours toward the sound of waves breaking on the beach and never reach the ocean, never even see it. Or you could hack your way through land that seemed flat, and fine for working with a tractor, and after a few feet find the ground falling away before you in steep gullies hidden by ten-foot-high tangles of *saboya* grass.

"Look," I said one day to Orestes as we wandered around in the middle of the farm. "This is madness. Let's not split it up yet; let's work it all together as a unit." Just off the trail that bordered the farm, on a ridge of land that ran parallel to the river, we had found what looked like about eighty acres of fine level land, and I had begun secretly to dream of getting hold of a small tractor. With a disking tractor we could get into that jungle and really raise hell in the way of an agricultural revolution.

"Whatever you say, Don Martín," Orestes told me. "I know we'll go along with whatever you think best. You know we've never worked together, and I don't think we ever can, but maybe it's time that we at least tried. But some day, some day, I want that paper in my hands that says I own a part of this." He pounded his bare foot down hard on the ground and looked at me with real affection and began to laugh. "Ay, *caramba*," he said, "to be the owner of my own land."

Eighteen-year-old Ricardo, the son of Jorge, the carpenter, came to the first meeting of the co-op and nearly destroyed it with one great blast. Ricardo was almost the size of a twelve year old, and almost as smart. Much of the time he walked around town badly scarred, having been hit with a frying pan or a bottle wielded by his *mamita*, a woman driven to violence. I didn't really know whose side I was on.

Ricardo was hopelessly in love with me, and he drove me right to the brink of insanity, because I could never escape him. He lived next door and was incessantly prowling around outside my house, calling through the bamboo wall and howling outside the kitchen, where the scent of frying rice made him bay like a wolf. He knew every move I made. Outside he guarded me. If a mosquito lit on me, Ricardo rushed over and, with a blow that sometimes knocked me down, saved me from malaria. The little cuts and bruises that I got from clearing jungle drove him to distraction, and he had to fuss over each one; he had to touch it, rub it, commiserate. He was like the younger, more shameless little kids in town who had never seen light-colored skin and hair and who were obsessed with touching me, equally repelled and fascinated by the hair on my arms, the hair on my head bleached by the sun, my bushy eyebrows. How many times conversing with a neighbor had I suddenly become aware of some six-year-old index finger delicately but with true dedication probing my belly button, exploring the mystery of my whiteness.

Well, I sort of loved Ricardo, too, though he had some pretty distracting habits. For one thing he was a very gassy kid; for another, he was always spitting. His spit-making machine was terribly overactive. If you were talking to him in one place for a few minutes, sometimes you could hardly get out.

Ricardo wasn't invited to the first co-op meeting, but he came anyway. Before calling it I went around and talked with everyone in town who sounded interested in joining. I tried to explain what a cooperative was, how it worked, how with union came power. I broke one stick as a symbol of individual weakness and then showed them that a bundle of sticks couldn't be broken. ("Sure they can," Wai said, taking the sticks from me and cracking them easily across his knee. "You just have to know how.")

All this talking took a couple of months. No one had any firm ideas about the co-op; they had never been in one, they had scarcely ever heard of one. Who did they want to run it? There was no consensus. They were wild to own land but suspicious of working together. They really didn't want anyone to run it. The idea of having a president who would direct them and assign them different work was a dismaying thought. Why couldn't Don Martín be president?

The problem turned out to be more basic than simply finding leaders; most of the people didn't even want certain of their neighbors in the cooperative, leaders or not. Wilfrido, for example, a very strict *Evangelista*, a man whose life was almost completely centered around God and the Bible, wanted to orient the organization toward the glories of God. And he didn't want Publio, Eugenio, and Crispín in the cooperative because they spoke so grossly and because about halfway through every fiesta they almost invariably ended up in jail for fighting or exuberantly yelling naughty words in the street. Publio, Eugenio, and Crispín were brothers in their early twenties; they

were charming fellows, but lazy and dedicated to their poverty ;
they never had the slightest interest in joining the co-op or
anything else. It was difficult for me to understand Wilfrido's
fear that they would enter the co-op and somehow destroy or
pollute it.

A lot of the people were afraid of Orestes ; they said he was a
troublemaker who would never cooperate with anyone. Almost
everyone agreed that Pedro with his twelve children had, out of
desperation, been driven to sharp ways ; they didn't want him
in the cooperative. A lot of people were bored with Alexandro
and the officious way he was handling the distribution of the
chicken feed. I too was a little bored with Alexandro, who had
turned sly and calculating ; he was making good money with his
chickens, but instead of paying his debts he was squandering
his money on a second woman in Esmeraldas.

Everyone was afraid that one or two men would end up
dominating the cooperative to their own advantage ; no one
would talk about who they wanted as a leader but only about
who they didn't want. Only Ramón had a positive idea about
who he wanted to be the leader. "I want to be president," he
told me. Ramón, I thought, was a little young and violent, a
little impatient, to lead the group through its first months. I
told him that I wanted Wilfrido for president but that I
thought he could be a good director.

"No," Ramón said. "You don't understand. I don't want to
be appointed president by you ; I want the people to elect me,
to want me, but later when I have proved myself."

I wanted Wilfrido for president because, although he was
slightly eccentric, he was, as everyone acknowledged, the most
serious and honorable man in town. He was one of those poor,
demented men who took the Bible seriously and actually tried
to live out the precepts of Jesus Christ ; they just don't hardly
make them like that any more. Wilfrido lived across the street

from me. He had run out of money building his house, and it had no front wall. I had a chance, along with everyone else in town, to observe him closely. When he wasn't working on his farm or shelling corn into a calabash, he was usually reading the Bible or praying. At night, long after all the lights were out, I could hear him whistling or singing the one hymn he knew. He lived much of the time in an intensified state of feeling close to ecstasy, balanced out by infrequent but violent depressions; then he talked about killing himself, about the crushing burden of his poverty, about the glory of God hiding itself in great crises of doubt. He had raised four children and sent them all through high school, but only by terrible sacrifice.

Finally it came time to call our first meeting. We had, I figured, about a dozen families. There was Jorge, the carpenter; old Wilfrido; three middle-aged women, all married, but to men too old or too sick to work; the younger guys from up the beach—Pancho, Wai, Alvarez, Ramón, and Orestes. There was Alexandro in town and his mother's current husband, old what's his name, and there was Pedro Castro who ran a canoe service into Esmeraldas on shares with Don Umberto, the rich storekeeper and cattleman across the river. Almost everyone showed up; we sat on stools and boxes in my bedroom around a single candle burning in the middle of the room. Jorge, who arrived first with his wife and Ricardo and who had had a couple of snorts of Cayapa, began to doze almost as soon as he sat down. By the time the last of the *socios* arrived and the meeting was ready to begin, he was sound asleep.

It was a lovely wild meeting; it started off bashfully and haltingly but built in intensity. There were first a few patriotic and stirring remarks by Wilfrido about the opportunity that lay before us and about all the hard obligations of union. He began to slip in a few cracks about his church and the necessity for a closer communion with God, but Ramón very nicely cut him off. This seemed to have a good effect on everyone, because each one now felt called upon to give his version of the same speech. Toward the end of this first phase three people were giving patriotic speeches at the same time.

I gave a talk on what a cooperative was, and how it would be possible if there was no panic for everyone to own his own land. I told them that I was looking for a tractor and that with it I thought a farmer could control ten times as much land with the same amount of work. We talked about community chicken houses and a cooperative hog project and about how maybe later we could start a store and break Alvaro's domination over their lives. There was another outburst of passionate speeches; for a while I thought Vicenta was going to break down and weep.

Then the time came to elect officers. No one said anything. Did anyone want to put forward a candidate? No one said a word. I suggested Wilfrido, Ramón, and Alexandro. The *socios*, like little automatons, nodded their heads in agreement, and each new director made a nice speech accepting the obligation unworthy as he was, and pledging disinterested vigilance in the furtherance of cooperative ideals.

"Now we need a treasurer," I said. This was a tricky moment, because treasurer meant money, and no one wanted anyone to handle the money. There was a long, long silence, and I asked, "Doesn't anyone have any suggestions?"

"I accept," Señora Carlina suddenly cried in a loud voice from a dark corner. Well, I thought, their way is as democratic as mine.

What happened next I'm not at all sure; I think someone made a remark to Alexandro, kidding him because he hadn't ended up with the treasurer's job. At any rate, Alexandro, his feathers well ruffled and his voice trembling with rage, got up and resigned as director of the cooperative. Immediately after-

ward Wilfrido stood, announced that he was mentally op-
pressed—sometimes not even in his right mind—and resigned
as director. Ramón got up and said that without the guidance
of an older head like Wilfrido he would be unable even to
consider being a director in the cooperative. There was a pause
as we all tuned our instruments for the last movement. It was
getting late; we had been talking for about two hours. We had
formed a cooperative and disbanded it. I was furious. Ramón
gave me a sly, quizzical look, and I whispered to him behind
Vicenta's back, "I'll talk to you later, buddy."

"Don't get excited," Machiavelli whispered back. "You
can't push yourself forward, you know."

The last movement was unexpectedly short because suddenly, in the midst of the dead silence that enveloped us,
Ricardo, who was unusually gassy that night, made his violent,
brutal, and simple statement. We sat there absolutely stunned.
Jorge woke up, blinking his smarting eyes, and smiled softly.
Ricardo, standing by his side, smiled an angelic smile of de-
tached innocence while we sat there staring at him; he was the
only one in the room, apparently, who had heard nothing. Four
teenage girls who had come to observe the meeting exploded
into hysterics and bolted through the door; for about ten
minutes we could hear them outside rolling on the ground and
screaming uncontrollably with laughter. The older members
managed to ignore the situation, although they were secretly
outraged. Unconsciously, I think, we were all waiting for The
Leader to show himself and save the situation.

Ramón began to talk now. He spoke about the necessity of
being rational, about the need to ignore all of the little tribal
resentments that each of the *socios* harbored. He said that we
had to learn mutual respect. He was proud, reserved, dignified,
altogether magnificent. We disbanded the meeting, but promised to have another session within the week.

"That was the damnedest performance I ever saw," I told Ramón later when we were alone. "Tell me, is there or isn't there a co-op?"

"Of course, there's a co-op," Ramón said. "And it's going to be a good one, too. And you know what, Martín? I'm going to be president sooner than you think."

La Cooperativa de Río Verde began to clear the new ground in back of town. We found after we had advanced ten or fifteen meters off the trail into the tangle of bushes that we had picked an area crowded with a tree called *chocho*. The *chocho* was a wandering, aggressive kind of tree with about twenty or twenty-five main branches growing from a common root, all of the branches very individualistic in their behavior and growing in a contorted, hostile way.

The ugliest thing about this tree was the rows of two-inch spikes that ringed its branches at three-inch intervals and the piles of dead spines that covered the ground around it.

Ramón was the only member of the co-op who owned shoes, and the *chocho* was a real problem for the others, who worked barefoot. Watching them work was like watching a slow-motion movie; the *socios* spent more time screaming "Ayee" and picking spines out of their feet than hacking away at branches.

By this time I considered myself pretty cute with a machete, and since everyone avoided the *chochos* I decided to concentrate on them. "You'd better not," Ramón told me. "The *chochos* are dangerous; you'd better stick to the weeds." I watched him working on one, and it seemed ridiculous. After cutting one branch he would walk around the tree for about five minutes stroking his chin like an old philosopher and looking for the next point of attack. I knew he was showing off for me, so I ignored him; after a few days I found that I could demolish one of the monsters in four or five hours.

One morning I had worked myself into the middle of a particularly large *chocho*, where, after hacking off the outer branches, I proceeded to work at its heart. Around me all ten *socios* were busily hacking away with their machetes, but secretly watching me, I found out later. It turned out to be a sort of magic tree, with each branch supporting every other branch

about ten times, so that nothing happened when I cut through one. I had the impression that I would cut through them all and that the tree would simply sit there, floating a few inches above the ground.

After about an hour I cut through the crucial branch, the big-daddy branch, the one that was secretly supporting and containing all the hidden tensions. There was a great cracking sound, and branches began whipping around me like enraged snakes. One branch swooped down and tore the knees out of both pant legs; in this same moment another branch came swooping down with a whistling sound and ripped the shirt right off my back, leaving the sleeves still on my arms. One branch dipped down and made the mark of Zorro on my forehead, and another one grabbed the machete out of my hand and sent it flying into the air.

All of this lasted about three seconds and was accompanied by the great sound of crashing and splintering wood—and the moans of the *socios*, who stood transfixed, watching me in the middle of this insane activity. A couple of the nearest ones, not really running because that was impossible but picking their way toward me as quickly as they could, began calling my name, and Ramón in a perfect rage was yelling, "I told you so; I told you so," over and over again.

When it was all over, there I stood, practically naked to be sure, but untouched. From about this time on the *socios* of the Río Verde co-op realized that I was too dumb and green to be allowed to work alone; afterward I noticed that whenever I headed up the hill with my machete someone from the co-op would arrive a few minutes later to work beside me.

We worked on that hectare—about two and a half acres—for over two months, at first one day a week, then later two days a week. We were in the middle of the rainy season, and the weeds grew up behind us almost as fast as we cut them down. A week after the *chocho* stumps had been severed, they sent out shoots of angry growth. We cut and hacked, cut and hacked, the people working in their rags, painfully picking their way through the piles of spines, and slowly, slowly, our hectare opened up. It was the wrong time of year for clearing jungle, but we wanted desperately to plant corn, and I think all of us figured that as a group we could dominate that piece of ground by brute force.

Finally, except for a dozen very large trees—guayacan, ebony, colorado—we reached the inside line. The ground was three feet deep in dead weeds and branches. Wai came up with an ax and felled the timber. Our first hectare, but what a mess. It was the custom to plant corn on ground thus cleared, but it seemed obvious that the yields would be minimal, and I refused to let them do it. "We'll have to burn first," I insisted, talking to the *socios* out in the field, where we stood in a drizzle of rain.

"It is hardly the custom to burn wet brush," they told me sarcastically.

"This is not the United States," Ramón told me. "This is the way we do it; you should have a little more respect for our customs."

"But that's the only reason I'm here," I told him, "to destroy your crazy customs."

Wilfrido and Vicenta sneaked out one day and planted corn in the few open spots where the fallen trees had not covered everything. The corn came up, but very tentatively, yellow and hidden in weeds.

Then, miraculously, the rains stopped, and the sun blazed in a clear sky; in three days of steaming the brush dried out. I went up to the farm and started piling brush and burning it. Wilfrido, passing by on the trail, stopped to talk.

"You can't burn in February," he told me.

"But it's burning," I said.

"Besides you're burning up the corn," he said. Actually, I had accidentally burned about three stalks of corn, but Wilfrido had an almost sacred respect for those puny, struggling plants, and he was distraught at losing three.

For a week I worked alone; no one would help me. Then one day, with hot sun and a strong wind off the sea, the brush caught hold and about a half an acre went up in one furious blaze. "*Fantástico*," the people said. "Imagine burning brush in February." They began to help me. Four months after we started to clear our first hectare, we had it burned and planted to corn. My God, but it was beautiful! And only sixty-one more to go.

Three months after the formation of La Cooperativa de Río Verde, we had cleared two and a half acres of land and planted it to corn and oranges. We had planted another two and a half acres, with the technical help of Forestation (a United Nations agency), to year-old teak trees, which, I kept telling the *socios*, in forty years would be worth approximately twenty million sucres. For people who had little idea where their next meal was coming from, who lived in the hands of God, and who didn't even plant coconuts because they had to wait three years for the first fruit, they received the news that in the year 2007 they would all be millionaires with a commendable degree of calm. Still, secretly, I think the idea pleased them, it was good for their egos.

The only *socio* who really got excited was Wilfrido, aged sixty-two. I had been talking to him about nutrition and protein requirements, and he was convinced that if he ate meat, cheese, and soybeans he could easily arrange to be on hand for that final climactic harvest. Poor Wilfrido, who had already lived twenty years beyond the average Ecuadorian life span. We sat down together one day after we had had a fine talk about the nine hundred years of Methuselah and figured out that on his 102nd birthday he would be worth around eighty-seven thousand dollars—if all the trees lived.

We were in the middle of the rainy season, in those months when clearing land is looked on as madness, and I soon realized that the *socios* were doing it as a personal favor to me. The rest of the people in the town, who were watching us compulsively and hoping desperately that we would fail, felt that the whole idea of the co-op was balanced on the edge of being either very dangerous or else very funny. Well, it wasn't funny to me,

although the madness and chaos of the meetings frequently had
me on the verge of hysterical laughter. (Or else so frustrated
that I wanted simply to bite someone.) On those days when we
worked together—the *socios* barefoot and in their oldest, most
worn-out work clothes, some of them working without breakfast, some of them women well into middle age, all of them
hacking jungle with their machetes, all of them stung by a tiny
ant called *candelilla* that dropped from the trees—I was often
on the verge of tears for them, especially after I realized that
so far they had little idea of what they were doing. Their labor
was, in a very real sense, an expression of confidence in me, that

naïve gringo from the Cuerpo de Paz who had said that he
could change their lives by (imagine it) planting corn on level
ground, where it would surely flood out, and by using a tractor.

The tractor was a real sore point. The only tractors they
had ever seen were the tremendous Caterpillars that passed

through town on their way to a road-building job. We had bought a disking tractor in Esmeraldas for about a thousand dollars (some of the people in San Francisco who had read about Río Verde had sent me cash, and a friend in San Diego had helped me arrange a loan with the Bank of America). Our tractor was a twenty-two horsepower, second-hand Allis Chalmers with almost enough power to pull the hat off your head. I had finally got it to Río Verde, but two months after the rains had started. I had rushed up on the hill for a disking demonstration to give them a little faith in its capabilities, and in the first two minutes I had got the damned thing stuck in a mudhole. It sat in the field all winter, gradually disappearing as the corn grew up around it, and everyone hated it because it wasn't a D-8; it couldn't build roads, pull stumps, or pull trucks out of the ocean when they fell off the balsa raft; all it could do was disk. Never having seen disked ground, they couldn't imagine why I was making such a fuss about it.

We planted the corn, and when it was shoulder high Don Umberto's cows found an open gate and spent a couple of days tramping around in the corn and licking the first green shoots off the orange trees. At night, lines of ants marched in and slicked up the shoots that the cows had missed. The doses of ant poison that we sprinkled around each tree seemed to stimulate rather than deter them.

We had meetings—sometimes once a week, sometimes twice a month—at which time I hoped we could talk about the work to be done, but the meetings were mostly psychological outlets for damaged feelings, as far as I could see. Everyone discussed, argued, justified, got his feelings hurt, resigned, accused, was talked back in; it was a real witch's brew, a fermenting, bubbling time when the resentments of years were aired and, I hoped, dissipated. An IBM machine would have been necessary to keep the membership list up to date, for every twenty minutes it seemed to fluctuate between five and fourteen.

When we finally got down to rational discussion, it was all organizational. Wilfrido wanted everything legal and formalized; he seemed to feel that getting things on paper would produce character changes. He suggested that the rules be written down and that all the *socios* line up, kiss the Bible, swear that they would obey everything, and then sign their names. But I wasn't about to write down rules in my exotic Spanish.

"Without written rules you've got nothing," Wilfrido insisted.

"O.K.," I said, "let's write down our rule that each month each *socio* pays six sucres. Do you think then that everyone will pay?"

Wilfrido blushed. This rule, like most of the others, was pretty much ignored, not, in many cases, out of willfulness but simply because thirty cents a month was more than a *socio* could spare.

After three months we were still without officers, and this drove Wilfrido crazy. "Why can't we wait?" I kept asking. "In a short time a leader will perhaps develop who you'll all want. For now we'll just work together *en familia*. In a family everyone has his job without signing any legal documents."

At the second meeting Alexandro, one of the leading members, failed to show up. He told a couple of his friends that he was not a machete man, that he wasn't going up the hill to suffer needlessly, and that anyway the idea of the people of Río Verde working together was unrealistic. "The whole thing will blow up in thirty days," he had said. Since Alexandro dominated his mother's second husband and Pedro Castro, they, too, decided that they wanted no part of the new co-op. The real reason why Alexandro eased himself out of the co-op was much sadder, and was based on the disintegration of our friendship. Over a period of eighteen months he had proved himself to be lazy and cannily dishonest; his system for attaining to the good life was simply to come by every few days and try to borrow a few more sucres.

At the third or fourth meeting Carlina resigned from the co-op. She had elected herself treasurer, but since no one trusted her, she had never been given any money to be treasurer of. It was just as well. Carlina was a hard worker, but she was also a shrewish, constantly furious, intemperate-talking woman who loved to start rumors and keep things stirred up. I felt a wave of relief as she sat there that evening telling us off and withdrawing from the organization. After she had finished with the co-op, she started in on me, giving me hell because her Heifer chickens were dying of cholera. She spoke very fast, very eloquently, and I couldn't understand it all, but her chief complaint seemed to be that I had no sympathy for the poor, only for the rich, and why weren't Don Rico's chickens dying when hers were? (Don Rico was the name that the more jealous people in town used for Ramón.) By God, if her chickens had to die, she wanted everyone else's to die too.

"For one thing," I said, "the chickens of Don Rico live in a chicken house where they belong and don't roam around eating garbage."

"And for another thing," she said with a malicious smile, talking faster and faster, "you picked out the biggest, healthiest chickens at the distribution for Don Rico. I'm a very frank person, and I believe in speaking openly."

"Well, you're talking pure *mierda* now," I told her, for actually Alexandro had distributed the chickens, not I. It was a big joke in town, because he had picked out the biggest for himself and had ended up with fifty-three roosters and only

seven laying hens. And Alexandro's chickens had had a touch
of cholera, too.

The co-op wasn't all chaos and slapstick. It was a group of
poor people who had never been to a meeting before trying to
learn how to act in a meeting. It was people who had never
thought of working together before, who were in fact repelled
by the idea, who had never thought that they owed loyalty to
anything larger than the family unit, being faced with a brand
new set of values. Trying to understand and work within these
absolutely foreign concepts was as difficult for them as calcu-
lus, for instance, to the high-school student who barely got
through algebra.

They were beginning to feel their power, too. For twenty
years Don Umberto's cows had roamed at will over the hills,
and every year they destroyed whole fields of corn or rice. Don
Umberto's cows were part of the reason why people didn't even
try to farm in the Río Verde area, for they were a humble
people and none of them would ever face up to a rich *hacendado* from Palestina like Don Umberto. But the sight of one of
Don Umberto's cows placidly eating orange trees was starting
to drive them to distraction. "Would you all sign a petition and
send it to Don Umberto?" I asked them. "Either keep your
cows out or pay damages."

"We sure will," they told me with heat, and I almost believed
them. And even if it wasn't true this year that they would dare
to face up to Don Umberto without being pushed to it (which I
wouldn't do), perhaps next year they would do it. If there was
still a cooperative next year.

□□

We were desperate for money. We had to buy land, and we
had to build fences, chicken houses, hog pens, corn-storage
facilities, a caretaker's house. We had to pay the caretaker,

and we figured we couldn't get a full-time man for less than five dollars a month. The aim of the co-op was to move a whole group of people out of poverty right into the middle of the middle class, with each family earning fifty dollars a month, about what a teacher or a policeman or an agriculture extension man made. And about six times more than the people were making to start with. But we had very little capital.

Using the large canoe and the Peace Corps outboard motor, we established a more or less regular passenger service between Río Verde and Esmeraldas, and special rental service for the farmers up the river who hired the canoe to take their products to market—things like pigs, avocados, lemons, coconuts, and oranges. We were also available for emergencies—the nineteen-year-old boy crushed by a falling tree, the kids suffering from some obscure jungle fever, the old men of forty out of their heads with malaria. We decided we would deliver anything for a small profit.

During the rainy season when the rivers were high and the beach washed away with flood water, we got almost all the business, but in the dry season there was enough risk in the ocean trip and enough possibility of getting soaked that many people preferred to take the truck, even though the trip by land was longer and involved more physical agony.

For sheer spectacle the truck trip from Esmeraldas to Río Verde was hard to beat. My first year in the village I almost always took the land route simply because I could never believe the previous trip. Could it be true? I wanted to see once more two bulls, a half-dozen full-grown market hogs, and eighty-seven people jammed together in a perfect blend in that two-ton truck, rocketing up the low-tide beach, everyone screaming and laughing with joy at the high speeds (up to thirty miles an hour), and to see again at fairly predictable bumps along the route the pigs or the bulls or a ton of coconuts falling off the truck in a trail along the beach. Sometimes when the tide was coming in the truck wouldn't even stop, just slow down enough to let the owner of the lost goods jump off.

It was an incredible trip compounded of blowing tires, faulty distributors, dirty or empty gas tanks, quicksand, land-slides, mudholes, and countless other unique and exotic factors. I made the trip a hundred times, and ended up perhaps 15 per cent of the time walking—sometimes, at high tide, practically swimming. But, of course, delightful as the trip was, you had to pay the price, which in my particular case was broken health. I used to crawl off the truck after some of those rides so shattered in mind and body that twelve hours in a darkened room was hardly enough to restore me for a tentative stroll around the plaza.

The risks in the canoe? Well, they were merely psychological; you only died a few of a coward's thousand deaths. The river mouth had been blocked by a spreading bar of silt and sand, and when the ocean swells reached shallow water, especially at low tide, they suddenly grew larger, broke, and rolled. When this was all mixed up with winds and riptides, the *entrada* at Río Verde was rather sticky and sometimes impossible.

One morning I found out just how sticky it could be. The co-op had been giving the *motorista*, Alvarez, hell because the canoe wasn't making enough money; we knew he was salting some of the profits away but couldn't prove it. On this particular morning Alvarez was making up for a couple of bad days by loading the canoe to the gunwales with pigs, boxes of empty Pepsi bottles, sacks of crude rubber, a couple of thousand oranges, and at least a dozen passengers. The sides of the canoe cleared the water by no more than three or four inches.

Moving under full power and at half speed, we steamed out to the *entrada*. It was blocked by rows of large breakers coming in at fifty-foot intervals, but there was so much money involved that Alvarez didn't dream of turning back. In fact, he didn't even maneuver; he just plowed into the first breaker, which broke over the bow in a solid wall of green water and completely filled the canoe. It also knocked the *ayudante* with his long pole out of his spot in the bow and onto a pile of chickens with their legs tied together, who had been thrown on top of the oranges.

We sat thunderstruck for about five seconds with the water up over our knees and the canoe beginning to swamp, and then as a group the passengers stood up and began to scream. The vision of a sinking slave ship rushed through my mind. There was something very touching and beautiful about this unself-conscious panic; the passengers were making fools of themselves, but with a sweet and natural simplicity. Maybe they knew something I didn't know, something about sharks or sea monsters. Surely they knew what I did know, that although we were a half mile from shore, the water was only waist deep, and even if we lost the canoe, all we had to do was wade ashore. The danger was all illusion, but it was mildly frightening to be so far from land and to be in the hands of Alvarez, who really didn't seem to know what he was doing. I decided to continue living repressed; I decided not to stand up and scream.

I stayed sitting down and screamed, joining with Alvarez, who was directing his fury at the *ayudante*, telling him for God's sake to get up out of that pile of soaked and squawking chickens and start bailing. For a few minutes, while we were getting the canoe turned around, we wallowed sluggishly in the sea with the waves pouring into the boat from both sides; but as much water was pouring out as was pouring in, and we were all bailing now, even the *ayudante* who was paid to bail. We steamed back into port and landed at Palestina, and everyone on the beach gathered around to laugh at us.

Standing by the truck and smoking cigarettes in long bone cigarette holders were two middle-aged women dressed in black satin. Their faces were deeply lined and heavily powdered. Their hair was swept back and up, sort of like Frankenstein's bride or like they were discharging great quantities of static electricity. They were gypsies, the only ones I had seen in Ecuador. They had the coldest, most corrupt and evil faces that I had ever seen on women. Meeting one of them would have been an overwhelming experience, but to run into a pair so evenly matched almost made you believe in a live and personalized devil, for with whom else could they have made a pact to give to their faces such diabolical casts?

We stood on the beach, the passengers and I, shivering in the wind while the canoe was bailed out. It is funny how cold you get at times, even though your feet are straddling the equator. Walter, the owner of the truck, came over to visit with me.

"You know what the gypsies said?" he asked me.

"So that's what they are."

"Twenty minutes ago when you left for Esmeraldas they said that you would make two attempts and fail both times."

"What baloney," I said. "They're only half right. The wind is too strong and the breakers are tremendous; we can't get through."

I looked down at the canoe; Alvarez had kicked out all the women and children and was motioning to me. "Come on," he called, "let's go."

"Are you kidding?" I called back. "It's way too rough."

"Come *on*, man," Alvarez said in a withering voice. "Don't talk *pendejadas*," and there was such scorn in his voice, such an explicit questioning of my manhood, that I simply crawled back in the canoe like a damned fool and didn't say another word until about five minutes later, with the canoe once more full of sea water and sinking in the *entrada* while waves crashed over us, when I found myself screaming at the *ayudante* to for God's sakes get up out of the chickens and start bailing.

Back in Palestina we all stood on the beach with chattering teeth as Alvarez kicked out the men passengers and prepared to make the trip with only the freight. I looked up toward the two gypsies, needing a sign, some indication of our star-crossed future. There they lolled, those evil-looking harpies, with the cigarette holders clenched in their teeth and the wind, blowing their dresses, making spooky and witchlike satiny sounds. My eyes locked in on one of the faces, and we stared at each other across that little stretch of beach. She was going to tell me something. What she gave me suddenly out of that cold, repellent face was a long, cold wink.

It was a gift, but what did it mean?

Was she moonlighting or was she telling me something about the third attempt? I turned away from her toward the canoe and stood there, trying to make up my mind. Then Alvarez came over and said, "Come on, Martín; we'll make it this time." Using the sweetness of his voice and that crazy wink as benedictions, I climbed back in the canoe; we sailed off for the *entrada,* and for once Alvarez was right.

But just barely.

□□

Within three months, the news that Río Verde had a new co-op had spread to all parts of the province, and people whom I had never met—agronomists from extension, officials from the Junta de Fomento (the Ecuadorian Department of Development), and small farmers from up the coast—would stop me on the street in Esmeraldas either to wish the co-op luck or to tell me that the coastal people were the laziest, most worthless people in the world and that no one would ever be able to help them. I had been listening to this sort of trash, 90 per cent racial, all my life, and it didn't much impress me. I had discovered that when I was forced by circumstances to eat the same things a poor man eats for more than a couple of days, I ended up not only lazy, but probably flat on my back in bed. And I was not burdened by the debilitating effects, as everyone was there, of a body crawling with worms—stomach worms, hook worms, kidney worms.

For the last twenty years Río Verde had been gradually losing its population and sinking into a moribund state. But suddenly an incredible thing happened. Three families who had heard that the co-op would give them land and money moved to town. The quality of the people who came was about as wild as the rumor, but we decided to try them out. Nilo and his wife lasted about two months and then drifted off again. Camilo turned out to be an alcoholic. Melchor never showed up except when he had to and then always ended up standing under a tree unable to think of anything to do.

We didn't know this when they arrived, and we called a meeting so that we could accept the applicants. The time had ripened; the old members felt insecure about these new people, and they began to elect officers. Everyone wanted Wilfrido for president, but he refused even a minor post, saying that he quite often felt he was losing his mind and that the responsibilities of the co-op would surely drive him over the brink.

Ramón then was the logical choice, and he was more or less given the post by acclamation; he accepted (modestly for him, who was beginning to realize his worth) and he threw me a secret look of joy and triumph, for he very much wanted a chance to be a leader in the town and to be loved by everyone. Jorge, the carpenter, woke up long enough to accept the post of vice-president and then dosed off again. Orestes was appointed first vocal—whatever that was. He was also asked to serve as a one-man vigilante, to look around for irregularities and dishonesties. He was perfect for the job; he was so suspicious that he didn't even trust his brother, Ramón. Vicenta, one of the two women left in the co-op, was asked to be treasurer.

Vicenta was fifty-four and married to a man close to eighty; he was unable to work and on the edge of senility. He sat in the sun all day—a tall, white-haired skeleton of a man with a caved-in face and rheumy, destroyed eyes—and waited impatiently to die, actually a little furious with God for making him wait so long. Vicenta was a serious and competent woman who, except for her sex and the customs of Ecuador, would have made a wonderful president; she earned money by washing clothes and raising chickens and corn on the steep, rocky hill behind her house.

Giving in to Wilfrido's insistence that the co-op be legalized and registered with the government in Quito, I asked Bill Binford, my Peace Corps Representative, to help me out. One day he arrived with Bob Jensen, a Volunteer from Seattle who was working with co-ops in Quito and who knew about the intricacies of their formation. They stayed with me for a couple of days, we had a meeting in which techniques of formation were discussed (which no one, including Bill or me, could understand past the first five minutes of a forty-five-minute list of prerequisites), and we appointed a committee to write up some regulations.

Wilfrido offered to head this committee, but after studying the government bulletins confessed that he was baffled. "I think I'm going crazy again," he warned me, giving me back the books. So much for Wilfrido's legalization syndrome; he never again mentioned the vital importance of written rules.

Bill, who sat through the meeting, like me, scarcely speaking

a word, was amazed and irritated by some of the *socios*. Nilo
and his wife, for instance, upon being invited to join the co-op,
had made an impassioned joint statement declaring their conviction that the co-op had to loan money to its poor members.
"But we're all poor," the other *socios* yelled, "and there's no
money in the treasury, anyway." This revelation didn't even
slow them up; they simply switched their emphasis from the
co-op to the rich gringos.

Wilfrido particularly irritated Bill. "I kept wanting to get
up and start screaming at that stubborn old man, 'Oh, *shut
up!*'" Bill said. And I, who really loved Wilfrido but who had
had the same impulse dozens of times through dozens of meetings, could only agree. "But he was much quieter tonight," I
said. "In fact the whole meeting was sort of dead. Jorge didn't
wake up once."

Binford and Jensen left, promising to come back in a month,
when we planned to measure the land and to have all the papers
written up and ready to send to Quito. Shortly after their visit
I began to get tired blood. I thought at first, though I was
rapidly losing my appetite, that it was because I couldn't seem
to find much food in town. The fish had stopped biting again;
the orange and avocado season had ended; it was even hard to
find bananas in the stores. Finally, with my blood getting
tireder and tireder and feeling so exhausted that I scarcely
ever got out of bed, I went up to Quito to see our friendly
Peace Corps doctor; the next day he diagnosed hepatitis, and I
was put to bed for a month.

In the meantime, Binford and Jensen arrived in Río Verde
to find the co-op in a state of chaos and on the point of
disintegrating. They told me about it when they got back to
Quito: the two hundred chickens in my bedroom were flying out
of the pen and making cross-country trips all over the house;

there was only about a three-day supply of corn; the canoe was running badly and making very little money; the co-op books were hopelessly fouled up; Baby, our purebred gilt, kept jumping out of her pen, running down the main street, and flipping old ladies over her head out of pure high spirits; and the *socios* didn't seem to have any idea of what was going on. What they were describing was a typical day in the life of the co-op. There wasn't any crisis; everything was going along just fine.

"We called a meeting," Bill said, "and I asked the membership how they intended to feed the chickens if you stayed sick and if the canoe didn't make enough money to buy corn, and they just sat there and stared at me as though I were mad. After a few minutes of deathly silence I suggested that each member chip in one hundred sucres to buy corn. My God, you should have heard them squealing and screaming. Only Ramón and Vicenta agreed that the idea was a good one.

"Orestes and Wilfrido were the worst. This time I really wanted to knock their heads together. Then Ramón got mad and said that as president he wouldn't stand by and see the animals suffer from hunger and that he would sell them first. More screaming; it was like that scene from the *Phantom of the Opera* when the chandelier falls down into the orchestra seats. I finally got them quieted down and decided to trap them.

" 'Look,' I said, 'instead of selling the chickens why don't we split them up among the membership?' Everyone thought that was a fine idea; it figured out to around twenty chickens apiece. 'Could you properly handle another twenty chickens? I asked them. 'Oh, yes,' they all said. 'And you,' I asked Don Wilfrido, 'could you handle another twenty chickens?' 'Yes,' Wilfrido said, 'I would find a way to take care of them.'

" 'You could all take care of your share of the chickens if you had them in your own houses,' I suddenly yelled. 'But none of you can take care of them in a community project? How come?' I really squashed them down.

"Jensen was hot too; he was jumping all over Wilfrido. Well, we almost destroyed your co-op, but if you ask me it needed a good shaking up. We ended on an inspirational note, and I think everything's O.K. But look, Thomsen, you'd better start teaching the membership to face and solve a few of their problems by themselves."

"Bill," I said, "Ramón's the only guy in town with one hundred sucres to put in the co-op. That's the truth. Half of the membership only eats one meal a day. And the reason they were so stunned by your suggestion is my fault because I have never mentioned the corn situation to them; if they knew how much corn those chickens were going to eat before they started laying, they'd all resign from the co-op. They just need help until the hens start laying; then they can walk by themselves."

Everything was not O.K. I found out a few days later when Ramón, who was worried about me, came to Quito for a visit. He described the meeting I had missed, saying that it was the wildest one they had ever had. In the middle of it, Jensen had gone over the line when he was arguing with Wilfrido. At one point, exasperated by Wilfrido's stubbornness, he had asked in a sarcastic voice, "*Y tu, ¿qué comes tu?*" (And you, what do you eat?), using the familiar form of address reserved for children, dogs, and very old and intimate friends. Wilfrido was sixty-two, and Jensen was in his middle twenties; for an older man to be so addressed, Ramón explained, was a grave and unforgivable insult. "Wilfrido is mortally wounded," Ramón said.

I went back to Río Verde after a month's rest to find that it was true. Wilfrido, with a drawn, sick face, resigned from the co-op. He was very nice about it but adamant as steel; knowing how stubborn he was, I only argued with him for the sake of appearances. Three days later Wilfrido's neighbor Isabela also resigned out of sympathy—which goes a long way toward proving the cloud-with-a-silver-lining theory. Wilfrido was the best *socio* in the co-op, but Izabela, who was in the middle of a disturbing menopausal time, was one of the laziest.

During the first months of the co-op I had tried to stay in the background as much as possible. I wanted some local leadership to emerge, and I wanted the *socios* to develop a sense of ownership and responsibility. But it was difficult. For a long time, for instance, the co-op's canoe was referred to as Martín's canoe, and the *motorista* came to me whenever he wanted permission to buy parts or to give some broke farmer a free ride into town. "Don't ask me," I always told him. "It's not my canoe." But it really wasn't anybody's canoe yet. No one wanted to take over and make decisions.

After Ramón was elected president of the co-op, he seemed to undergo a profound character change; he quickly took over as a leader and began to direct things, a little strongly at times, but always with fairness. At night when he came to visit he often spoke of the satisfaction he was getting from being a leader and how he wanted to serve and be respected by the community. "Listen, Martín," he told me, "I'm really in love with the *cooperativa;* I can't sleep nights thinking about it. And not just for us and how it can change our lives, but for you, too. I want a great success for the *cooperativa*, and I want everyone in the Quito office to know about it and be proud of you."

Not at all aware, apparently, of the delicacy and vulnerability of his position, Ramón began to manage. He fired Alvarez, one of his best friends, from the canoe for stealing money and not taking care of the motor. He planned the work on the days when we gathered as a group—Vicenta to water the oranges, Camilo and Rufo to cut fence posts, Wai to split bamboo—and he tried with the same indifferent success that I had had to get everyone to grind his share of the corn.

A few other, apparently disconnected, items will provide a background for what happened to Ramón after he had been president for a couple of months:

Item One. The elections for *alcalde* of Esmeraldas were scheduled to take place, and Alvaro, the main storekeeper in Río Verde, who had been pledged to support Chiriboga (who was emphatically *not* a Communist, he said, but a Radical Revolutionary Anarchist), switched in the last week before the voting to Dr. Salas, the Liberal candidate. (The philosophical position of the Ecuadorian Liberal party was slightly to the right of that of the John Birch Society.) In return for switching his allegiance, Alvaro was promised a place on the city council. Chiriboga was narrowly defeated, and Alvaro, on the winning side, began to feel like a real power in the community.

Item Two. We had experimented in the co-op with a plan for buying rice, sugar, and cooking oil in bulk and selling it to the *socios* for a small profit. The plan had not worked because the stuff arrived just before a big fiesta, and we had sold on credit. We had a very hard, unpleasant time collecting (Jorge and Nilo never did pay). But the idea was a good one, not only because of the reasonable price but because of the honesty of our scales. Even though the plan had not worked out well, we were talking about starting it again—this time on a strictly cash basis—and it was, of course, a real threat to the storekeepers and their 100 per cent markup. Alvaro especially was displeased with the co-op's growing feelings of power and independence.

Item Three. Coming down the hill into town one evening I ran into Alvaro. He was building a horse corral out of split lengths of bamboo. He was putting his corral in the exact spot where we planned to build a new reservoir for the town. When I explained this to him, he told me to confine my efforts to the co-op and not to butt in in matters of the town.

"I'm just trying to save you the trouble of having to tear down your corral," I said.

"Well, you might order up on the hill, but you don't order here on municipal property," Alvaro told me. "Just leave me alone."

Item Four. Someone broke into my house while I was gone and stole my cameras, one of which was a brand new Canon that I had bought in Panama, and the pride of my life. The robbery was particularly depressing for me, since I suspected everyone in town and everyone felt so guilty that for two weeks no one would walk into my house. I hated them all for a while; my ego was really bleeding.

Several weeks passed. Then one day the schoolteacher told me that he thought he knew who had stolen the cameras.

"Yes," I said, beginning to sweat. "Tell me."

He hesitated for a long time and then said, reluctantly, "Well, it was your right arm."

And that could only mean Ramón.

"No," I told him. "I don't believe it."

"I heard it in Mate. I can't mention any names, but this party saw Ramón give the cameras to Otilio, the *contrabandista*, on the dock and heard him tell Otilio to sell them for what he could get in Colombia."

"No," I said. "I can't believe that; it's not true." But I was shaken by the number of details and the presence of a witness. I went up to the farm and sat there alone all afternoon. I felt two years of work disappearing down the drain if it were true; I wouldn't be able to stay. But then I thought about Ramón and what I knew about him, and I realized that it was a lie. Ramón had not stolen the cameras; I would have bet my life on it. And aside from all of Ramón's qualities, the story didn't hold water; not even an idiot would walk out on the dock in the presence of a third party and sell ten thousand sucres' worth of stolen property.

I went home and fixed supper. Ramón always showed up in time for a cup of coffee; I wanted him to know that he was a suspect in the big camera robbery, but I didn't have the guts to tell him. When he came in I told him he'd better go talk to the schoolteacher.

His face was sick and gray when he returned a half hour later, and he went out on the porch and sat in a corner; he just sat there shaking his head.

"How did the story get started?" I asked him.

"I'm just figuring it out," Ramón said. "The only time I talked to Otilio was in Esmeraldas. It was that damned Vicenta. When you were sick in Quito I arranged with Otilio to meet him in Mate on his way north to Colombia. I'd borrowed some money from the co-op in Esmeraldas to buy corn, and I wanted to buy a little contraband because I figured I could double the money first and then buy the corn. It was a good time to do it because you were gone and couldn't talk me out of it. I walked up the beach carrying a little waterproof bag with a rain cape, some old pants, and a sweater in it for the canoe trip. It could have looked like the cameras, I guess.

"And I didn't meet anyone but Vicenta; she was up at the point digging oysters off the rocks, and she asked me where I was going. Well, when you're in contraband you don't tell anyone; I said I was going to Montalvo to buy corn. Oh, that damned woman, that damned Vicenta. And I thought she was my friend."

"You're not the only one with troubles," I said and told him about the strange hostile encounter I had had with Alvaro earlier. He left but he was back at three o'clock in the morning pounding on the door. It was the first time I had ever seen him drunk, but he had done a wonderful job of it.

"Listen," he said. "I went to the police when I left here, and you know what, they think I stole your cameras, too. My God. My God, the whole town thinks I stole those cameras. And the police said I had many enemies in the town; they said the *socios* are talking in the street against me, that I act like a grand man, that I order everyone around, that I am stealing money from the canoe." He sat down in the middle of the floor, grabbed his head, and began to weep. "And all I wanted was to help, to work for the co-op," he cried. "Oh, this damned town; how I detest this dirty little town."

It was drunken weeping, and it didn't last very long, but even at that it was hard to take. Ramón left finally, after listening to a little talk on patience, on the fickleness of people, and on the importance of playing life cool. He agreed with me, I thought, but at 5:00 A.M. I was awakened again by the sounds of brawling outside the window and discovered Ramón and Alvaro being separated by their friends, both of them dead drunk but trying to get at each other's throats. I got Ramón into the house on the pretext of taking care of his shirt, but he wouldn't stay. "You can't fight for your good name," Ramón told me, "but I sure as hell can. He says you're a bad man, a Communist, and nobody in this town is going to talk against you." He wrestled his way to the door, but at the bottom of the steps he turned and gave me a sad, bewildered, drunken look. "It's a bad time for us, eh, Martín?"

"Sure," I said, "but don't let the stupid people of the town destroy you; in ten days this will all be a joke."

"Perhaps you're right," Ramón said, staggering off down the street. "But right now it's not a joke. And right now I'm going to punch Alvaro in the face."

I never did find out who stole the cameras, although several months after the theft Alexandro went into business on a rather impressive scale. He bought bolts of cheap cotton or gabardine at wholesale prices in Esmeraldas, children's reject T-shirts (with messages like "Seattle World's Fair" or "Davy Crockett" or "I'm a little athlete" printed on them), and other shoddy merchandise that he peddled up and down the river, accepting chickens, cacao, or pre-Incan artifacts instead of money and making an exorbitant double profit. On about his fourth trip his canoe tipped over, and he lost everything. He almost never came to the house any more. He began to talk against me quite openly in the street, and he developed a subtle and two-faced loathing for Ramón.

The first year I lived in Río Verde, I had always left the key to my house with Alexandro. But I had missed little things, things of no consequence actually, and had started leaving the key with Ramón. It was shortly after this that the cameras were stolen, and I was more or less convinced eventually that Alexandro had done it out of jealousy, and to let me know what could happen when he was no longer in charge of my house.

□□

In Río Verde humility was a virtue; no one wanted to be a boss—or to be bossed, for that matter. When I tried to get the town to clean up a site for a new lagoon, I found out that even the president of the town junta wouldn't order a *minga*. Yet from July until the end of December, when the coast dried up, there was no water in the town; the river was low and became a part of the ocean. During the first months of the dry season the only water in town came from two small ponds about a ten-minute walk from town. The women and children spent about 40 per cent of their time either carrying water to their houses in little two-quart gourds or else hauling dirty clothes up the hill. In October even the ponds went dry, and all the

town's water was hauled in canoes from above the low-tide line
four or five miles up the river. Then it cost five cents for a
five-gallon tin of slimy green liquid, which surely made it the
most expensive water in the world.

Just a hundred feet past the last house there was a natural
site for a reservoir, a small valley bottom between two hills. It
would hold five times the water of the mudholes if it could be
dammed off. I talked to Señor Haas in Esmeraldas, the president of Fomento. He came out one day to examine the site and
agreed to send one of the highway Caterpillars for a day when
the place was cleared and burned. First, though, the townspeo-
ple must get together and do the work.

I had talked to just about everyone in town about the new
pond. Except for Alvaro, they all wanted the new lagoon,
especially the women; and especially during the dry season.
The women said they would do anything to get a pond close to
town. When the inspector of schools arrived and called a town
meeting to explain why one of the teachers who had inexplicably quit his job would not be replaced (it was inexplicable only
until one of the local girls turned up pregnant), I used the
meeting to talk to everyone as a group. I asked to hear any
dissenting thoughts about a new lagoon so that we could all
discuss the problem together. But there was no dissent. A
scowling Alvaro, standing in the doorway of the schoolroom
while I was speaking, disappeared at some uncertain moment,
and everyone else clapped and cheered when I said that the
whole thing could be arranged.

"There's only a couple of things," I said. "First, we'll have
to clean and burn all the brush so that tractor can get in to
work, and then we'll have to build some sort of a spillway so the
dam won't wash away in the first rains." Actually, there was
little need for the people to clean the weeds out first, but I
wanted to involve them as a group in a community project, to

give them a sense of ownership in the new lagoon so that they wouldn't think the whole thing had simply been a gift from their government.

"*Magnífico*," everyone yelled. "You can count on us." The women in the back row rose as a group, cheering, and Señora Florinda began blowing me kisses. "Don't worry about Alvaro," a few people told me in privacy later. "He's an *hijo de la grandíssima*." Well, yes, Alvaro was that, but he was also the principal storekeeper in town, and there was scarcely a family that didn't arrange forty or fifty cents' worth of credit with him almost every month. I wondered if he would use this as a weapon to defeat what I took to be the aspirations of the people.

My credit, for instance, was cut off the very next day. I sent little Daniel to buy me a bottle of beer from Segundo, who was out of beer. I sent him to Alvaro's then, and he came back, terribly embarrassed, with the *noticia* that since I had seen fit to go first to Segundo's for my beer, Alvaro no longer wanted my business. *Bueno.* It was developing into a stimulating situation; I began to feel like a typical villager with his grudges and resentments. I had been in the town for over two years and now I had an enemy. It made me feel a little less bland, and I determined to be worthy of Alvaro's hatred.

The time arrived to organize a *minga* to clean up the little canyon. Ramón advised me that the usual way was to talk to the *Policía Rural*, who would arrange a date and then order the people to appear. I went down and talked to the *Rural*. "Why, yes," he'd be enchanted to call a *minga*. But could I speak first to the *Teniente Político*, who would write out an order authorizing the *minga*? A couple of days later I finally got hold of the *Teniente Político*. Yes, it was a wonderful idea, this new supply of water for the town, but actually it would be much better if I talked to the president of the town council, Tomás Plaza. He could write out the order; it was really a job for the junta.

The town council of Río Verde. I began to taste the flavor of defeat. When Don Julio had resigned as president of the junta the year before, the town fathers had elected Wilfrido, Atoniel, and Tomás to head the council. But no one in the whole town had showed up for the first six meetings, and Wilfrido, in a fit of disgust, had handed in his resignation. After six more meetings no one attended, Atoniel resigned, leaving Tomás as president by default. Tomás was a son of a family from Palestina, that little town across the river where everyone from Río Verde was either a thief, a drunk, or a bum (just as everyone in Río Verde knew that everyone from Palestina was either a thief, a drunk, or a bum). These convictions were absorbed with the mother's milk, so I didn't expect much cooperation from Tomás.

"You've got a wild dream," Tomás told me. "To hell with it. I wouldn't raise my finger for this dirty little hole."

"But you're the leader of the town, the president of the council."

"Listen, as far as I'm concerned there is no town, no council, and no people, just a group of brute animals. Forget about that lagoon; you'll get no cooperation, and besides in the first rain the whole thing will wash away and destroy the school."

A few minutes later from my window I watched Tomás and Alvaro drinking a Pepsi together and laughing.

I had from time to time had similar thoughts about the town, but had consoled myself with the fact that if the people *were* capable of working together there would be no need of a Peace Corps Volunteer. It was the most anarchistic place I had ever seen, and this fragmented quality, while the curse of the town, was also one of its charms. You couldn't help but be impressed by these people, these grandsons of slaves, who bowed to no authority whatsoever and who lived a life so fiercely independent that they couldn't unite even to keep themselves from being destroyed. It was as though they had reacted so violently to the memory of their enslavement, which had ruined their culture, that now they couldn't exist within the shadow of an outside discipline. It was indeed a shattered culture—a town without lights or water, without decent houses, medicine, education, a

town isolated from the rest of the world—and, most amazing of all, there were no plans to change anything.

I had a long talk with Wilfrido and explained that all the officials in town had somehow been subverted by Alvaro. My position in town was delicate, and I didn't think it wise for me personally to try to organize a *minga*. Wilfrido, who was very anxious that we build the lagoon, promised to help. He talked to Atoniel, and they set a date for a *minga* and told the people that on Wednesday at 10:00 A.M. they were to gather with their machetes.

On Wednesday at 10:00 A.M. Wilfrido and Atoniel arrived

with machetes. The three of us worked for a couple of hours, and all this time I was building up a head of steam. We had bypassed what little authority Alvaro could have used to prevent the construction of the lagoon and had met up with that curse of the coastal areas, the basic and terrifying lethargy.

"Let's go," I said, finally. "Let the town die of thirst." This was about the most shocking thing that happened to me in Río Verde; it was something that I could scarcely believe. It rankled as nothing else had rankled me, and I became quite neurotic over the situation. A month ahead of the winter rains, the tractor arrived from up north, heading for the winter pasture; the crew had celebrated the completion of the summer's work the night before in Rocafuerte, and they entered the town like a catafalque, the raised bulldozer blade carrying half a dozen sleeping workers. They scattered to the different *salones* in town and continued the celebration, and the women began to stop me in the street to ask if the tractor would make the lagoon.

"No," I told them. "It appears that there is no interest in this town for a lagoon. Perhaps some other year."

The women waited a couple of days, thinking perhaps that I would weaken, and then they organized a *minga* of women to do the work that their husbands hadn't done, but by this time it was too late. Early one morning the *gabarrón*, the barge that carried the trucks across the Esmeraldas River, showed up; it loaded the tractor and the still-celebrating *tractoristas* and disappeared down the coast.

For forty years, at least, the rainy season had arrived at 9:00 P.M. on Christmas Eve. But that year something went wrong upstairs. Even the monthly showers of autumn disappeared, and Christmas Eve was bright and clear, except for the usual fog of alcohol in the street. The mudholes had gone dry in October, and there was literally no water in the town except what was brought down in canoes and sold by the gallon at the dock. When the women washed clothes they piled the dirty bundles on their heads and marched four miles up over the hills to the next river to the north, but this was a job for the strong and the young; we all began to smell a little like goats, and my romantic dreams were involved with nothing more sensuous than the feel of cool, clear water on my face.

Ramón, as president of the cooperative, decided at some moment in February that he would be a town leader. "Actually," he said, "the *cooperativa* is the only thing in this town that is united and strong. When the tractor comes back I think that we should build the lagoon and just throw it in the faces of the town as an act of insolence. Will you help?"

"No," I said, "I won't help, but I think it would be fine if the co-op wants to give the town a lagoon. I'm not thinking of the town but of the co-op; the fact is that the old lagoon on top of the hill now belongs to the co-op, and if you can build a lagoon closer to town then the people won't be coming up on the farm to steal all your crops."

So the people did get a new lagoon. They got it the same way they got their light plant that didn't work and their dock that stood high and dry at low tide: by sitting on their haunches and doing nothing. Some irrational part of me hoped that the rains would not come and that the lagoon would sit there forever as it was to begin with—completely dry.

🔲🔲

Two years after I arrived in Río Verde to live, the time had long passed when my presence was looked upon as something exotic or extraordinary. I was a fixture in the town, and the population no longer gathered on the dock to cheer and wave when I left or returned, and at night the house was no longer filled with people sitting around on stools and boxes watching me opening a can of tuna fish or sending billowing thirty-foot flames into the darkness as I tried to light that mad Portuguese stove.

I was pretty much accepted by the town; I even had enemies. But I was still something quite special, unique, and apart from the town's life, and perhaps only Ramón knew that I had more than my share of faults and that under certain conditions of duress I could be a quite ordinary old son of a bitch.

From the first I got emotionally involved in the town and its problems; I was aware of the dangers in this but unable to do much about it. I promised that I would stay in Río Verde past my original contract if it seemed that I could keep on working with the people and if the Peace Corps would let me. The truth is that I couldn't face the idea of leaving. I was caught in one of those terrible love-hate relationships with the town, and I got in the habit of awakening every morning at 3:00 A.M. and lying in the darkness, frustrated and furious, cursing the lethargy of the people, the degradation of their poverty, and my own inability to do anything about it.

But I was lucky, because to a great degree I was sustained and guarded by Ramón. He had come to my house one night in those first months and said, "I want to change my destiny; tell me what to do." He had come with such openness, such innocence, such complete trust and friendship that even in my worst moments of isolation or depression, I could never think of leaving the town except as an act of betrayal.

Along with his friendship, though, he also brought me his problems—every damned one. I was his friend, and helping solve his problems was one of friendship's obligations. I suppose that in a way, being weighed down, sometimes almost crushed, by his burdens—his poverty, his troubles with Ester and her family who robbed his corn and his coconuts, his friends who wouldn't repay small loans, landowning aristocrats who treated him contemptuously, not realizing that he was no longer a poor beach *zambo*, his neighbors who poured boiling water on his pigs, etc., etc.—I was in a sense relieved of my own problems, for which I substituted his.

Then, after almost two years, a frightening thing happened which seemed for a time to open an abyss between us and to throw into a despairing light the difference in our cultures and our sensitivities to life. It had to do with Ramón's dog, Tarzan. When I first came to Río Verde, Tarzan was Ramón's most cherished possession. Not counting his wife, a little tilting house not even eight feet square made of bamboo and balsa chunks off the beach, and a rotten canoe which threatened each day to split in two (and finally did), Tarzan was just about all that Ramón owned.

He was a miserable, dun-colored mongrel, emaciated with hunger, yappy, and suspicious. His only good quality was an absolute devotion to Ramón; he ignored or assaulted everyone else. Flea-bitten and mangy, his ribs standing out, detested by the whole town, he walked at Ramón's side; from this central position he made forays, chasing horses and nipping at their heels until they bucked and reared, attacking small children on the beach, running the local chickens to exhaustion. Out of every twenty-four hours he spent at least eighteen barking. He had a reptilian face, with his eyes too close together and slightly crossed so that he seemed half lizard and half idiot. At mealtime he lay at Ramón's feet and received fishbones, bananas, and a few grains of rice.

Whenever Ramón left the town by canoe, Tarzan, mad with grief, would stand on the very edge of the dock howling to the sky, and finally would fling himself into the river. When Ramón had business in Palestina and had to cross and recross the river several times in one day, Tarzan, crossing and recrossing behind him, tallied up miles of swimming. During the rainy season when the river was at flood, the poor demented dog would dive off the dock and be swept almost out to sea.

During my first months in the town, when no one knew why I was there (occasionally including myself) or what the Peace Corps was or whether I might actually be a spy, I worked almost exclusively with Alexandro and Ramón. Everyone else was cautious and watchful; special security police even came from Esmeraldas to check my papers. I used to work almost every day at Ramón's, hoeing out jungle, and after four or five months Tarzan decided that I must be part of the establishment. At first he tolerated me, then he grew to look for me; finally, goofy with love, he didn't know who he belonged to.

By the end of the first year Tarzan spent about half his time with me. We hunted rats together or chased *juantas*, and at night he stood outside the house barking until 2:00 A.M. or prowled around in the kitchen tearing open sacks of dried milk or stealing bananas. I had a rat problem, but it sank to minimal proportions when compared with Tarzan's nocturnal depredations.

There were many days in that first year while Ramón was moving out of his poverty when he had to sacrifice everything to his long-range goal of economic independence. There were weeks when he ate only one meal a day, at two or three in the afternoon, a dish of potato or yuca soup, enriched perhaps with a penny's worth of cheese or noodles, and a steaming dish of boiled platano. It got so that I could more or less gauge the daily condition in Ramón's house by the arrival or nonarrival of Tarzan.

The dog, ribs jutting out, stomach drawn up, and yellow eyes glowing with emotion, would arrive at the house and curl up under the bottom step. When I came in from work I would feed him bananas if I had any, or if I had any money I would go to the store and get him some Río Verde bread, little pretzel-shaped constructions as hard, tasteless, and nourishing as rocks. Sometimes Ramón, tottering with hunger, his ribs only slightly less protruding than Tarzan's, would show up to borrow a nickel for noodles or potatoes.

Tarzan, split in his affections, began leaping that ten feet off the dock whenever either of us left the town; it was a local attraction. Whenever he met me on the beach I had to go through the ritual of having my face licked, my hands lightly bitten, and my clothes covered with wet sand. I think it gave Ramón satisfaction to share the lunatic affections of his dog with me. I'm sure he was convinced that I was equally enraptured with his miserable dog, because when he wanted to frighten me after an argument he would always threaten to trade Tarzan for a cow, one of Ramón's more insane delusions; no one in his right mind would have traded the horns off a dead cow for old Tarzan.

Halfway through my first year the rainy season and the corn-planting season arrived. In this zone man, using a machete as his only farm tool, is sentenced to eternal poverty, since the violent growth of weeds during the winter rains limits the amount of ground that he can tend to about two acres. Hoping to convince the farmers that with chemical sprays they might double their farm acreage with about the same amount of work, I got a three-gallon, hand-operated back sprayer and a gallon of 2-4-D from the office in Quito and gave a few demonstrations on weed killing. This project wasn't entirely successful, aside from the prohibitive cost of the spray. Ramón, for instance, was too emotional in his approach, dashing through the crooked corn rows, and stopping from time to time to pour gallons of weed killer on particular plants that he didn't like. Much of the corn, too, was planted on steep hillside ground, the slopes littered with downed tree trunks and sprouting stumps; it was almost impossible to walk through the rows without a

weight, let alone with forty pounds of spray material fastened
to your back. At the end of the spraying season there was still
almost a quart of 2-4-D left, and Ramón had it under his
house.

When the new corn was harvested and his chickens were
laying, Ramón became the richest man in town. His income
jumped from around eight dollars a month to more than thirty.
But he was like every other man in the world too suddenly
released from poverty. He began to blow his money. He bought
new clothes—beautiful, shimmering neon-colored pants, bras-
sieres and panties for his wife, a switch-blade knife, a two-band
radio. He began to lust to own a horse, and against all my
advice spent five hundred sucres for a young mare which he
called Esperanza, "Hope." He hardly ever used the horse except for dramatic exhibitions on Sunday evenings, when he
rode up and down the street in town; his main interest seemed
to be in fattening her up and making her beautiful.

I had suggested rather obstinately that he use this money
instead to hire workers to clear more jungle land, to plant more
corn, and to think about two hundred chickens instead of one
hundred, but he was consumed by the furious joy of being rich,
and he didn't want to think a whole year ahead. What was the
good of having money if you couldn't be happier by having it,
and if you couldn't spend it royally? He was loaning money to
all his friends, those outrageously poor fishermen from a little
farther up the beach—of whom, a year before, Ramón had
been the poorest. He took a real joy in playing the *patrón*,
really rubbing it in.

(My sense of angry frustration was a little blunted by a
memory of my own irrational attitude toward money. Once in
Chico, California, after years of poverty trying to raise alfalfa
for a profit, I had taken the first money that I didn't need for
actual survival and blown twelve hundred dollars in one mo-

ment for a Capehart phonograph. It symbolized for me some final happiness, a triumph over several years of stunted living, and all of the *haute bourgeoisie* virtues. It was a great, glowing 78 RPM machine that weighed at least a ton, and that was the year Columbia came out with the 33 RPM long play. How I grew to hate that monster. It used to chew up quantities of Red Seal records and, if the top weren't firmly closed, spew them out in small fragments all over the living-room floor.)

Well, I was pleasantly surprised at the care Ramón lavished on Esperanza. In a couple of months she had fleshed out into a stylish-looking animal, her coat deep, rich, and glowing with health. The strangest thing of all: she was absolutely free of *garrapatas*, those pin-point-sized ticks that infested and cursed the land and grew to dime size on the host's blood. All the horses were covered with them.

"How often are you using Negubon?" I asked Ramón one day. "She doesn't have a tick on her."

"I'm not using Negubon," Ramón told me. "I'm using 2-4-D; it's really wonderful stuff, isn't it?"

"But that's for killing broad-leafed weeds," I cried, "it's not for killing bugs on horses."

"Well, I'm using it, and it works fine."

"But it could be dangerous; you've got to respect the printed directions; some of these chemicals are fatal."

"Oh, Martín," Ramón said, "don't talk foolishness; I've used it at least four times, and the mare is fine."

Three or four months later Tarzan showed up at the house, much thinner than usual, if such a thing were possible. He had a dazed, glazed look in his eyes and a faltering control over his hind legs; when he tried to run his rear end kept collapsing. I thought for a while that one of Ramón's neighbors—who used a machete or pots of boiling water on animals that came near her kitchen—had hurt Tarzan again, but Ramón explained that there was nothing wrong with the dog. He had been weakened by flea bites, Ramón explained. He had bathed the dog in 2-4-D, and now all the fleas were dead.

"But you've killed your dog, too," I told him in exasperation. "Look what you've done; he's dying."

"Oh, Martín, calm yourself," Ramón said. "Just wait a couple of days; he'll be like new."

"Well, at least pack him home," I said. "I can't stand to have him here dying all over the place."

"He walked here, let him walk back," Ramón said coldly.

"But he can't walk, he's dying."

"He can walk; how else did he get here?"

For two days Tarzan lay outside in the sun in back of the house by the new co-op chicken coops. At night I carried him upstairs, and he slept under the bed, staggering into the kitchen about once an hour on his poor destroyed legs to knock over bottles and empty marmalade jars, but his heart wasn't in it.

On the third day I carried Tarzan that half mile up the beach to Ramón's house. The dog didn't seem to be suffering, but it bothered me to have him in the yard, and it bothered me that Ramón hadn't showed up to care for him. He was not my dog, and I didn't want to be burdened with his death. I wanted Ramón to be burdened with his death; I wanted him to suffer a little.

Tarzan made it back to my house one more time before he lost his sense of balance entirely, dragging himself by his front legs up along the sand and over the piles of balsa logs at the edge of the beach, through the salt grass, up through the main street of town, and then up the hill. It took him all night, and I found him in the morning lying underneath my bottom step softly wagging his tail. He wouldn't eat, but he drank water, and he slept all day. Late in the afternoon I paid

Ramón's brother, Rufo, a nickel to carry the dog back to Ramón's house. I was gone almost all day working on the co-op farm, and I thought the dog would die a little happier on Ramón's porch, a part of the familiar things he knew.

About a week later Ramón invited me for lunch; it was the time of *puja*, the ebb tide in the two-week cycle when the rocks at the point lay exposed, and I knew that we would have lobster or oysters, those crops of *puja*. I headed down the beach, anticipating a feast.

In the old hog pen fifty feet from Ramón's house, lying in his own filth, his body a mass of open sores and maggots, lying where I could see he hadn't been moved in a week—Tarzan. He raised his head at my voice; his eyes were filmed over and blind; his body, which trembled violently with the effort of moving his head, was wasted. He wagged his tail a couple of times and dropped his head. Choking with rage, sorrow, and guilt, I climbed over the fence to touch him and talk to him.

From the house they all watched me in consternation— Ramón, Ester, Ester's mother and brother. Ramón called for water and brought me a gourd full.

"Get out of the pen," Ramón said. "Wash your hands; you can get sick touching something so diseased."

"Why haven't you killed him?" I asked in a choked voice.

Ramón looked back at me without understanding. "Get out of the pen and wash your hands."

"When did he have water last?"

"We give him water every day, Martín. Now, for God's sake, get out of the pen."

"But why don't you kill him? He's yours; he depends on you; you're responsible."

"Come on, Martín," Ramón pleaded. "Lunch is all ready; we're having your favorite—lobster. Come on, wash your hands."

I grabbed Ramón by his shoulders and started shaking him. "Listen, Ramón, answer me. Why is he still alive? Why haven't you killed him?"

The question shocked and embarrassed him. "I'm not the type who goes around killing his dogs," he said. "What kind of a man do you think I am?"

We stood there for a long minute staring into each other's eyes, really separated. This unacceptable possibility was already rushing through my mind, that perhaps the dog was mine, that in the long night's journey as he dragged himself up the beach to my house the ownership of Tarzan had irrevocably changed, but I immediately twisted this guilt onto Ramón. I felt a real loathing for him, for the whole barbarous country. I kept wanting to tell him to go to hell and then walk away. The one truth that for two years I had not had the strength to face, that I had been unable to accept—that one day I would leave this place and never come back—this truth flashed across my mind stripped of its terror.

We were standing there staring at each other like strangers, and Ramón's face was very troubled. He said my name a couple of times. "Martín, what's wrong?" He held the *mate* out before him, still offering me the water. After a while, trembling, I took the water and washed my hands.

Part Four: 1968

*W*E WERE in a time of relative tranquillity. Most of the co-op members were showing up on Mondays and Friday to clear jungle; no one was suffering from hurt feelings or threatening to resign; the chickens were laying eggs, and everyone with a few exceptions was grinding his share of the corn for them. Baby had nine pigs one night, and Cara de Angel, our other Berk gilt, was coming into heat with terrifying regularity; it was almost time to breed her. Our plans for building up to a herd of ten sows looked bright. With the egg money we were paying cash for feed, lumber, and repairs to the tractor; we were even paying off a few old bills. It was a time so tranquil and hopeful that even I knew it couldn't last.

Something strange and secret began to happen in La Cooperativa de Río Verde in those days just before we established the co-op grocery store. At night lying in bed I could hear the *socios* underneath my window sitting around endlessly discussing a new co-op project until ten or eleven o'clock. Their voices were full of a new excitement, and there was much laughter.

After about the fourth such meeting, eighteen-year-old
Goya came to the house and said that he wanted to be a *socio*,
too. Goya? A *socio*? He was about the most languorous kid I
had ever met; he could sleep any place. There was hardly a
moment in the day when you couldn't stumble over him grace-
fully covering the steps of one of the town's stores, conserving
himself under a palm, or half hanging out of a window. Goya?
Something was surely in the air. It seemed that the co-op was
beginning to catch on, and that the *socios* were beginning to
understand what it was all about. I didn't know what their
project was, but I was delighted that they were planning something by themselves and without me.

Now, Ramón came to confer about a matter of the utmost
importance. We were arriving, he said, at a momentous period
in the co-op's history, with great success just around the corner. Even the nonmembers were beginning to realize what the
co-op could do to improve the life of the whole town; there was
much less antagonism toward the co-op. There had never been
so much union, so much enthusiasm, among the *socios*.

"Why?" I asked. "It will still be many months before all the
bills are paid and the hog pens built? And what about Goya?
He says he wants to join the co-op."

"Yes," Ramón said. "Goya is crazy to join. Well, I'll tell
you. We have a new project. We've been talking about forming
a *cooperativa futbol* team with uniforms, a captain, and a
madrina—everything well organized, everything pretty and
nice. You know."

"That's great," I said.

"Yes," Ramón said. "It will draw us all closer together, and
the *socios* will have more interest in the organization. There's
only one problem, naturally—money."

This was the beginning of a series of conferences and meetings which lasted all week. We met every night, and something

happened that had never happened before—all the members showed up. It was decided finally that the co-op would buy the football, the uniforms, and a pair of football shoes for Wai, who had been elected captain (it would all come to around thirty dollars); that a formal challenge to play would be sent up the river to the San Vicente team; that Vicenta's daughter, eighteen-year-old Bolivia, would be the *madrina*, the god-mother; that we would buy a *vara* of satin ribbon upon which would be painted "La Cooperativa de Río Verde" to be pinned across Bolivia's breast; etc., etc.

Wai, the captain of the team, went through a complete character change. He had never had much interest in the co-op, having confided to one of his friends after a few drinks that he had joined only because I wanted him to and he hadn't wanted to hurt my feelings. But now the idea of owning a pair of football shoes subverted all of his cautious antisocial instincts. Wai, who was the town's strongest and most spectacular player, had never played football with shoes. With his great, square, calloused toe he could kick a football unbelievable distances; no one seemed to mind that his aim was a little shaky. Pow! Wai kicked; the ball would go sailing across the field high above the tops of the trees and disappear in the jungle. *Fantástico! Viva* Wai!

Walter Pata, the town baker and our newest *socio*, wrote out a formal invitation to San Vicente and brought it to me to be copied on the typewriter. Wai, Ramón, and Walter signed it, putting in all the curves, slashes, loops, and curlicues which surround a formal signature and almost blot it out. Ramón and I went to Esmeraldas and bought twelve uniforms—red and yellow striped shirts, white cotton trunks, red and yellow striped socks, a red and yellow referee's whistle. We bought the biggest football shoes in town for Wai's great feet. Mondays and Fridays Goya would show up with his machete at the co-op farm, where you could almost invariably find him leaning against a tree while the other *socios* cleaned out brush.

"You know," I told Orestes one day, "I think the only reason Goya wants to be in the co-op is for the football uniform."

"But of course," Orestes said. "What else? But it *is* a great thing, the uniforms. It's the first time in history that Río Verde has had a football team with uniforms, and they're talking about it all up and down the river, all up and down the beach. Now, finally, they know we have a *cooperativa;* now they know."

A messenger in a canoe arrived from San Vicente, accepting the Río Verde challenge and announcing that the team would arrive on a Saturday afternoon about five in anticipation of a Sunday contest. The Río Verde team smiled indulgently at this informal way of accepting, cynically amused that it was not nicely done with a formal letter. "Oh well, what can you expect from *montuvios?*" Ramón said. "They don't even have uniforms." *Montuvio* means something like hick or country bumpkin.

Another meeting was called; the visiting team had to be bedded down and fed. They must find enough woven mats. Each *socio* pledged twenty-five cents to buy fish and rice, and the co-op would supply two dozen eggs for breakfast. Vicenta would prepare the meals. It was decided to impress the visiting team by making a bucketful of lemonade to give them during the half period—with ice.

"Why don't you really impress them?" I asked. "The co-op could contribute a couple chickens that aren't laying, and you could serve them chicken soup for their dinner on Saturday."

"Oh, no!" several *socios* cried. "They live far enough up the river so that sea fish will be a special treat." Chicken was going too far; it was food for the rich or for a very solemn occasion. But Ramón didn't agree. He got up and gave a talk about the dignity of the co-op and about the necessity of showing every-one that we were a rich and important organization.

"The idea is a good one," he said. "We'll do it; we'll give them chicken on Saturday and then they'll know who we are."

Ramón was president; there were no dissenting voices.

Saturday noon a block of ice arrived on the truck from Esmeraldas, and Vicenta and her daughters began cooking pots of chicken soup. The whole town was restless; a crowd of people waited on the dock to receive the visiting team—notably obvious: Wai, dressed in a heavily starched and sparkling white shirt. Five o'clock came, but no team. Six o'clock. The sun set, and it grew dark. Ramón, who had visualized the drama of meeting the team at the dock and formally escorting them to Vicenta's house for chicken dinner, was furious. "Those damned farmers," he said. "They have no sense of propriety. We'll wait until seven, then to hell with them; we'll eat the chicken ourselves."

But at seven o'clock, in pitch darkness, two canoes loaded with *futbolistas* pulled up to the deserted dock, and a crowd of small boys running through the street announced their arrival. Ramón refused to greet them. He sent Wai down to the dock, and we heard later that after everyone had eaten Wai slicked up all the food that was left. No one drank much that night; everyone wanted to be clear-eyed and coordinated for the big contest.

At 2:00 P.M. on Sunday the cooperative had its finest mo-ment. Dressed in their red and yellow uniforms, the *socios* gathered outside the store and lined up to march to the football field, an area hacked out of pigweed behind the school. Bolivia with her satin ribbon and a bouquet of flowers led the parade; at her side was Wai, who carried his football shoes still packed in their box. Next Ramón and Orestes, the president and the vice-president, and behind them in the degree of their importance the other *socios;* at the tail end but walking like a king, Goya, all black skin and white teeth and red and yellow stripes. They were so happy, so splendid, so proud and dignified that I could hardly stand to look at them.

They marched around the field two times, very serious in their splendor, and the people of Río Verde were absolutely dazed. Señora Florinda, who gives penicillin shots to everyone who has anything wrong with them (science's answer to the witch doctor), a woman who had never had much use for the cooperative, was carried away. *"Viva la cooperativa!"* she cried. Everyone joined in. Now the visiting team paraded, but they were abashed and self-conscious; there weren't four football uniforms in the bunch. The teams met in the middle of the field; each team gave three great shouts; the rules were discussed and the referees chosen. Wai put on his football shoes, and the game began.

Of course, with Río Verde referees, one using a red and yellow whistle, there was never much doubt about which side would win. But for the first few minutes I held my breath, because a horrifying thing happened. The great, splendid, graceful Wai was moving around like a crippled idiot. He stumbled when he ran; he picked his feet up high in the air when he tried to walk, as though he were just learning or as though he were walking through high grass. He kicked at the ball, but missed completely. He did get in a couple of spectacular punts, but they were meaningless demonstrations of sheer power; they impressed the crowd but slowed up the game since the kids had to beat the jungle looking for the ball.

Río Verde scored the first goal, and San Vicente the second, but it was disallowed by our friendly referee. A drunken spectator, a traitor because he was from Río Verde, got punched in the face by Ramón for insisting that the second goal was good, and there was a short, inconclusive scuffle at the far goal post.

Bad feeling developed; both teams were furious. Río Verde scored again and broke San Vicente's will to fight.

After the half period and the iced lemonade, the game went on, but it was all anticlimax—hot sun, exhausted players, red and yellow shirts coated with dust. Wai had discarded his shoes and loped around with easy grace, but his heroics were no longer needed.

"Well, Martín, how did you like the game?" one of the *socios* asked me later back at the co-op.

"If you all worked as hard as you play," I told him, "you'd be millionaires."

"They're mad at us now," Ramón said. "They say the referees were bribed, that the lunch was no good, just fish and rice, and that the lemonade didn't have enough sugar. They say the cooperative is a crummy outfit."

"Graceful losers," I said.

"*Montuvios*," Ramón said. "What can you expect?"

Each team proceeded to celebrate with a few glasses of *aguardiente*, but in different *salones*, and at five o'clock, ignored, the visiting team climbed into their canoes and paddled back up the river. The moment of glory passed, but I still remember with emotion that parade of beautiful *socios* as they marched around the football field that day—united and cooperating at last.

A week later everything was back to normal. Goya resigned from the cooperative; we paid him ten cents an hour for his work, the usual wage, deducting the cost of his football uniform. The outboard motor flew to pieces one day as we went up the river looking for bananas for the pigs; the chickens got diarrhea and stopped laying; the *socios* weren't coming to work.

Yes, everything was back to normal, but they still talk in the town about the time that Río Verde showed San Vicente how things should be done, and about how beautiful the team looked that day. "And the chickens," Vicenta says. "One hundred sucres worth of chickens; *dios mío*, chicken for twelve men. Have you ever heard of anything to match that?"

◻◻

In many ways Wai illustrated all the great qualities of the typical Ecuadorian coastal *zambo*. In retrospect, I remember him at a few intense and very separate moments of his life when all his dignity, or frailty, or vulnerability stands out, and he moves in memory as though under a bright spotlight. Men like Wai, who represent all of the qualities of their race, all of the secret aspirations of their people, inspire myths.

Walking up the beach one Sunday morning to visit with Ramón and Ester, I noticed Wai standing at the edge of the waves visiting with a neighbor, Oriano, the old *carbonero* who earned his living making charcoal out of scrub hardwood in back of town, whose hair, skin, and ragged clothes were impregnated with the black dust of his trade.

Wai was facing the sea and his neighbor, and seemed to be dividing his attention between them. Suddenly a half-dozen swift movements changed him from a man indolently visiting with a neighbor to a man violently paddling out through the breakers in a *bongo* scarcely longer than himself. The change was so violent that I felt as though I were watching a strip of film which had been badly spliced, with certain essential material removed.

Two hundred feet out past the last line of breaking surf, Wai stooped, took up a harpoon, and hurled it into the sea. The whole action was one smooth continuity, an action so economical, sure, swift, and pure that watching him I felt that all the years of his life had been distilled into a technique as perfected as the technique of a great artist, a Horowitz or a Cezanne.

In two minutes it was begun and finished; as I came up to them a couple of his kids had rushed down into the waves to pack off a twenty-pound *pargo*, a red snapper, its round side pierced in the exact center like a target. Wai, breathing evenly, slightly bored, completely relaxed, his expression tranquil and unchanged, was visiting once more with his neighbor. As I passed them they nodded gravely and wished me a good morning.

I was invited to Wai's house for the fiesta of La Virgen de Carmen, probably the most solemn and important of the religious festivals in Río Verde. It was always given both in Wai's house and in the house of Crucelio's parents farther up the beach. Months before, Wai's house had been washed away in the high tides, but for the last few weeks he had been working frantically to finish his new house, and I suddenly realized why. He had to be ready for the fiesta when all the people in town would arrive, as they had done every year through all the years of his life.

In one corner of the main room a shrine had been set up with pieces of balsa off the beach; twenty or thirty penny candles blazed around a cheap lithograph of the Virgin, her weeping eyes raised to heaven and her bloody heart, hanging outside her robes, pierced with knives. Streamers of tissue paper threaded on fishline—white, red, green, purple, all faded—hung in loops and festoons. The candles supplied the only light in the room.

It was an entire night of drums and chanting, pure African, and there were words in the precise rite that no one understood any more. It was a night of growing intensity, and in a certain sense it belonged to the women. They directed and controlled the pace of the ceremony, chanting at first individually or in pairs, and then, losing themselves in some religious vision, their eyes rolled back into their heads, dominated by the drums, more and more of them joined in. Finally the women, singing in unison, moaning and hollering, stamped their own domination over the drummers. The men remained in the shadows, drinking quietly, not singing at first, but gradually giving in to the beat. Their drinking was careful and controlled; it was a religious drunkenness, and the *puro* that they shared, passing the glass from hand to hand, was only a springboard into a sense of looseness and ease.

By midnight the joint was jumping.

About one o'clock, Ramón, Orestes, Rufo, and I visisted Crucelio's house for a while. It was half a mile up the beach, at the bottom of the cliffs that form the point of Río Verde. The same thing was happening there, but the house was a little closer to Rocafuerte, and families had come down from the farms along the Río Mate, so the house was slightly more crowded and the people a little more rural. A seventeen-year-old boy had shot himself in the foot with an "unloaded" shotgun just before we arrived. We offered to take the boy in the canoe to Esmeraldas, but no one had money for a doctor, and they didn't want to move him in the night air, and, well, no one ever looked for a doctor until rigor mortis had begun to set in.

We went back to Wai's house, and the whole coast was throbbing with the sound of drums, like a heartbeat, and the wailing sound of the singing women. At Wai's the situation was getting complicated. Alvaro had arrived, and he was stupidly drunk and a little pugnacious. He had collected a group of cronies with the aid of his bottle and was making sarcastic remarks about Wai and the disappointingly poor quality of his fiesta. Wai, who couldn't stand complications and didn't understand what was going on, had a confused and distracted expression on his face. The news that Crucelio's house was filled with people, and that later they would all eat pork, further depressed him. He began to drink more than he should.

Alvaro hated the cooperative, and he couldn't stand to see Wai, Ramón, and Orestes standing with me as we listened to the music. He tried to get Wai to join his little clique of friends, but Wai as host was busy with many things, and he drifted away.

About three o'clock in the morning Ramón found me in the crowd and asked me to go to Wai. "Have you got any money?" he asked me. We found Wai squatting in a corner of the room almost in darkness with his hands over his face, his hands and face glistening with tears in the candlelight.

"What's wrong with him?" I asked Ramón.

"Well, first he's drunk," Ramón told me. "But it's on account of Alvaro. Wai charged food at the store last month and hasn't paid. Seventy-five cents, and Alvaro is insulting him about the debt. It's just incredible. Here, tonight, of all places."

I loaned Wai fourteen sucres, told him to pay Alvaro immediately, and went back to the music. About five minutes later Alvaro, who hadn't spoken to me in three months, sought me out in the crowd. He was terribly agitated, his face flushed and sweating. He realized that he had done something inexcusably crude, something that had been predicated on Wai's inability to pay.

"All I want is a little respect," Alvaro yelled at me over the music of the drums.

"You're absolutely right," I yelled back.

"Just a little respect," he yelled. "Just not to be treated like dirt. I just want a little respect."

"You betcha," I told Alvaro. "That's what everybody wants, Alvaro. You've hit on one of life's secrets."

I moved away from Alvaro. He was under a terrible pressure

to act, and I was afraid that Ramón, who was standing with us, his fists clenched, guarding me, would do something crazy. Actually, we were all a little drunk, but more from the music and the power of the night and the drums than from anything else.

About four o'clock, as I was planning to leave, Ramón once more sent me to see Wai. I stepped outside for a moment first and almost urinated on Alvaro, who was lying in the yard sound asleep. Wai was out in the kitchen where the women were fixing a breakfast of chicken soup and rice. Wai asked Ramón and me to be the guests of honor and to eat with him at the table. After we had finished eating, the three plates would be washed and the three next most important guests would be served. Wai offered his invitation very badly. He was not so much drunk as under some curious strain, as though he were being driven two ways at once. His speech was thick and foolish; then his face crumpled with grief, and the tears rushed out of his eyes; a moment later he was kneading his fists and trembling with anger.

"What's wrong, Wai? Tell me what's wrong."

"It's that Alvaro," Wai said. "That damned Alvaro. Coming here like that; humiliating me because I'm poor, insulting me in my own house. And there's nothing I can do; he's a guest under my roof; the house is his. After you and Ramón have eaten I will invite Alvaro to eat. And what I really want to do, my God, what I really want to do is smash his face in and pick him up over my head and throw him through the door. And I can't do it; there's not a thing I can do. I think I'm going crazy."

"Take it easy," I said. "Just wait a little while longer until we get the co-op store started. You won't have to buy anything from Alvaro then."

"Yes, Martín, for the love of God, Martín, let's start that

store." The idea picked him up, but only for a while. Later Wai sadly and abstractedly dripped tears into his chicken soup as the great fiesta of La Virgen de Carmen slowly became history.

Another vivid memory of Wai is concentrated simply on his face, and more precisely on the whites of his eyes. (Actually, since this memory involves my spookiest experience in Ecuador, it is probably—aside from a few bombing missions over Berlin during the Second World War—the most intense and vivid memory of my life.) Ramón Prado, Ramón Arcos, Wai, and I had gone about sixty miles up along the Ecuadorian coast in our motor canoe to pick up a purebred boar that Heifer Project had given us. It was a gray day of winds and rain squalls, but traveling north we rode with the sea, and the trip was uneventful except that as we entered the Cayapas River through the breakers we were circled by a couple of tremendous sharks. It was one of the few times that I had seen sharks in Ecuador, but since I had a phobia about them, an irrational intimation that eventually they were going to get me, simply watching those quick evil fins cutting through the water was more or less traumatic. I sat in the canoe as we passed up the river through miles of mangrove swamp and thought about the Winslow Homer painting of somebody famous being eaten by a shark.

With the crated boar loaded in the canoe, we headed back. It was getting late but we didn't have the money to stay away from Río Verde overnight. About five o'clock we reached the river's mouth and the open sea. The wind had risen and the breakers were tremendous; at the sand bar the ocean was a wild confusion of river flood, riptides, wind, and breakers. A couple of hours later, screaming and laughing and dancing with relief, they would all agree that it was the worst sea they had ever been in and that they had all expected the canoe to break into pieces, but now no one said a word.

Traveling on the sea, I had long before simply put my life in the hands of these fishermen, who lived on the sea and who knew more about it than I would ever know. But this time I realized that they needed a little well-thought-out technical advice. After about forty-five seconds in the ocean, tightly grabbing the sides of the canoe to keep from being washed out, I turned to Ramón Arcos and screamed, "For God's sake, turn around!"

"You can't turn the boat in this!" they screamed back at me.

I had been sitting on a cross beam in the middle of the canoe where I could watch the pig in his crate and the scenery along the river as we traveled home, but now the scenery was a little too real. The sight of the waves crashing over the boat was too agonizing to watch; the first couple of waves, solid gray walls of water, had half filled the canoe, and out as far as I could see breakers were lifting and crashing, a desert of white, white spume blowing off the tops of the lifting breakers. I turned my back on this horrifying spectacle; it was entirely unacceptable.

The new view was no more satisfactory. Ramón Arcos, soaking wet and trembling violently, was manhandling the motor, tense and balanced; there was a look of intense concentration on his face, and since I had never seen much of anything on his relaxed and languid face before, it was like seeing him for the first time. There was a concentration so profound that it drew a man out of himself, made him more than human, and gave to the most ordinary face a kind of dignity and beauty.

Ramón Prado, like me unable to do anything but simply live through the experience, had like me decided not to face it. He had gone into a trance; he had pulled a large piece of heavy plastic over his head and body like a shroud and disappeared into a fixed immobility. I had the feeling that he had left the canoe and gone somewhere else to live for a time.

Wai, grasping the side of the canoe with one hand, was expertly bailing water with a large calabash. He was stripped down to his underwear and soaking wet from the seas that rushed over the canoe every time we hit a swell. His face was set and expressionless except for something in his eyes. It was quite dark, but each time he bent down to fill his *mate* with water, his face came to within a few inches of mine; every few seconds I found myself staring into the softly glowing whites of Wai's eyes. His eyes never left the front of the canoe, and after a time I found that I was interpreting and anticipating every rush of sea, every smashing wave, through some almost imperceptible look of pain or terror in the eyes of Wai.

He stooped to fill his *mate*, and his face obliterated everything, filling the limits of my vision; then something terrible and unacceptable appeared in his eyes. About three seconds later the shuddering canoe lifted and rose and rose and rose; a sheet of solid water slammed across us; then the canoe dropped brutally onto the surface of the sea. Up in the bow, under the boar's crate, the canoe had developed a three-foot-long crack, which none of us would know about until much later.

We were tossed about for an interminable time, perhaps forty-five minutes, but after the first few minutes a curious thing happened. My own personal experience, filtered through Wai's consciousness, became aesthetic. It was all more real, more intense and beautiful, than reality, almost religious. I was alive and part of everything—the dim shore obliterated by night and spray, the half moon hanging in clouds above the black clouds above the black hills, the wild sea, the destroyed canoe, the sleeping boar, my three friends, Ecuadorian fishermen trembling with cold and terror. I even accepted the sharks and the knowledge that they were out there waiting in the breakers.

A couple of hours later, in normal seas and screaming with

laughter, we ate cheese and bread, coconuts and bananas, as we toured down the coast. At midnight, still exultant, we crossed over the sand bar at Río Verde and floated into the harbor of the black, sleeping town where we lived.

□□

Shortly after I arrived in Río Verde, the young *mocho*, Crispín Bagui, had the inspired idea of building a dance hall and drinking parlor in town. Counting his mother's dance hall and drinking parlor just four houses up the hill from my house, there were three others in the town. Prorating dance halls and drinking parlors on a per-family basis, about every eight families in Río Verde had their own place of worship. The *mocho* had a good money-making idea, and only Wilfrido and the local Peace Corps Volunteer were distressed by his plans. What made the whole idea grisly was that Crispín began to build this newest cultural center a little less than three feet from the west wall of my house.

After about two months of building, he ran out of money and put the uncompleted structure up for sale. Wilfrido (who was still a member of the co-op at that time) and I—both a little hysterical, I'm afraid—began suggesting at ten-minute intervals that the co-op buy the building and convert it into chicken coops in back and a grocery store in front. Perhaps Wilfrido, a strict *Evangelista*, had moral reasons for not wanting this fun palace built. Not I; all I wanted was the chance to sleep nights, lulled to sleep by the sound of waves lapping the shore or the Voice of America.

To the poor of this area who lived by fishing and farming, owning a little store was an ultimate goal, the top rung on the ladder of life's aspirations—*una licencia para bagar*, as some of the more cynical people said, a license to cool it, to live lazy.

But it was more than that; there were subtle volumes of Latin status in this dream that I, being a non-Latin, will never understand. In Ecuador there was nothing intrinsically noble about physical labor. For a man who sweated and suffered with a machete for his life, a store was a symbol of the middle class, the crowning glory, as high as he would ever dare to aim without being presumptuous in the eyes of God.

At any rate, the idea of actually owning a store galvanized us, and we saved our egg money for a month and gave Crispín the forty dollars that he asked. For over a year we worked on the building, buying bamboo for the walls or thatch for the roof whenever we had a little money. We had three hundred chickens in the back, one hundred of them in the kitchen area of the house itself. There were great wooden boxes to store the corn we hoped to raise; one section in front was walled off for co-op meeting (those violent, exhausting, therapeutic events), and another section was reserved for the store.

It was going to be a new kind of store, I explained. I wanted to destroy the strictly noncompetitive Latin idea, with prices gauged as high as the traffic would bear. For instance, the storekeeper in Palestina, Don Umberto, had floating prices, and the older the product, the more it cost. "I've got to make interest on my investment," he would explain, handing across the counter a rusty funnel so full of holes that it was useless and for which he was asking 300 per cent more than the Esmeraldas price. We would cut prices on everything, making a maximum of 10 per cent profit; we would not only serve the whole town but also make twice as much on volume as the other storekeepers with their exorbitant markups. It was an exciting concept.

We sawed and hammered and dreamed, buying six pieces of lumber at a time for shelves, doors, a sliding window above the

counter. Then one day, right out of heaven, my dad sent me
two hundred dollars; I lent it to the co-op, and Ramón and I
hurried into town to buy stock for the new store.

We came back with the canoe loaded—sacks of rice, sugar,
potatoes, onions, flour; tins of lard, kerosene, instant coffee,
tuna fish, and sardines; little piles of things that poor people
buy—milk of magnesia, pain pills, hair oil, fishhooks, needles
and thread, children's copy books and pencils, straw hats, a
dozen machetes, animal crackers, buttons, penny candy, poi-
sonous-tasting colas, bottled mineral water used almost exclusively as a medicine for sick kids, yeast, salt, cloves, cumin,
peanuts. Deodorant. That's just about it. Oh, yes, *beer.*

The members of the co-op were wild with excitement. Alvaro,
the thieving storekeeper at the foot of the street who had been
awaiting this moment with a boiling hatred for us—and with
terror, too—began spreading the word that Ramón, like the
gringo, was a practicing Communist determined to destroy the
tranquillity of the town, and that a revolver bullet or a good
dose of 1080, the rat poison generally used to kill dogs and
wandering pigs, was what he needed. Ramón began to carry a
butcher knife in his belt and to leave town for his house up the
beach before full darkness.

During the week that the *socios* met nightly and fought over
who would manage the store, I was left in charge. Finally I was
removed by the *directiva* because I kept selling three animal
crackers instead of two for the penny that the children
brought. But that week was a revealing and confusing time for
me. Because we were selling only to the poor, everything had to
be converted from pounds or sucres into ounces or centavos.
Everything was bought as needed. Brown sugar for the breakfast hot drink was purchased at 6:00 A.M., enough for that
meal; rice was bought at 11:30 A.M. and again at 5:00 P.M.
Women who lived a mile away shopped themselves or sent a

child three times a day. A typical sale: a penny's worth of onion, two pennies' worth of rice, and a sixteenth of a pound of lard—this for a family of four, their meal made more filling by boiled platano and, depending on that day's luck, fish or shrimp.

We were buying rice at that time for 1.30 sucres a pound. It is the basic food of Ecuador, and in order to dramatize the low prices in our new store we were selling it for 1.40. Alvaro had been selling rice for 1.80. He had been buying potatoes for eighty sucres and selling them for two hundred. We cut his price by one hundred sucres and still made 10 per cent, including the cost of transport. We sold *bombolinos*, little wrapped pieces of hard candy, for half price compared with Alvaro, and we sold over one hundred the first day; Alvaro's normal sales on *bombolinos* could never have been more than six or eight a day.

Business was so brisk that on the third day we had to return to town for more supplies. In those first days we captured almost 100 per cent of the town's business, and on Saturday, the day when the farmers came to town to buy their week's supplies, we sold over thirty dollars' worth of groceries, a staggering sum.

Alvaro was out of his head with worry; he couldn't take his eyes off our store and the lines of people who, embarrassed to pass him, would cut through the pigweed in the town plaza to buy from us. We were watching his reactions, too; he seemed to be losing weight, a good thing we decided, since he had a sloppy, drooping paunch, the only paunch in town. We heard rumors that he was planning to move his store to Palestina, and one day in desperation he loaded a canoe with sacks of staples and went paddling up the river, crying his wares, with small success apparently, for he only did it once.

Walter Pata, one of the *socios* but also a good friend of Alvaro, was talking about the situation one night. (He had remained loyal to Alvaro and bought nothing from our store except cigarettes, a puzzling thing since our prices were so much cheaper. Then Orestes explained that Walter's wife, Tiodora, washed clothes for Alvaro and his family and was in an excellent position to steal food from his store; they could therefore see no advantage in buying from the cooperative.) "But what is Alvaro going to do?" Walter wanted to know. "He's not selling one hundred sucres a day."

"It's simple," I told him. "He's going to have to compete with us."

This came as a revelation; Walter sat there for a long time shaking his head, as though I had struck him between the eyes; after a while he strolled down to Alvaro's and had a long talk. The next day Alvaro was selling rice for 1.40 and potatoes for one sucre. He still had an advantage over us, for his scales were rigged to show a pound of weight for twelve ounces of groceries, but since the people were wise to this technique, we continued to receive about 75 per cent of the town's business.

After four or five months our sales had leveled off to about eighteen dollars on week days, double that on Saturdays, and double again on feast days. Easter week, for example, was a period of heavy compulsive eating, and a month before the holiday everyone was looking for work in order to have a little cash in the house. In four days during Easter week the store sold almost six thousand sucres' worth of delicacies like tuna fish and sardines, luxury foods considered much too expensive for daily consumption.

The management problems had leveled off, too. At first I wanted each *socio* to spend his share of time in the store, but this created too many problems, the main, unspoken, one being that no one trusted some of the *socios* in a job that offered such hidden and forbidden rewards.

We gave the job to Rufo, Ramón's youngest brother, and I

thought he did well. But he gained about twelve pounds the first month. Ramón insisted that he was stealing, and we finally caught him red-handed. Three times! In the same week Rufo had other problems, no doubt brought on by his improved diet. He was eighteen years old, as innocent as an angel, but absolutely consumed by the burning passions that were beginning to control him. One night he tried to act out one of his fantasies, and the next morning Señora Carlina stormed up to Ramón to report that Rufo had hidden in the rafters above her daughter's bed, and when everyone in the house was asleep had begun whispering hot words of love. "Either he leaves town or he goes to jail," Carlina yelled. Ramón and Orestes held a family council, and young Rufo was banished from the cooperative and the town.

Poor little hot-blooded kid! For a while he wandered the streets of Esmeraldas like a ghost looking for work. Another of his last week's capers had been to steal fifty cents from some work pants hanging in my house when Ramón had sent him up to feed the baby chickens living in my bedroom. Each time he saw me he was so ashamed he would run away. He finally got a job at fifteen dollars a month as a helper on a freight truck running between Guayaquil and Esmeraldas. But he still ran when he saw me.

After Rufo was dismissed, we made Eloy the storekeeper, raising the wages to eight dollars a month. He was young and scrawny, too, when he went to work, but after three months he was gaining weight and beginning to flesh out into another Alvaro. He insisted that he was not stealing, that he ate only the broken pieces of animal crackers, the fragments that he couldn't sell. The story was slightly far-fetched, but the store was making about sixty dollars a month, and I kept telling the board of directors, "Let's not rock the boat." Eloy was as honest as could be expected. Poor people steal; this is a trait they have in common with the rich, whose thefts vary only in the degree of the necessity and the quality of the theft.

🔲🔲

During the time that I was recuperating from hepatitis in a Quito pension and going crazy with boredom, I had heard from another Volunteer that AID, our government agency that handles the disperal of funds to developing countries, had a special nest egg set aside for Volunteers with projects that badly needed financing. The rumor had it that AID was interested in projects where a small cash outlay would yield quick and dramatic results. I lay in bed for almost a month constructing a quick and dramatic plan for changing the faltering Río Verde cooperative into a dynamic, pulsating organization with fifty acres of cleared land ready to plant to corn.

The heart of the plan involved an eight-hundred-dollar grant of the taxpayers' money for the rental of a D-8 Caterpillar to clear out the stumps from the land that we were opening up with machetes. I had spent three months up on the farm with a crowbar digging out the stumps from a half acre, but the work was painful and impossibly tedious, and the *socios* refused to help me. With the land cleared we could use our disking tractor and start preparing a seedbed; without the big Cat to clear the land we would either have to do it by hand (which nobody was about to do) or else wait ten years for the stumps to rot out.

I went up to AID and talked to Mr. White and Mr. Brown. "I understand that you're looking for projects that with a very little investment will show quick and dramatic results," I said. "I've got just the project for you."

"Well, no," one of them told me. "We've changed; we've finally decided that there are no quick, dramatic solutions. We went that route and ended up with nothing."

"Actually," I said, "this plan isn't so awfully quick and dramatic; you might in fact be a little excited by its slowness and lack of drama."

They were interested; I wrote and rewrote the plan on special government forms about four times and had five-hour-long sessions with Mr. White, Mr. Brown, and on up to Mr. Grey. Just before I went back to Río Verde, Mr. Grey took me in to see Mr. Green, who approved the plan but told me not to expect the money immediately. "It sometimes takes a couple of weeks," he told me. How this madman escaped from the loony-bin and got a job with AID must surely make a fascinating story for anyone who has the facts. Or was it simply that he meant to say "years" and the word "weeks" slipped out instead?

I went back to Río Verde, called a special meeting of the co-op, and told the *socios* that if they would clear fifty acres of land with their machetes, pile the brush, and burn it, AID would come in with the Cat. We would accomplish ten years of work in one great, beautiful, painful spasm. We had a dozen members at this time, and each member would have to clear about four acres of jungle. They all grew pale and stole secret glances at one another; the enthusiasm that I had hoped to hear was missing, but no one objected either. Ramón came to me later and said I was placing a killing burden on the people, but at the meeting he defended the idea with a couple of dynamic speeches as emotional as Knute Rockne's halftime remarks.

Up until then we had been working as a co-op on Mondays and Fridays. These were machete days. The extra work of caring for the chickens and the pigs was theoretically divided up among the *socios* and done on the other days of the week. Actually, I was a little disgusted with the membership, since on work days we always quit at noon after three or four hours,

everyone promising to return immediately after lunch. But no
one ever showed up to finish out the day. I told them now that it
was essential that we stop fooling around, that we had to put in
eight-hour days. We were well into June, and by December the
land must be cleared and burned.

Everyone agreed to work full days and stop fooling around.
The meeting was held on a Saturday. On Monday about 75 per
cent of the *socios* showed up; they came quite late, worked
about three hours, and gradually disappeared. By 11:30 I was
alone.

Secretly I was glad. We were in the middle of the dry season,
and there was little to eat in the town. I had been working
beside them all morning having eaten nothing for breakfast but
several cups of coffee and a half-dozen bananas; I was dizzy
and trembling with hunger. But I decided to play out my role,
and I weaved down into town, righteously indignant, and
looked up Ramón. I found the President and four other *socios*

in the *bodega* underneath my house where we stored piles of
bunched bananas for the pigs; everyone was eating ravenously.
It was after noon, and it was the first food that any of them had
had all day. Without saying anything I sat down beside them
and started putting away the bananas.

We called another meeting to discuss the food problem, and
a primed Ramón suggested that each *socio* contribute one
sucre, a nickel, each work day so that Vicenta, our only remaining lady member, could buy rice, fish, and platano to cook up
on the farm. I thought that a hot lunch would not only bring in
more members and give them more strength to work, but also
capture them during those noon hours when they tended to slip
away and disappear in the weeds. Maybe they couldn't work
eight hours, but they might work six.

Everyone agreed that this was a good idea, but only Walter
handed over his sucre. *"Bueno,"* Ramón said. "Monday morning when we go to work everyone bring his sucre so Vicenta can
buy food. Agreed?"

On Monday morning four *socios* failed to show up for work,
and those who did come didn't have any money. Ramón returned Walter's sucre, and we all marched up to the farm
where we worked for four hours on empty stomachs.

"What happened to Santiago and Wai and the others?" I
asked Orestes. "Why didn't they come to work?"

"I guess they didn't have a sucre and were ashamed," Orestes said.

This proved to be the case, because at the next meeting
Orestes made a little speech. "If you haven't got your sucre
don't miss a day of work on account of shame but come anyway
and we'll share what food there is." This made Santiago furious, and before walking out on the meeting he accused Orestes
of mocking his poverty. He stood outside in the darkness talking loudly to himself about the rich *socios* and the poor *socios*,

and a disturbed Orestes, listening, looked at me and said "???"
with his eyes.

The co-op about this time was beginning to divide into two
groups. The "rich" *socios*, working faithfully, had begun to
accumulate three and four times as many hours of work as the
"poor" ones. Any co-op profits would be divided according to
the number of hours each member had worked, and I had been
warning everyone that it was quite possible that three or four
socios would end up controlling everything.

We moved on into the dry season. The lagoons dried up;
even at the lowest tides the river could never clean out the salt
water. There was no fruit coming down from up country; the
season of oranges and avocados had long passed; even platano,
the staple food of the coast, became scarce, and we sometimes
went a week without bananas. All the trees along the coast lost
their leaves and went dormant; even the fish stopped biting.

I didn't adjust very well to the new situation. Unlike the
people of Río Verde, I was used to eating something every day.
I was living on bread and strawberry jam brought in from
Esmeraldas, Pepsi Cola and animal crackers, rice and eggs;
rice was the only item in my repertoire that wasn't in the
luxury class. I think that for about six months the people in
the town more or less lived on rice and *cocada*, a paste-like
sweet made of raw cane boiled down and mixed with grated
coconut.

I started to lose my leaves and go dormant. Trips to Quito
became a secret vice. Every three weeks or so I would take off
for Quito to talk to the AID officials, and also to consume huge
quantities of roast chicken, T-bone steak, and chocolate sundaes. Mr. Green, it appeared, was on a five-month vacation in
the States; he would return about two months too late to do our
cooperative any good. The other officials were sure that things
could be worked out, but apparently it wouldn't be as simple

and clear-cut as Mr. Green had led me to believe. Was the co-op legalized? AID would hand out no funds until this was done. With whom was I affiliated? I would need letters of recommendation from agricultural extension promising to supervise the co-op. Could the Peace Corps promise to replace me in Río Verde at the termination of my contract?

About this time the President of Ecuador got riled with the American ambassador and gave him forty-eight hours to get out of the country, and the Ecuadorian Navy impounded a couple of United States fishing boats that were violating Ecuador's ocean. Some of the San Diego fishing companies wrote to their congressmen, suggesting that Ecuador was a country of pirates and that war should immediately be declared. AID, sitting in the middle of all this, grew nervous and uncertain. Each month from May through November I arrived at their offices, slightly bloated from roast chicken or roast beef, and explained that time was running out. In December my plan was approved. I talked to a Mr. Black. "I've got good news for you," he said. "We've got an approval on your project. Unfortunately, we don't have any funds. When will we have funds? Ask Congress. They're not too hot on foreign aid right now."

After that AID began to lose *its* leaves and go dormant.

Throughout this period, the little co-op was clearing jungle with machetes; I had promised that AID would help if they would work hard. By December, if everyone made a supreme and killing effort, we could move out of this stone-age agriculture, this farming with a machete and a sharp stick, into—well, into 1930 agriculture, at least.

But we had to clear enough land to make it worth while to bring the tractor out from Esmeraldas, across two rivers and up the thirty miles of beach. It would cost about a hundred dollars just to get the tractor to Río Verde, ready to begin work. I was pushing the *socios* shamelessly, sulking when they promised to work and then didn't show up, getting mad at them when they quit early, pleading the case, giving them long, boring talks on the necessity of suffering Now, sacrificing Now. I was like a one-man symphony orchestra; when the flutes and violins didn't work, I was blaring trumpets and percussion. I tried to shame them or inspire them or obligate them in some way to cut down fifty acres of jungle. As I think back on that time, it occurs to me that they must all have thought I was quite mad.

There was hardly anything to eat in the town, and we were caught up in a monumental lethargy. The Italian priests who dominated the religious life of the province of Esmeraldas sent a fresh, plump brother out to take charge of the mission in Palestina. He had little money and to a large degree depended on the goodness of his parish; he lasted about four months, and when he was recalled he had lost about forty pounds and a good deal of his vocational calling. It wasn't that the people didn't want to feed him; it was simply that there was nothing to share, and many of the people were filled with shame and humiliation when the brother, vacant-eyed and ribs jutting, left the town.

It was the bananas that saved my life. When it was possible to buy them, I could generally manage to move around, but it meant eating bananas all day. (And I thought Ricardo was gassy!) Trying to set an example, I was clearing land on a daily schedule, and it became a fascinating problem in internal combustion to stuff bananas into myself and see how far I could go. Two bananas would get me up the hill to the farm; five bananas would fuel me up for forty or fifty minutes of low-keyed work; one banana would get me down the hill again to the Pepsi Colas and the animal crackers. When I went to work mornings, I had bananas stuffed into every pocket, pants and

shirt, the precise number counted out beforehand. Sixteen bananas would carry me through to noon if I didn't work too fast
or if the hordes of sons and grandsons of Sebastián Bagui
didn't shatter all my plans with their hungry cries as I passed
the last house on the street.

But being hungry wasn't simply losing my energy and
reaching a moment about eleven o'clock in the morning when I
ran out of energy and had to sit down every five minutes to
plan the next move, like a mountain climber at eighteen thousand feet. There was also a growing mental depression, a gray
fog of hopelessness that grew in my head each day; I could feel
myself getting stupider. Things became incomprehensible and
irritating. I snapped at the *socios* when they did dumb things,
even though I knew they were as hungry as I was and that they
were frantically combing the beach for something to give their
children.

I began to get furious letters from my friends and family
asking what was wrong, why didn't I keep in touch? I would sit
down, write "Dear Father," stare at the paper for fifteen
minutes, and then say, "Ah, to hell with it," and go take a nap.
It wasn't only that I couldn't think of anything to say; writing
a letter also involved finding the envelope, steaming it open,
addressing it, stamping it, getting it into the mailbox. The
whole thing was impossibly complicated.

Afternoons I usually stayed in the house and either slept or
just sat on a stool staring out the window at the ocean. I lay on
the bed and between naps read a book called *The Economics of
Subsistence Agriculture* in five-minute periods of comparative
concentration. Slowly I came to realize that the author was
writing about us in Río Verde when he said that a majority of
all the farmers in the world—perhaps 90 per cent of the self-
employed farmers in Africa, Asia, and South America—their
caloric intake limited to a bare subsistence level, worked no

more than three or four hours a day. There is only so much
energy in a dish of rice and a piece of fish. There are just so
many miles to a gallon of bananas—not one foot more.

I don't know why reading this in a book gave me such
satisfaction, seeing it all spelled out in graphs and statistics,
but it came to me as a revelation, this terrible truth that I had
known since arriving in Río Verde. And seeing it written down
wiped away my last lingering feelings that Ramón and his
two-hour naps after lunch, or Wilfrido sitting on a box all day
in the shadow of his house without moving, or all those
hundreds of men whose faces I had seen looking out the windows of little bamboo farmhouses up and down the river
through those long afternoons, were manifestations of laziness.
No, they were manifestations of exhaustion, in the case of
Wilfrido—an old man fading and aging before our eyes—a
moral exhaustion so consuming that he had to fight the impulse
to kill himself. I was making a hundred dollars a month. My
hunger was in varying degrees experimental and masochistic,
and resulted from laziness, bad planning, and affectation. I was
like a six-year-old kid playing doctor; I just wanted to see
what it was like.

But projecting my own lethargy, exhaustion, and mental
depression onto my friends, who weren't playing and who went
through this seasonal hunger every year of their lives, I began
to see in them such qualities of heroism and endurance, such a
wild and savage strength, that it about broke my heart with
pride for them.

Poverty isn't just hunger; it is many interlocking things—
ignorance and exhaustion, underproduction, disease, and fear.
It is glutted export markets, sharp, unscrupulous middlemen, a
lack of knowledge about the fundamental aspects of agriculture. It is the witchcraft of your grandfather spreading its
values on your life. It is a dozen irrational Latin qualities, like

your fear of making more of your life than your neighbor and thereby gaining his contempt for being overly ambitious.

There is no single way to smash out and be freed. A man has to break out in a dozen places at once. Most important, perhaps, he should start breaking out before he is six years old, for by then a typical child of poverty in a tropical nation is probably crippled by protein starvation, his brain dulled and his insides eaten up by worms and amoebas. No, more brutally true: if he is a typical child, an average child, by six he is dead.

To work harder a man has to eat better; to eat better he has to produce more; to produce more he has to work harder. And all of this is predicated on a growing knowledge of nutrition, basic hygiene, and the causes of the diseases that ravage his body; an understanding of agriculture and a respect for new farming techniques, new seeds, new ways to plant, new fertilizers, new crops.

Craziest and most interesting is the problem of incentive. Many of the people in Río Verde, for instance, aside from wanting more food, prettier clothes, and the money for doctors when they needed it, couldn't think of any good reason for not being poor. They didn't want anything. Perhaps a radio, perhaps a horse. To talk to a man about tripling his income to three hundred dollars a year was to fill him with confusion; he got nervous; he started to laugh; he wanted to go get drunk. The poor man from the moment of his birth was so inundated with problems, so deprived, that to end up wanting things was a form of insanity. What he wanted was to stay alive another day to tell jokes and visit with his friends in the sweet night air; he wanted new pants for the fifth of August fiesta, another pair at Christmas, and a house full of food for the Easter *Semana Santa;* he wanted ten sucres from time to time so that he could drink and dance and feel cleansed of life. Ramón with his composition roof was *egoísto,* the maverick; roofing a house with Eternit that would collect rain water, in this town of thatched roofs, had separated Ramón from the people. Ramón wanted a million things—a refrigerator, a larger house, a store-bought bed for the son he expected, and, not least, the respect of the middle-class storekeepers in Esmeraldas with whom he had done business all his life as just an undifferentiated shadow in the doorway, another beach *zambo*.

Ramón didn't want to be poor any more, and he was riding for a fall. The people had a growing contempt for his ambition and his aggressiveness, and he, a growing contempt for their lack of drive, their acceptance of the old ways. The time will come when he will have to find a middle-class environment where he can be at ease.

We cleared land until late November. By then I was aware that AID would probably not help us, or that if they did it would involve months and months of conferences with every gringo in the AID mission, from the office boy on up to the remote and invisible high mucky-muck. I needed the money in December, in thirty days. When the rains came our farm would turn into a mudhole, and the tractor would have to wait another year. It had been some time since I had pushed and raved at the *socios*. They had suffered, some of them, way past what anyone could reasonably expect, working without eating, sweating through the long morning hours. I was terrified that after all this work I wouldn't find the money, and I didn't know what I could say; they had too much faith in me. "Gringos never tell lies" was a sort of Ecuadorian truism, at least among the rural people who didn't know any better.

In December we burned the brush on the farm. We didn't have fifty acres cleared, but we had close to twenty, and it looked tremendous as it stretched away from the dry lagoons at the top of the hill down toward the ocean. For three weeks we burned brush, and the *socios* were exultant over what they had done. Picking their barefoot way through the thorns and stickers that covered the ground, they would pause in their work, shade their eyes, play-acting, and look out over the ocean and yell, "Here comes the *gabarrón* with the tractor; here comes the tractor."

The shrimp boats were out there and the canoes of the fishermen with their feed-sack sails, but there was no *gabarrón* and there was no tractor, and after I talked for the last time with AID, I knew that there never would be.

So I went to Quito and talked to Eric Hofman, the Peace Corps director for Ecuador, about the dilemma I was in. (I didn't realize it at the time, but this was the beginning of a weird period in my Peace Corps experience when, instead of working at the village level, I was skittering around at the national level talking with everyone from the vice-president of Ecuador and the provincial governor and senators, right down to the president of the municipal council.)

We had run out of time, and I was desperate with worry and frustration. A good part of my frustration was built around the placid attitude of the *socios* in the Río Verde co-op, who, since I had told them so, knew with a kind of religious certainty that old Martín was going to get the tractor.

Eric listened to me and promised to seek a solution if one existed; he wrote a couple of letters to Washington and sent word to me one day that the Peace Corps rules contained some unknown paragraph regarding "Project Development" and that he would be sympathetic to giving me the money I needed. I figured that about four hundred dollars would do the job. After nine months of negotiating with AID—an endless series of conferences, letters, and reports—the straightforward simplicity of the Peace Corps offer was dazzling in its beauty.

The Peace Corps was not a give-away program, Eric explained; the Peace Corps rarely felt the necessity for investing money in the projects of Volunteers. At the same time they did not want to see the collapse of my project. If I were sure that the work could be done for four hundred dollars, I could have it done. I would submit a detailed bill in duplicate to the Peace Corps office, and it would be paid.

I rushed back to Esmeraldas with some notes of introduction to the commanding officer of the Ecuadorian Army construction battalion and began negotiating. The commanding officer was a very nice guy, who indicated from the first that he would be interested in working with the co-op. I explained that we had a limited supply of money, and he began cutting the price per hour. He sent his operational major out to Río Verde to look over the ground. We had enough money for four days of work plus one hundred dollars to get the Cat out to Río Verde and back again. In four days, the major said, he could do it all.

There was only one big problem. How was the Ecuadorian Army going to get an eight-ton tractor across the Río Verde to the co-op farm? Some of the people from Palestina had built a large balsa raft for ferrying trucks across the river, but it had recently broken loose, drifted out to sea, and been dashed to pieces in the waves. Major Cueva, who had come up to check the road and the smaller balsa raft that we had, refused to consider putting his Cat on it. I couldn't really blame him, nor could I blame his reluctance to take seriously my suggestion that he wait until low tide and drive the Cat across the river on the sand bar about a quarter of a mile from shore.

There were two possibilities open to us; we could build an enormous new balsa, which might take months, or we could make a deal with Fomento to rent their barge-like ferryboat, the *gabarrón*, to bring the tractor up along the coast. I knew the chief engineer, or thought I did, but we arrived at a bad time. The office was swirling around in an internal civil war, with three chief engineers trying to get control of the department. No one really knew who the chief was. When I told them that we only had a hundred dollars to pay them for the four trips that the *gabarrón* would have to make, they seemed to lose what little interest they had. "Four trips to Río Verde at five hours a trip comes to around six hundred dollars," Don Maximiliano explained, shaking his head. "And then there are the tides to consider and the fact that taking the *gabarrón* away would leave the whole north coast isolated from Esmeraldas."

I didn't bother to point out that the whole north coast had been isolated from the beginning of time until about six months previously when the *gabarrón* began to operate, nor the fact that normal traffic for the *gabarrón* was one truck going out from Esmeraldas to Río Verde and one truck coming in. Instead I worked out a subtle timetable based on the night tides for that week, which proved that they could do our job and still be available through the daylight hours of heavy ferry traffic. But this didn't impress anyone very much either. Ingenero Montaño, who appeared to be the chief engineer on the day that I submitted this particular plan, told me that he took a rather dim view of scheduling nighttime ferryboat rides out in the middle of the ocean with his nice new *gabarrón*.

Another two weeks had gone by in these negotiations with Fomento. I had been so sure after my talk with Eric that everything would work out that this last, unexpected impasse was totally depressing. I began to develop muscle tics around the eyes and neurotic symptoms of abandonment and persecution. I knew most of the important businessmen in town by this time, and I got in the habit of stopping by to tell them my problems and ask for advice. I buttonholed the senators and the candidates for the senate in the new elections that were scheduled and asked them to help me. I felt like a professional beggar, but without shame.

By then it was mid-January, the very middle of a rainy

season, which so far hadn't materialized, but light rains were beginning to fall from time to time, and the whole coast lived under an ominous black cloud cover. I was like someone who, living at the foot of the Johnstown Dam, sees the first cracks appearing, and each morning I awoke expecting to see the downpour of rain that would flood the farm and put us out of business.

One night at the theater I met Don Julio Estupiñan, the vice-president of Ecuador, and he suggested that I write a letter to the board of directors of Fomento. Until then I hadn't known there was a board of directors. I wrote a passionate letter; I sang the national anthem accompanied by a chorus of thirty thousand; I blew the bugles of the national dream; I mentioned the aspirations of the poor and the glowing place of the cooperative movement in the national development. I also made clever little references to the general conviction in Esmeraldas that the authorities neglected the province and used provincial tax money in the capital instead of here. I took a rough draft up to Copérnico's feed store and asked him to make it grammatical, suggest any additional suitable rhetoric, and type out a copy that I could present at Fomento's next meeting.

"I agree that your Spanish is incredible," Copérnico said, "but I wouldn't dream of changing a word; it's just incredible enough so that you might possibly get your *gabarrón* after all."

"No," I said, "I no longer have any illusions on that score."

"I had no idea a man could say so many things using only the present tense," Copérnico said. "May I have a copy for the files?"

I left the typed letter in the Fomento offices, where I was promised that it would be discussed at the next directors' meeting. At low tide I hopped on the truck and went back to Río

Verde. As we crossed the river I dropped a sly hint to the captain of the *gabarrón* that, if he could talk his office into a trip to Río Verde, a grateful cooperative would, no doubt, want to express its gratitude in a way that he would understand. The captain had a drinking problem which had been well-known since the night, a few months before, when he had parked his *gabarrón* against the bank during the river's highest flood and had later spent three weeks with a crew of ten digging a forty-foot-long channel to get his boat back in the river. I conjured up for him a picture of a long row of *puro* bottles. It was the last trick in my bag; I couldn't think of another thing to do.

When I got back I explained to the *socios* that there was no way to get the tractor to Río Verde, and that we had better start thinking about planting corn the old way, planting it as we could among the tree stumps. There was a rumor that Fomento was going to provide a new *gabarrón* for Río Verde and bring it out in July. "Next December," I said, "we'll really give her hell."

It was raining a little every day, and I realized that in a very few days it would be too muddy to work the Cat. Everyone in town except the co-op members was planting corn; the main street had water standing in the ruts, and the little kids began bringing me pieces of pre-Incan pottery that had been washed out by the rain. Things continued as normal; we went up the river one day and bought bananas for the pigs; another day we went fishing.

I had been back about a week when I woke up one morning to the sound of children running and yelling in the street; it was just getting light and a faint drizzle of rain was falling. I got out of bed and went to the window. Everybody was yelling, "The *gabarrón*, the *gabarrón*. It's coming. It's coming in." I rushed to the kitchen and looked out to sea over the thatched roofs of the town, dark and glistening in the rain. There, just coming through the breakers at the river's mouth, churning through the waves at a brave three knots—the *gabarrón.* And loaded on it the tremendous bulk of the army Cat. I stood there transfixed watching it, not believing it. From an unidentified spot in the room I began to hear a funny sound, the animal sound of someone gagging, choking, and gasping for air. At first I was too preoccupied with the *gabarrón* to pay much attention, and then slowly I directed my attention to this peculiar sound that was coming from somewhere in the room, somewhere quite close.

Suddenly I realized that it was me. It was embarrassing. I got control of myself and instead of making all those crazy, gasping, animal noises I just stood there at the window watching the *gabarrón* pulling into the harbor and bawling like a baby.

In four days the Cat filled in the potholes and took out all the stumps, pushing them into great piles at the edge of the jungle. It was a moment of real triumph. And I had another moment of triumph, too, before the luck changed.

Our own tractor had been sitting in the corn field since the day we had brought it home. It was very small, old and beat up, and there was a monumental immobility built into its design, so that when it was at rest you couldn't imagine its ever moving. It had to be hand cranked, the tires had to be pumped up every five hours, the governor was sluggish, and it jerked, belched, and hiccuped as it rolled along; the children, it appeared, had used the gas tank as a piggy bank for sticks and dirt.

For a year no one had had a kind word for that poor tractor, not in town, or in the co-op, or in agricultural extension, or in the Peace Corps. Every time a Peace Corps Representative got ready to leave Río Verde after an inspection tour, I would receive a few concluding words: "Now, as for the tractor, why don't you think about selling it? Seriously, don't you think it's just a little small?" Bill Binford, the deputy director, had sent me an ad torn from a magazine which showed a guy dressed in a Civil War uniform sitting on a six-inch-high tractor with sword raised, screaming "Charge!" It was funny, but my laughter was a little forced and high-pitched.

But finally we were disking land, and the tractor worked. I was torn between the urge to get the land disked and my desire to take off a few days for a trip to Quito to yell in Bill's ear, "I told you so; I told you so!" We had twenty acres to disk, and it took a couple of weeks. But the rain held off and finally, for the first time in the history of the world, our corn land lay there torn open and ready to receive the seed. A couple of rains dampened the ground.

On Monday and Friday mornings the *socios* planted corn behind the tractor, using string to mark the rows. Contrary to their age-old custom of planting three seeds on top of each other on a thirty-nine-inch square, they were at my insistence putting one seed in the ground at about eight-inch intervals. Watching everyone working from my tractor seat, watching the field fill up with rows of corn, was an unreal, almost surrealistic experience; like the *socios*, I was filled with that irrational and insane belief that now everything was going to turn up good. Twenty acres of corn; nothing could stop us. Millions of small, dun-colored butterflies fluttered up in front of the advancing tractor like a celebration, like an unfurling of flags. I don't think it ever occurred to me in those days, not once, that those millions upon millions of butterflies were the mamma worms that would destroy our crops.

There were about ten more good afternoons, golden afternoons when I walked through the rows of newly emerging corn, alone up on the hill with the little town below me, sleeping, and the open curve of beach swinging away to north and south. We had a 100 per cent stand, but I walked through the field every day looking for the first worms that would mean we had to begin spraying. News of the field reached some of the farmers to the north, and they came down to look at it. We had long, happy arguments about the spacing of the seed, and although nobody went away convinced by my theory that doubling the amount of seed and spacing it more rationally in the row would double yields in this leached soil, at least they were excited by the idea and determined to watch the field.

One midnight in the middle of March the gods, aware of my overweening hubris, began to grind me exceedingly fine; unfortunately, they ground everyone in the cooperative exceedingly fine, too. The heavy rains of April arrived in March, starting off with three days of solid rain, floods of water that smashed all but the oldest corn into the mud. We lost 25 per cent of the corn and all of the last-planted seed, which rotted in the ground under a half-inch crush of cement-like soil. When the ground had dried out, we disked up about five acres and re-planted it, and late one afternoon, caught up again, I walked out to look at the older corn. It was half eaten up by worms; not the worms of California that one occasionally finds chewing away in solitary self-satisfaction in the heart of the corn; these were tiny maggots, twenty to a stalk, that ate out the core and shredded the leaves. In three days they could destroy a field.

The unscheduled rain of March had dispirited the more flighty of the *socios*. Replanting corn was something they had never done before; it depressed them. It was necessary to launch an all-out war to win the battle of the worms, but it was impossible to rededicate and enflame the *socios*. The situation was too obviously the will of God. They would work Mondays and Fridays, and the fact that the worms would consume a whole field between these days was sad but irrelevant. Spray corn? They had never sprayed corn before, the idea was loco. Wasn't it possible that opening the ground with the disk was an inconsidered action that had released these billions of butterflies that now laid eggs in the corn? And why in the first place had I wanted to plant corn on level ground? The hillside corn wasn't afflicted with worms.

But the hillside corn *was* afflicted with worms. All along the beach I had seen corn with the leaves tattered and dying and a good percentage of the crop eaten away at the base of the stalk. It was the dry season, I tried to explain; normal rainfall would have killed the worms or at least have minimized their depredations. "Well, if that isn't the will of God," the *socios* said, changing the subject without knowing it. I had given up trying to convince them that killing worms with DDT was more effective than talking it over with San Pedro; this was blasphemy. At these moments, an outraged Ramón, trying to think of the worst word he knew, would look at me with his black eyes blazing, and then, almost afraid to use a word so strong, say it anyway, "Why," he would say, "you talk just like a *Mason*."

For a month we worked every day. When we weren't spraying, we were replanting. We sprayed with DDT, Aldrin, Malathion, Dipterex, Chlorodane, BHC, and Parathion. The butterflies flew through the mist of the sprayer, smiling gaily and waving their hands. "Go ahead and kill us," they screamed. "But for every dead comrade there are ten thousand more coming in from the woods on the left flank." And they weren't kidding.

We were saved by the arrival of the winter rains, gentle, steady rains that lasted a week and washed the corn leaves clean and drowned the butterflies in all their millions. We ended up with about an 80 per cent stand, exhausted but triumphant.

After a week of rain, a drought set in, and as it dragged on and on things looked more hopeless than ever. I was terrified for some of the *socios* like Vicenta, Orestes, and Ramón, who had sacrificed their own private plantings this year and had spent their time on the co-op farm. And I was sick of some of the other *socios* who were dropping out of the organization or staying and making problems just for the fun of complicating the situation. I used to sneak away and go up into the corn, sometimes half a dozen times a day, but after a while the sight of it, shriveled and drooping, put me into a condition of physical shock; it made me weak to look at it. Still, like a flagellant fascinated by his own blood, I couldn't seem to stay away.

Vicenta found me one afternoon sitting on a high stump in the shadows of the wall of jungle at the edge of the farthest row of corn, high up where I could look out over the tops of the dying stalks. "Oh, what a sad face," she said. "What are you thinking about?"

"I'm thinking about the last days of the *cooperativa*," I told her. "It's been two days since anyone's sprayed the worms. What's wrong with everyone?"

"Oh, Martín," Vicenta cried. "Let it go; let it go. No one thinks it's your fault. And we all know that the spraying does no good."

"It's better than just sitting on your *nalgas* in the house," I said.

"You can't go against the will of God," Vicenta said. "Now, Martín, I'll tell you a secret. I'll tell you how to kill the worms, though as you can see now, the problem is one of rain not worms." She explained that worms had to be collected from the four corners of the field and from the center of the field, and that when these worms were held over a slowly smoking fire in the kitchen of your home, all the worms in the field would die.

"But that's witchcraft, Señora Vicenta, and you know I don't have much faith in your magic charms and *brujería*."

"*Brujería?*" Vicenta said, shocked at the word. "No, it's just a secret, one of God's great gifts of goodness; I have seen it work many times."

Somehow I felt better after this conversation; I had been harboring a growing apprehension about the stupidity of the people, a feeling that I was living in an irrational town where everything was slightly out of focus, distorted. It was comforting to be able to pin down a particular witch's tale so that I could say to myself, "Well, what they're doing or not doing is stupid, but at least there is a reason."

At night now I would suddenly start fully awake to the sound of a family of rats chewing things in the rafters above my bed. This chewing that electrified me so sounded exactly like rain falling on the corrugated iron roof. Later, the family grown, a teenaged rat fell into my water barrel, the last few gallons of good water in the town, and all night long as he splashed and drowned I dreamed of rain splashing onto the dusty rows of corn. Asleep I would hear water splashing on the ground and be filled with a wild joy until I realized that it was only my next-door neighbor urinating out of a second-story window. Some nights a half-dozen drops of rain would hit the roof like drops of lead shot, and I would lie there listening to the babies crying up and down the street and waiting for the rain to fall. Or, waiting for the rain, listen, perhaps once a week, to some drunk kid being packed home weeping and screaming in the street.

A week-old newspaper arrived, and we read about the drought; it wasn't just Río Verde that had gone under. In Loja the people were selling their children before they died of hunger; autopsies on the ones who had died revealed stomachs

full of roots and dirt. In Manabí a whole people was moving
out, the crops dead, the streams dry.

"Tell me the truth," I asked Orestes one day up on the farm,
standing at the edge of the dead corn rows. "Do you really
think that God is just and kind and that He is worried about
you?"

Orestes laughed nervously. "Don't tell Ramón," he said,

"but I sort of think like you at times; maybe we have to be punished for being so bad, but what about the kids, why do the little kids have to suffer?"

We stood there watching the dark rain clouds coming in from the ocean. For two months we had broken our hearts watching those damned clouds. For sixty days we had studied the sky and sixty times had said, "You know, it really looks like rain tonight. I think we'll get it tonight." The corn was gone; we had lost it. Maybe with luck we would harvest fifty sacks instead of the five hundred we had planned on.

"Well," I said, "the rain won't help us now; it's too late for rain now."

"Yes," Orestes said. "Next year we'll have to plant earlier, don't you think?" And then after a long minute he said, "Now you tell me the truth. Are you really a Mason like Ramón says, or are you a Christian? Is there a God?"

"Yes," I said, looking at Orestes and the dead corn and those tantalizing whore clouds. "I think there's a God, but I just don't think He's very nice."

By the time the drought had finished off the crop, the co-op was in its death throes. Orestes, Ramón, and the Señora Vicenta stood like rocks of loyalty while everything crumbled around them.

Wai was the first to leave. He was waiting for me at the store at lunchtime when I returned from spraying corn. He was drunk and aggrieved—in other words, everything was normal. He no longer came on Mondays and Fridays to plant or weed corn, but sent his young son, Clever, in his place. He had heard that some of the *socios* felt that this was unfair.

"They're talking about me in the street," he said. "It appears that I am a bad man for sending Clever. There's only one thing to do, retire from the *cooperativa*."

"You're not a bad man, Wai, but if you start sending Clever then Orestes will send his five-year-old Carmen and Vicenta her six-year-old grandson; in a while the co-op will be just a bunch of little kids, and you know that won't work."

"No, no, no," Wai said. "I don't want to argue; there's only one thing to do, retire." He began to blink his eyes and pass his hands distractedly across his face, and I knew he was getting ready to cry.

Actually, it wasn't only the *socios* who were going through a panic; I was in a state of panic myself. I was really running scared. For over two years I had been organizing the co-op, getting land cleared, setting up pens for pigs and houses for chickens, and all of our success was predicated on at least five hundred sacks of corn a year. I had gathered a group of people who trusted me, and I had promised them that if they changed their stone-age agriculture, I could show them how to dominate their poverty. "To lick this poverty you have to produce more than you can eat; you have to have production," I kept telling them. But the corn was dying, all the work had been for nothing; it looked as though I had simply burdened my friends with thousands of hours of senseless labor that would yield them nothing.

Leaning out my window one night in the darkness, I had heard Orestes talking about me with someone. "Oh, that Martín," he said. "He's *terrible*. You know, he's never told us a lie; he's really a serious type. I'd follow him right to hell." I had sneaked back into bed and lay there staring out the window, shaken; I didn't feel up to the challenge of being considered infallible. I had been under cruel and terrible pressure for several months, ever since I had promised that the army would clear our land. Now I felt drained and bankrupt, used up.

A month earlier Wai had come to the house drunk and aggrieved. He had just heard that because many of the *socios* weren't grinding their share of the corn for the chickens, the *directiva*, out of desperation, had decided to fine each weekly failure with two hours of work. Wai hadn't ground his corn for five weeks, and so he got drunk and told me that there was only one thing to do, "retire from the *cooperativa*." I had spent three hours closed in the house with that magnificent, stupid, weeping man as he poured out the drunken heartbreak of his poor, doomed life—all of its injustices centered at this moment on ten stolen hours of his sweating labor. Finally I gave up and put his ten hours of work back in the book and talked him into continuing as one of the *fundadores de la cooperativa*. But this kind of afternoon left me exhausted and destroyed, as though after a fifty-mile hike. You can't move in too close to poverty, get too involved in it, without becoming dangerously wounded yourself.

Now Wai was back, ready to weep again. He wanted to be reasoned with, complimented, comforted, and told strongly that the co-op was good and that he should stay on as a *fundador*. But God help me, I didn't have the strength to hold him up; I was tired of packing that man on my back, exhausted by his lack of comprehension, his stupidity. If I told him anything, I would have to tell him that the crop failure had left the cooperative only as strong as each *socio*'s capacity to keep on struggling for another year.

So when he said that he had been insulted by the gossip in the street and that there was nothing to do but retire, I just stood there coldly and agreed with him. "You're absolutely right," I said. "The *cooperativa* is for people who trust each other and work together and suffer together and don't run around making crazy problems every five minutes. I don't blame you; I think you ought to renounce." He gave me the incredulous look of one betrayed, and he moved back a step, stunned. I shook hands with him very formally and went next door to my house to fix lunch. He stood outside for about five minutes, and then he was gone. I wanted him in the co-op, of course; I wanted him to come back, but under his own power, using his own reasoning.

At five o'clock he was back all right, really drunk now, weeping like a baby, bawling in the street, yelling at Ramón that he was a thief, that he was stealing eggs and money from the store. And that Orestes was a thief, too, and perhaps even Vicenta, who was always hanging around the store. It was an ugly and uninhibited exhibition, and it left us trembling with shame for him because Wai was a fine man and very much loved in the town, and it was bad to see a good man humiliate himself.

A week later Alvarez left town to work on a cattle ranch up by the Colombian border. Well, *vaya con dios;* Alvarez was always leaving, and no one expected much from him, though we did feel a mild disappointment, a vague sense of betrayal. If we solved all the problems of the co-op he would be back. But now he said he had to make a living; he couldn't just stick around and starve to death. You couldn't blame him, really, although he could have stayed and fished and made as much as he would make at Las Peñas and perhaps on Saturdays gotten just as drunk besides. But fishing, that's a hard life.

Santiago followed him. Nobody blamed Santiago. Nobody ever blamed Santiago. As a child, according to Vicenta, he had had typhoid twice, and the fever, well, it had affected his mind a little. Santiago was in his early thirties, but he had the dazzling smile of a child, and he was childish too in his simple, innocent, and delighted reactions to life. He didn't know how to hide anything, and his feelings came out without shame. If you put your arm around him, he laid his head on your shoulder, his face full of joy, and began to pet you. Most everyone in town was very tender with Santiago. His father had always adored this youngest son, especially since, through the grace of

God, the typhoid didn't take him, and this doting adoration of his father had sustained Santiago through everything. "I am loved," his face said, and he accepted everything—the rags on his back, the sickness of his children, the days of hunger—with an inner grace, a tender joy, and that terrible unaccusing and accepting smile, the Christ's smile of a fool.

Alone at night, trying to sleep but thinking about this maimed man and the other confused and frightened *socios* and the other people in the town, an unthinkable suspicion began to grow in my mind. There was an irrational element in the way these people faced their problems. The truth was that if Vicenta hadn't told me what the town felt about Santiago—that he was mad, that his poor brains had been cooked by burning fevers and his reason destroyed—I would never, comparing his actions with those of anyone else in town, have been able to tell the difference.

Was it remotely possible—was it humanly possible that the whole town . . . ? No, stop thinking. Let's listen to the Voice of America. The burning cities, the rotting dead, the speeches of politicians, the crack of assassin's bullets—all put me to sleep, my perspective widened to accept the essential insanity of the whole world.

Twenty-year-old Aladino tried to charge a cigarette at the co-op store one day, and his brother, Eloy, the manager, told him that since he was already fifteen cents in debt no more credit could be advanced. Aladino, insulted, said that he was resigning from the cooperative. He sat all day on the steps of the store mumbling to anyone who would listen about this last unbearable indignity, and it was strange and disquieting to see him so sullen and angry. Usually he was as serene as Santiago, his face slashed with two rows of teeth so large, white, and perfect that they gave his expression an unreal radiance.

We called a special meeting of the cooperative with the idea of publicly rebuking Eloy, though this plan was risky; an insulted Eloy might feel called upon to resign, too. But we were saved by a customer who captured Eloy's attention; while we were berating him in the candlelit darkness of our clubroom, he had slipped out to sell a nickel's worth of cigarettes and didn't hear us. In the darkness, off in one corner, Aladino's teeth began to glow; his dignity had been saved.

But, my God, wasn't it ridiculous, this useless, churning, endless stream of pettiness and passion? And how vulnerable, how fragile had become this crazy little co-op, to be threatened by one lousy cigarette.

To form a legal cooperative under Ecuadorian law, a minimum of eleven *socios* was required. Our cooperative had finally shrunk to four: Ramón, Orestes, Vicenta, and Eloy. And the only reason Eloy stayed was that we were paying him to be storekeeper. This left Ramón, Orestes, and the Señora Vicenta to do all the co-op work—grind corn for the chickens, cut grass, haul bananas and water for the twenty-five pigs, buy supplies for the store, repair the outboard motor, a million other things. There was no water in the town. We gave the pigs water from the muddy lagoon on top of the hill until it went dry; after that we had to buy water from the kids who brought it down in canoes and then haul it in buckets a quarter of a mile up the hill to the pigpens.

Eloy was excused from all these chores. He worked from five in the morning until nine at night, slept on a grass mat on the floor among the piles of platano and bananas, where he was available all night to sell single cigarettes or bottles of cola to people who couldn't sleep. We paid him almost eight dollars a month, and, being the only man in town with a job, he rapidly turned into Río Verde's man of distinction. The way he was gaining weight was terrifying; for probably the first time in his life he wasn't hungry. While we couldn't prove it, we knew why he was growing so fat and glossy; we didn't buy his wild tale that he was only eating the broken animal crackers. *Carajo*, nobody can gain five pounds a month on just animal crackers.

In a poor town the storekeeper is a man of power, and I watched in fascinated dismay as scrawny little Eloy bloomed with the power of his job. There were many stories in the town concerning which women had sold themselves to one of our competing storekeepers for enough groceries to keep their families, and on a more innocent level the same thing began to happen in our store. All the young girls in town suddenly fell in love with Eloy; some of them weren't so young. You could usually see a couple of them hanging around on the store steps saying cute things to Eloy and blinking their eyes ecstatically. Why not? Eloy was the kid with the Cokes, the chocolate, the crackers, and the credit.

For three years I had been in more or less the same position as Eloy, but on a much larger scale, and for three years I had been obsessed with trying to define the realities of my position in the town. What *is* love? If it is the answering of one's needs, is it any less legitimate if those needs—grounded in hunger, disease, and desperation—are centered on your strongest personality trait, the money you carry in your pocket?

This is one of the Peace Corps traps. It can be absolutely shattering to the ego to realize that it isn't your own inherent lovableness that has all the people in town wild with passion for you, but rather the one hundred dollars a month that makes you by far the richest and most powerful man in town, the new *patrón* whether you like it or not, and the only one who can in some measure solve the problems of their despair. Or even with a phrase, a "No, I haven't got any," condemn their fevered children to death.

As Peace Corps Volunteers we come to give of ourselves, but we are almost all a part of the Puritan ethic, and we make rules and set limits as to what we will give and on what terms, and what it is legitimate to ask of us. We want to be loved because we're lovable, not because we're rich gringos. But the people in the town don't know the rules. After six months, when they know that you're not there as a spy or to exploit them or to live apart from them, they claim you; they want to touch you, watch you when you eat, own you; they want to be Number One with you; they want you to solve their problems. They start twisting the relationship around trying to make a *patrón* out of you, and it takes another heartless year to convince most of them that you aren't a *patrón*.

Well, it had been a good many years since I had thought myself very lovable, and I escaped to some degree this trap of shattered ego. I was lucky; I had found a village of people so poor and simple, so engaging, that I had been more interested in my feelings for them than in what they thought of me. And frankly, after eighteen years of farming in the Sacramento Valley, that terrible life-consuming rat race, I was desperate enough to accept almost any human relationship on almost any terms. Love is love, I decided. Just take it and don't analyze it away. "You're my friend; you're good; you give me pennies," some nameless kid from down the beach told me. My God, what is love in this whorehouse world of poverty? And was I shocked because I could buy love or because I could buy it with pennies?

As far as I could see, Eloy accepted his new position in the town with a minimum of inner conflicts. In a few months he turned from an anonymous kid into a self-satisfied, slightly arrogant, sleepy-eyed young man, well fleshed out, with fat, pouchy, chipmunk cheeks. He had beer parties for his friends in the store at night, and those of us outside could hear muffled laughter and watch thick clouds of cigarette smoke rolling out from under the locked door. The next day he would deduct a few bottles of beer and a few cigarettes from his wages, but we wondered how accurate he was.

He dressed in his best clothes and wore the only pair of shoes he owned, shoes which he had always saved for the days of fiesta. Studying Eloy in his new role was like watching a younger Alvaro, the paunchy, raunchy storekeeper down the street who hated us so because he no longer fully dominated the town. I thought of one of the Peace Corps definitions of itself, "an agent of change," and shook my head helplessly. When you start bringing about change you often wonder what you've set in motion. I had been so anxious to get new money into the town, to get families earning more, that I had scarcely thought about the new problems that new money might bring.

I watched Eloy as he gradually lost his innocence, as that eight dollars a month put unbearable pressure on him and twisted his character. Each month the store made about five dollars less, and we heard rumors that Eloy was making small loans to the farmers at 40 per cent interest. He was a sharp kid; he learned fast. But I realized that his days as a *socio* were numbered, that when he lost his job in the store he would never go back to the menial labor of hacking out jungle with a machete on the co-op farm. He was much too grand for that.

□□

There was an insane quality to the poverty in the town, some black secret that lay just outside the mind's acceptance. Carlos Torres' new baby developed lockjaw from an umbilical infection and died twelve days after it was born. Such a stupid, unnecessary death. I raged at a group of ladies gathered on the steps of the co-op store. "But didn't you know that the last eight babies born in town have all died?" No, I hadn't known. The death of babies was so inevitable that it wasn't even news.

Unless, like Walter's wife after her miscarriage, the woman's sanity was threatened, and she just lay in the house and screamed and screamed hour after hour. It was sad, but it was diverting, too. That night the crowd, instead of gathering on the dock, moved up the street and stood outside Walter's house. "*Hombre*, such a tiny woman, but the lungs are well developed, no?"

Santiago came to the house to borrow $2.50. His two children had the measles, a disease which was about 50 per cent fatal in this area. I told him to talk to Ramón and have the canoe take them into an Esmeraldas doctor. "No," Santiago said, "they can't be moved." They'd be O.K. if they lived through the night, but he didn't think they would. They were sick in the house of a friend in Chungillo twelve miles up the Río Mate, and Santiago had walked in and out twice that day looking for money and medicine. He was very tired but completely serene. Before starting back he visited for a few minutes in front of the store. He had just gotten the good news from Esmeraldas that his father and brother, who were attacked with machetes by a couple of drunk *montuvios*, were much better and might be coming home soon.

A fellow from two miles up the Río Verde arrived drunk and wild and was chased out of town at the point of Lucho's revolver. But, as though he were determined to find death, he later threatened one of Nelson's balsa-mill employees and ended up dead, his head sliced down the middle like a melon. I listened to Ramón, who had delivered the casket in the co-op canoe and had seen the body and the brains spilling out. Later I listened to Aladino, the dead man's cousin, who with the rest of the town gathered at the graveside to watch the autopsy—the chest cavity opened and the top of the head sawed off, all in accordance with the law.

I began to be aware that in the town there was scarcely a

moment when a baby's crying didn't fill the air, and there was a resemblance between the violence of the babies' furious raging cries and the violence of machetes slashing through flesh. Like a revelation, I suddenly realized that these screams were the screams of human beings learning about poverty. They were learning about sickness and about hunger; they were learning in a hard school what they could expect from life, learning to accept their destiny and the futility of revolting against it. They were being twisted and maimed. They were being turned from normal human beings into The Poor.

After the age of six they are ready for life, and as for being poor, they know all about it; there isn't a thing they don't know. There are no more tears. They play quietly, gravely in the dirt before their houses, and there is something terrible in their eyes, a kind of blindness. For years they will go without weeping, and then a strange thing happens. At about the age of nineteen the boys discover the healing and magical release of alcohol, and until they are about twenty-four or twenty-five whenever they have the money they drink cane alcohol almost as a rite, seeking out the purging relief that comes in those few minutes just before unconsciousness when everything concentrates in a flashing, searing point—all the hopelessness, the misery, the stupid deprived past, and the stupid endless future. They want a pair of shoes or a little silver ring or a Japanese transistor radio or maybe just a pair of pants that isn't worn and patched. They want to go to the movies in Esmeraldas and sit in the sweet obliterating darkness with a bag of *caramelos* watching Hercules slaughtering the Romans. They want to get married. They want to get out of their father's house, away from the endless bickering.

"Oh, *puta*," they yell in the street. "Oh, *la gran puta*." "Oh, great whore," they yell in the street. They are screaming at life in a paroxysm of rage, accusing life of cheating them. The tears gush out of their eyes, they roll on the ground, beating the ground with their fists, chewing the earth. "Oh, *puta*. Oh, PUTA. Oh, *Gran Puta*, LA GRAN PUTA!"

After about twenty-six all the revolt is burned out of them; by that time they are beginning to get old. They finally accept their destiny. Or, if they can't, I guess they take up their machetes and go out looking for it.

And this thing about the town that I had been afraid to think, the town's black, unspeakable secret? They mentioned it on a news broadcast one night, sandwiched in between the stories of wars and riots, announcing that 60 per cent of the world's children were suffering from protein starvation and that this deprivation in the first five years of life permanently and irrevocably destroyed up to 25 per cent of a man's intelligence.

Twenty-five per cent.

If 75 is the I.Q. in the town, what is the medical word that describes this poor, doomed people, this wasted human resource living out its unproductive destiny in the impregnable prison of a destroyed mind, in a twilight, idiot world where nothing really makes much sense?

□□

I had always been afraid to start a fishing project in Río Verde because of our isolation from the Esmeraldas market, the surrealistic transportation, and the conviction that a good percentage of our catch would arrive in an advanced stage of putrefaction. But with the co-op in ruins, I had a terrible sense of failure, of time running out on me, and I began to consider some of the riskier possibilities. One morning I awoke with a fishing project fully developed in my head.

It was indeed risky; it was complicated and expensive. We would need a small boat, an inboard motor, nets, long lines, an ice house, and later perhaps, if we could prove a production of four or five hundred pounds of fish a day, a little second-hand double-transmission pickup truck. I talked the idea over with Vicenta, Ramón, and Orestes, and met with a desperate enthusiasm; they, too, had been considering the future with real terror. Another dry year would destroy the town; it seemed foolhardy to depend entirely on agriculture. I asked them to discuss the plan with the retired *socios* and with the fishermen in town; perhaps we could get the co-op started again. That night about twenty people gathered in the darkness outside the store, and Ramón, amazed, rushed in to tell me that they wanted a meeting.

So we had one, and we decided that instead of paying our debt to the bank, a debt already two months overdue, we would use the money from the nineteen weaner pigs that we had ready to sell and buy a boat. We changed the name of the cooperative from "La Cooperativa de Río Verde de Agricultura" to "La Cooperativa de Río Verde de Agricultura y Pesca," agriculture and fish, and the next morning at six o'clock Orestes, Nona, Miguel, and Carlos dragged me into Esmeraldas to start looking for a little fishing boat.

"Oh man," I thought, shaking in my boots, "here we go again."

The cheapest boat we could find in Esmeraldas was a second-hand sailboat about twenty-five feet long. It was beautiful, but the price was five hundred dollars. We figured that we had five hundred dollars for the boat, the motor, and some long lines. Back in Río Verde we had defeated conversations. Ramón (and Bill Binford) thought we should prove the fishermen's enthusiasm in the canoe before spending great sums of money, but the old canoe had been through some extremely rough seas, and the outboard motor was becoming flighty and uncertain. I was afraid to encourage a project so dangerous. The idea died for a month or so, but the necessity to think of something still remained.

One day on the beach in Esmeraldas I ran across an old whaleboat lying upside down in the sand. It was about eighteen feet long and had been used some years before by a small shrimp-buying combine that had gone out into the sea to buy shrimp from the fishermen in their canoes. It was old and abandoned, but Orestes and Miguel and some of the local Esmeraldas fishermen thought that with an overhaul and a good little inboard motor we could at least get started and perhaps in eight or nine months save enough money for a proper boat. Joe Haratani, soon to be the new Ecuador director of the Peace Corps, and my new Representative, Craig Damstrom, drove out in the jeep, and we walked around the old wreck. "Isn't it beautiful?" I asked. They didn't think so; they were far from hopeful and counseled caution, but I was running out of time and was desperate to get something started in Río Verde that would bring in money during the dry months when it is impossible to farm. There was no time for caution. I talked the co-op, or what was left of it, into the idea that the boat was a poor man's practical beginning.

With only six months to go before my Peace Corps contract expired, I left Río Verde for two months and went to Esmeraldas to live. I was to oversee the installation of an inboard motor in the boat. If it worked, we would have to figure out how to get hold of nets or long lines, but we were only strong enough to dominate one problem at a time. I was getting as fatalistic as everyone else in town, and I figured that the only way was to charge ahead, putting our faith in a benevolent God to come up with something at the proper time.

Months before, I had made friends in Quito with Arthur Fried, an American businessman, and his wife. They sold farm machinery and motors, and had spent many years in Ecuador; they were that rare thing, American business people who had a deep love and respect for the people of the country. One day when I was telling Arthur about the impossibility of getting a good fishing project started because of the extreme poverty of the village, he had offered to sell us a small gasoline engine at a special price, with no money down and an unspecified number of months to pay. Now I took him up on it, brought the new engine down on the bus, and engaged the best naval mechanic on the beach.

At the time I left Río Verde, things were getting rather psychotic. The co-op had only three practicing members. The ones who had dropped out, convinced that we would never have a success, were torn between their desire to slip back in as members and their desire to destroy the organization completely. They had expected that the loss of the corn crop would cause everything to fold up, but we kept going. In June we had a batch of baby pigs ready to sell, we were disking up the farm ground getting ready for the December rains, and the fields looked beautiful. We had a hundred chickens just beginning to lay. Everything was still in a delicate state of balance: the egg money went to buy groceries for the store; the store money was all invested in concentrate for the pigs; and it was still six months until the rains would come. But it did look a little less hopeless. Alvarez hinted very delicately one day that he had never actually retired from the co-op and that he still considered himself a member. Orestes cut him off brutally.

"I've got 1,400 hours of work written down now. How many have you got? 150? 160? If you come back in, I'm getting out. I've been taking care of those pigs, hauling water, grinding corn for the chickens for the last six months. Where were you, Alvarez, *amigo?* You didn't show up once."

Ramón backed his brother. "The co-op's done," he said. "It's finished. We're not taking anybody back, not anybody. Look, I've let all my own work go just to keep the co-op going, but I wasn't doing it for a bunch of lazy people. I was doing it because Martín wanted it done that way, and I was doing it for my own future."

I tended to agree. We decided then that if we could start a fishing project it would be entirely separate from the farm, with new members, but that since it would be financed with co-op money it would be controlled by the existing members. No one thought much of the idea, since Ramón, Orestes, and Vicenta would be the directors of the fishing boat. But no one else seemed willing to get involved.

Since the beginning of the co-op, Alvaro had whispered that the farm, the store, the tractor, and the animals were mine and that I would never be crazy enough to turn these things over to the co-op when I left. It was hard to prove him wrong, because we still owed Alfonso almost forty dollars on the final land payment, and we couldn't produce a deed in the name of the co-op until this was paid. Of course, we didn't have any legal papers on the pigs or the chickens. Everyone in town was aware that my time was running out, and they reacted in different ways, from the tearful, almost suicidal, gloom of Ramón to the ecstasy of Alvaro and his clique.

Now Alvaro came up with a more subtle angle, the truth. "When the gringo leaves," he told everyone who would listen to him, "everything will be owned by just those three; they'll own this town, practically. And they've done all this with everyone who ever helped in the cooperative." It was true. We had had fourteen members at one time. The three of them alone could never have built the store, the chicken houses, and the pigpens, and cleared the land. But everyone had known that this could happen. We had made the rule at one of the first meetings: anyone who retired from the cooperative would be paid two

sucres, about ten cents, for each hour of work. This was the
going rate for farm labor. And one of the main reasons for the
co-op's difficulties had been the thousands of sucres that we had
had to dig up to pay off the retiring members. We still owed
almost seventy-five dollars to a half-dozen former members who
were beginning to harass us, telling us that if we were honest
and sincere about paying them off we ought to sell the breeding
stock. It would have meant the destruction of the co-op, which,
of course, they realized. I vetoed the idea.

"What are you going to do with your tractor when you
leave?" Don Julio asked me one day. "I'd like to make some
arrangements with you."

"It's not my tractor," I told him. "I've said this a thousand
times. It was never my tractor; it belongs to the cooperative."

He looked at me as though I were putting him on. "And the
outboard motor? That belongs to Point 4; I know you can't
leave that here."

"Yes," I said, taking pleasure in his displeasure. "The motor
is four years old; it has been written off the Point 4 books; it
now belongs to the cooperative."

"And the farm?"

"And the farm."

Twenty people cornered me on the street that week. They
wanted to know if it were true that Ramón, Orestes, and Vicenta were going to be the owners of everything. "But, of
course," I said. "They're the co-op now, aren't they?" This
prospect was depressing to everyone even to the three *socios*,
who began to realize just how delicate their situation had
become.

We added up the assets of the cooperative one night. After
subtracting debts of a thousand dollars, we discovered that the
organization was worth close to six thousand dollars. With
good management it could earn around four thousand dollars

every year, figuring in the store, three hundred chickens, and
six sows. In the two years since we had contracted to buy the
land its value had doubled, thanks to a local cotton boom.
Every shopkeeper in Esmeraldas with a little capital was looking for the kind of acreage that the co-op owned. It was prime
cotton land.

□□

I went to Esmeraldas, together with Ramón, Orestes, and
young Teobaldo. We spent three days on the beach in Las
Palmas, the port of Esmeraldas and the barrio where all the
fishermen lived, scraping the old paint and digging the dried
caulking off the boat's cracked and dry-rotted sides. Ramón,
very much the country hick since everyone knew he was from
Río Verde, dickered with every boat carpenter in the port to
get the rotten planks replaced, the seams recaulked, and the
boat repainted. The best price we could get was forty dollars,
which was actually quite outrageous, as we found out later
when we put the boat in the ocean and spent 20 per cent of our
time bailing water out of it. We consoled ourselves with the
certainty that if the rich gringo had done the dickering it
would have cost eighty dollars. But our project was under way,
so the three of them went back to Río Verde.

It took a month to put the motor in the boat. Hell, it took six
days just to line up the motor with the propeller shaft. I spent
weeks looking for cheap second-hand propellers, used reduction
gear boxes, and all the other stuff we would need to go speeding
through the water in search of the white whale. Actually, I
didn't do much, but I had to be at the boat all day every day
inspiring the carpenter and the mechanic to work together.
There was a subtle conflict of status there that I never did get
to understand. Each one called the other "Maestro," but with
an underlying sarcasm.

Every few days Orestes or Ramón would bring money from the baby pigs we were selling. Eventually, it came to around five hundred dollars, and little by little I spent all that, plus another hundred dollars that some friends in California had sent us, plus whatever I could spare from my living allowance.

It was a good two months. It was good to get away from the town, a sort of preparatory weaning for me as well as for my friends. I was still close enough to know what was going on out there but far enough away that I no longer felt so emotionally involved in the things that happened. I discovered that I didn't really miss Río Verde, discovered, in fact, that I had had it there. It wasn't the people in the town who bored or enraged or terrified me, it was the town itself, the capacity of each individual to submerge his personality as a part of the town and to display all of the worst mob qualities. There were certain people who I deeply loved: Ramón, Orestes, Vicenta, Wilfrido, Wai, Pancho, Teobaldo, Ester, Aladino, Santiago, Ricardo, Gloria. And there were many others too, who—if I had no great love for them and had never worked with them—offended nothing in me. They were good people. But with the exception of the women, and perhaps Teobaldo and Ricardo who were still kids, too young to have developed the Río Verde syndrome, I was convinced that you couldn't put any five of these people in a room together for, say, three hours, and expect five live people to emerge. You would open that door to a flood of blood and the moans of the dying.

Toward the end Ramón, Orestes, and I were obsessively engaged in an analysis of the town; it was almost all we talked about. I, of course, as a Volunteer who had failed to bring about any great change, had to find in the town itself the reasons for my failure. I took this failure placidly enough; I think I had to because another, really terrible, problem was beginning to emerge: my success. I had helped change the lives of Ramón, Orestes, and Vicenta, had helped bring them so far along the road out of poverty that their position in the town was becoming insupportable. I felt like a guy from AID who had come out to visit me in Río Verde one time in those last months. He had formerly been a missionary in Ecuador, an *Evangelista.* I took him across the street and introduced him to Wilfrido, the only Protestant in town, and later, perhaps out of some necessity to be unpleasant to one of the guys who hadn't helped us with the tractor the year before, I jabbed at him a little. "This is what you've done," I said. "You've taken the best man in town, the hardest working man, the most honest man, and you've separated him from his culture. He lives

completely isolated in this lousy little town, the only non-Catholic on the beach, the only True Believer, and he's a joke to the town. Everyone thinks he's crazy."

"Yes," my friend said. "That's why I left missionary work. I came to realize that I couldn't be responsible for wrecking the lives of people with promises of paradise, making their whole lives miserable in the certainty of saving their souls. I came to realize that people had to find happiness within their own culture."

"Ever since the priest damned the town," Orestes began one day as we were sitting around our whaleboat waiting for the carpenter to show up.

"What?" I said. "When was all this? I never heard about that."

"You mean, truly, that you hadn't heard?" Orestes asked in amazement. "I thought everybody knew. About a year ago on the end of the dock one Sunday morning? It was the priest from Palestina. He stood there with a cross raised up over his head and he damned the town, he put a curse on the whole town."

"No," I said with a horrified laugh. "I don't believe it."

"It's true," Ramón said. "Half the town saw it. The cross raised above the town. And in the name of God Almighty, and His son Jesus Christ, and in the name of the Sanctified Spirit, he put a curse on the town."

"Why, that neurotic old bastard," I said. It must have been true; thinking back, I couldn't remember having seen the priest in months nor had I heard the bell tolling at the little bamboo church next to Pablo's *salón*.

"Have you ever heard of such a thing?" Orestes asked. "We're really screwed." He said it with a sad, fierce pride.

"And do you believe it? Do you believe that God has gone out of the town?"

"It's very possible," Ramón said.

"And you, Orestes?"

Orestes shrugged, thinking. "I don't know," he said finally. "Was God ever *in* the town?"

My place in Las Palmas had been vacated by Tom Brigham, a Volunteer who had terminated the month before. I had the basement rooms of a cement house with electric lights, a toilet and a shower, a bed with a mattress, a butane cooker, and screens on the windows. There were two separate rooms with two beds in the extra room, and friends from Río Verde often came and stayed with me—mainly, I think, since Río Verde had been without water for months, to take a shower and feel clean again. Santiago, who had hardly ever left Río Verde, came in three times in two months, feeling very much the *montuvio*. He always slept with a large knife in his hand, as though he expected almost anything to happen in this great metropolis.

When I had company we went to the shows at night, had good dinners with meat or chicken, strolled in the square beneath the trees watching the tall, proud girls in the soft night. We ate candy bars, listened to the music which poured in a deafening flood from every store, chatted with friends as they promenaded up and down the main street, drank cold Pepsi or little cups of terrible black coffee as strong as the priest's curse. And it was wonderful.

Months later when I would hear Frank Sinatra singing "Strangers in the Night," the essence of those evenings would suddenly come alive in my mind, and I would start gasping for breath, a victim of nostalgia. It was one of the jukebox records in the ice-cream parlor where the teenagers gathered and where we joined them for a few minutes almost every night for a dish of chocolate ice cream. Through the years I had had a dozen hours-long discussions there with the young students, the rebel element who used to love to goad me about Vietnam, to express their fury at the dominant world position of the United States and the mystical love they felt for Che Guevara.

In the early mornings I would take coffee down on the beach and look north past the banana boats loading their cargoes, past the rocky point across the river covered with dormant and leafless trees, to the distant point of Río Verde, softened and almost invisible in mist. Looking toward Río Verde I felt nothing. She was like a faithless lover to me, and I was in the midst of forgetting her.

I was helped in this by my work on the beach and by all the new people I was meeting. The fishermen were fascinated with the idea of using motors instead of sails for fishing far out, and while they agreed that it was the best way, they were divided in their opinions on our particular motor and boat. Most of the more progressive people with a wider experience told me that the motor was much too small. It was their word against Arthur's, who had seen hundreds of this same type motor used in Peru.

I could speak Spanish by then and felt no constraint with new faces. The fishermen were friendly and talked at length, spending whole afternoons at the boat while the carpenter bored new holes in the hull and plugged old ones. We talked about the dangers of fishing for one-thousand-pound marlin in canoes, and I developed a mild contempt for the American sportsman who goes out in a yacht and risks nothing but a fifty-dollar charter fee and a few hundred feet of line; these guys were risking their lives every day. We talked about the wildness of the sea, the deaths of their friends, the perfidy of the fish buyers, the criminality of poverty. And women, of course. With fishing out of the way, we talked about sex, normal and perverse, for hours—long, hilariously vulgar stories about themselves and the people in the town. Out past the point was Río Verde, and I looked toward it a hundred times a day, not rejecting it, but simply looking toward it, no longer possessing it. I wondered if someone was grinding corn for the chickens or if Vicenta was still bringing grass to the pigs. I imagined not. Well . . . tough.

I made friends with a couple of Americans. One of them was Tommy O'Rourke, the local millionaire, a difficult, sarcastic guy to know, a man with too much power, but basically very honest and good-hearted. He had been king of the town too long and made no effort to ingratiate himself with anybody, and at first I couldn't get along with him at all. He never let me talk, but one night I called him a cranky old bastard, probably the first time in twenty years that anyone had dared to say such a thing. He gave me a funny smile and a look of incredulous amazement, and after that we were more or less friendly. He was the largest exporter of bananas in the province and employed thousands of men.

There was another American, Burt Scott, who operated a fleet of shrimp boats with an American partner in Guayaquil. He ate in the same German restaurant where I took dinner. He was a great reader, and we spent hours talking about books. After the years in Río Verde it was like a fresh wind blowing through the mind to hear the names of books again.

The restaurant was on the beach, and we sat outside in wicker chairs and watched the sailboats leaving with the offshore night wind, their lamps clustered together closely as they disappeared into the night, beautiful and vulnerable as fireflies on the great expanse of tranquil sea. And off to the north in the darkness Río Verde slept, that faithless lover. Sleep, whore.

After dinner, as I walked down the beach the three or four blocks to my house—past the beach *salones* where tourists ate shrimp cocktails, drank beer, and listened to marimba music, a dying music of the coast, true African music of pure rhythm —I would be aware of Río Verde out there in the darkness, and I would say to myself, "But I *don't* hate Río Verde; I *don't*, I *don't* hate Río Verde," and I felt like a character in a Faulkner novel, my blood contaminated and damned, still involved in the town, destroyed somehow by the curse of that fanatic old priest.

I was in the Las Palmas house the day that Ramón came back from Guayaquil with Ester and his month-old daughter. He had never thought of having a daughter; his mind had been full of the son he wanted—to be named Martín and to be sent to California at age six to live with me and speak only English and to come back to Ecuador at twenty-one as a doctor or a veterinarian. Now he came to the house proudly triumphant and introduced me to Martita; it was as close to Martín as he could get, and the memory of that son had already left his mind.

Normally, month-old babies are not my cup of tea; they are too breakable. But Ramón's Martita was something else. She had a face so broad and fat, cheeks so chipmunk pouchy, and skin so flawlessly beautiful that I couldn't resist her. I was moved to cries of admiration by the close resemblance to both Ramón and Ester, this only intimation of immortality.

Ester, whom I hadn't seen for six weeks, was completely changed, her youthful beauty gone forever, as though she had presented it as a gift to her child. She was much stockier, the young matron, her face serious and full of different thoughts. I asked her why she looked so different, and she smiled shyly to show me her teeth. She told me that the doctor had made her have six teeth pulled before the baby was born. She had a plate now, and all the gaps in her mouth were gleaming white, but it was strange how she had aged.

Since the last eight babies in town had died at birth or shortly afterward, I was terrified to see them heading back to Río Verde. I was full of advice, admonitions, worryings. For years the jealous town had referred to Ramón as *su hijo*, your son, and now I realized it was true and that an inconsiderate son had made me a grandfather. But they had become serious people, they told me. They boiled all their water, and they were going to boil all the baby's dishes; they had a schedule of vaccinations; they had a baby bed, special blankets, mosquito netting, and a paper in the doctor's hand which explained the first year's diet. They had even bought an iron, an essential item the doctor had insisted, for sterilizing diapers and killing the little *garrapatas* that survived a washing. I rushed down to the Catholic bookstore for a couple of books on child care and told Ester to memorize them. (These soon became best sellers in Río Verde.)

Ramón came back from Río Verde ten days later and told me with glee how the town had reacted to his child. They had been thunderstruck by the baby blankets and the bed. The weight of the child, her violent health and vigor, had appalled them. Ramón was the first man on the whole stretch of beach who had ever sent his wife away to have a child. He had spent three thousand sucres on the doctor, the hospital, the dentist, and the baby's accouterments, a sum that had actually just about put him into bankruptcy, but the stunning effect when he mentioned this sum in the street made it worth every sucre to him. A baby in Río Verde cost fifty sucres for a midwife and a couple of hundred sucres more invested in a bunch of chickens to feed the bedridden mother. Ramón's triumph was somewhat spoiled by the town's insistence that I had paid all the bills, but actually, aside from a small contribution to help him buy the baby's bed, I had done nothing.

Thinking about this and about what had motivated Ramón to change his style of living so completely, it occurred to me that two forces had dominated his life while I was there: his love for me, and his wild delight in mocking the town, shocking the town with his splendor.

◻◼

It was on some saint's day, the saint who protects sailors and fishermen when they are out of sight of land, that our whaleboat was finally ready to try out. I had been trying to think of a good name to paint on the boat's stern, but the only really appropriate name, "La Grand Cagada," the great bowel movement, was too vulgar to register with the captain of the port. This was, however, its unofficial name, and instead we painted "La Tortuga Coja" in great red letters. The crippled tortoise.

Ramón had come in again for our moment of triumph, and since there was a regatta that morning—with canoe races, football, and much serious drinking in Las Palmas—there were crowds of people gathered on the beach to watch our maiden voyage. The fishermen in Río Verde had said that the boat must take them out five miles, into the deep water where the marlin lived, and it should make at least five knots. I had a lot of reservations by this time about our motor and was secretly convinced that three knots would be our maximum speed. Three knots would have delighted me.

What happened as we poled out from shore, started the motor, and shoved into high gear was simply incredible. The boat sped along at about one-third knot through the little inner harbor lined with people watching us. At the point, we hit a breezy spot, at which moment, still heading west, the boat slowly began to drift backward toward the east. It would have been bad enough on a normal day, but this catastrophic exhibition before the whole town was devastating. "For God's sake," Ramón yelled at the mechanic, who was managing the rudder, "let's land this disaster." We made a wide turn and twenty minutes later had retraced the hundred yards or so. The mechanic and the carpenter joined the fiesta; Ramón, depressed into a catatonic silence, went back to Río Verde.

We never did properly analyze the reasons for this fiasco because everyone in town had a different idea. The propeller was too large; the propeller was too small; the propeller was not set deep enough in the water; the shape of the boat was bad and impeded the flow of water; the motor turned too slowly; the motor was too small; the reduction gears were making too much friction. We had spent half our money by this time, and I was afraid to begin experimenting, or rather to continue experimenting. I was pretty sure that the boat was too big and the motor too small.

Later that night I discussed the consequences of my ignorance of boats and motors with Tommy and Burt. They had always kept aloof from this fishing project, insisting that if one wanted to fish in the deep sea one needed to do it properly. They talked in the neighborhood of four thousand dollars for a boat and a diesel motor. Now they gave me their little orations again, but this time Tommy told me that he had a rebuilt Volkswagen automobile engine sitting in his warehouse that he would give us.

So the whole operation began again. It took another month of looking for new reduction gears, a battery, a starter, a new propeller. Finally, in the first days of August we found ourselves on another maiden voyage two miles out in the ocean pooping along at about two knots. We were all together again: Ramón, Orestes, the mechanic, the carpenter, and two teenaged mechanic's helpers. We were all depressed. The sea was not really rough but great quantities of water were breaking over the bow, and we were all wet.

Then the moment arrived. In one three-minute period the following things happened: the throttle fell off the motor, the oil filter slipped out of sight between the motor and the sides of the boat, the fan belt broke, the exhaust pipe, red hot by then, gave a final little effort, and the boat burst into flames. Dead in the water, we began to drift toward the rocks on the north side of the river. Ramón threw the anchor overboard, and the chain broke. We had reached the end of our fishing project. Just before we crashed into the rocks, a little boat from Manta, reacting to all those wildly waving shirts, came along and pulled us back to Las Palmas.

The next day the three of us went back to Río Verde.

We made one last attempt at fishing. While working on the boat in Esmeraldas I had become friendly with the Esmeraldas fishing co-op, and the members offered to loan us one of their nets. Made of nylon, it was about a hundred yards long and weighed a good two hundred pounds. We brought it out to Río Verde and spent a week and about ten dollars repairing the broken mesh and putting new lead weights and balsa floats on it. One night Ramón, Orestes, and Roberto, a fisherman from Esmeraldas who had come to show us how to handle the net, went out into a rough sea in the canoe. They came back about four that morning with a long split down the bottom of the canoe from the battering of the waves, completely exhausted and half terrified from the experience. They had laid out the net three times in three different spots and had caught one *pargo* that weighed twenty-one pounds. We sold it to Nelson, the owner of the balsa mill, for two dollars. So our fishing project, which had cost us about seven hundred dollars, wasn't a complete loss after all; we had something to show for it.

By then there wasn't much time left; in three months my contract would expire. Six or eight months earlier I would have found the idea quite terrifying; now I accepted it with an equanimity that really irritated Ramón and Orestes. There wasn't time to start anything new, nor did I have any new ideas or any enthusiasm to begin working outside the cooperative.

I made out a list of twenty things that had to be done in the co-op before the rains started, and they were final things that,

when completed, would make an operational entity out of the
organization. And we even did some of them in those last few
weeks. We replastered the cement water-storage tank that I
had made the year before, built a wooden top for it to keep the
turkeys from jumping into the water—or, just as bad, standing on the sides facing out with their rear ends facing in. We
roofed the sows' farrowing house with palm leaves and pieces of
balsa, built wooden gutters to catch rain water, began to build
a wooden form for the new cement water tank at the pig house,
and disked up most of the farmland again.

Except for two or three things, the final months rushed past
in the usual tranquil way. The ugliest incident, which dramati-
cally clarified Ramón's position in the town, took place about a
week after the canoe had been damaged in the sea. Ramón and
Orestes still had faith in the net; they wanted to try it out
again on a calmer night, in a good canoe and a couple of miles
farther out. They talked to Otilio, who lived up the river but
kept a canoe in town. He told them to go ahead and use his
canoe.

One night about two I awakened to yells and curses in the
main street. There was a certain way of slapping a machete on
the ground so that it cracked like a pistol shot. I had never
heard a machete handled this way except in moments of rage,
and then it rang out like a war cry. I could hear these sharp
slaps mixed with the furious yelling of drunken voices. One of
them sounded like Ramón, and another sounded like Carlos
Torres. I had a sense of foreboding. Unless he were completely
insane with drink, Carlos, a coward, would never dare attack
Ramón. Ramón seldom got drunk and when he did, insulted or
humiliated, he felt some inner necessity to act violently, and
was a complete ass. I lay in bed listening, and I could hear
someone running furiously up the hill. I figured it must be

Ramón because he was the only one who lived on the hill, and I guessed that he was looking for a machete. Behind him, mocking voices.

I got up and stood in the window and watched two extremely drunk citizens, surrounded by a small group of spectators, walking toward the co-op store and the tractor, which was parked beside it. It was Carlos Torres and Ramón Arcos, both with machetes and both of them, minds completely blown, screaming obscenely for Ramón Prado. They danced around the tractor, transferring their fury from Ramón to the machine, slashing a tire, the headlights, the gas tank, and then they started throwing bottles and rocks at the store. I wasn't about to go out into that wild darkness of whistling machetes and flying objects until Ramón appeared again, running down the street—and stopping to slap his machete on the ground— screaming in fury, "All right, you sons of bitches, let's play!"

I had to go out then and prevent the flow of blood. It was hardly necessary; most of the crowd, friendly with Ramón, or at least outraged by the insane violence against the tractor, gathered around him and began pleading for restraint. And even that was hardly necessary, for with Ramón's first savage rush the two drunks broke and ran. I got the machete away from Ramón, threw it over the door into the locked *bodega*, and tried to get him into the house, but he was too wild. We were all holding him back; he was completely distraught, out of his head. Finally, unable to endure it, he fainted dead away, and for nearly a minute he lay in the road like a dead man.

It is almost impossible for me to write about this night, and I would much prefer to leave it out of this account of my life as a Peace Corps Volunteer. There were a thousand other nights in Río Verde which I have scarcely mentioned, when we lounged quietly on the steps of the store listening to the radio, or sat around the table in the house making conversation, that in fairness ought to be weighed against that brutal, revealing night.

I had never had a friendship with Carlos Torres; he had always been repellent to me. But Ramón Arcos and I had been friends. And in truth this hatred which had come boiling up was directed against me as much as against Ramón. Some of those rocks and bottles had hit my house.

What had caused it all? Ostensibly, it had been Otilio's canoe. Ramón Prado had told Ramón Arcos over a friendly glass of *puro* that he was going to use Otilio's canoe with the net one night. Ramón Arcos had pointed out that Otilio had left the canoe in his care and that nobody was going to use the canoe without a written *permiso*. Take it from there.

But more profoundly this hatred was rooted in the jealousy toward the farm that the three *socios* controlled. The other people had been deprived, they were not a part of this monstrous richness, and their resentment was directed not only toward Ramón but toward me, who had organized the co-op and had made such a situation a reality. The failure of our plans for fishing had been more disastrous for the people in the town than I had realized. Carlos and Ramón Arcos had both wanted to be invited to fish with the new net. Ramón and Orestes had ignored them; they would fish by themselves; they were angry. When the net had arrived had anyone in the town offered to help them repair it? And since no one had raised a finger, why did they feel insulted at being ignored? The two of them, against all their instincts and the whole social fabric of the town, had exhausted themselves in this insane cooperative which had been built to unite the town and to exist for everyone. And now they were through with the town; they would work for themselves.

The other side of the coin. The gringo. All he did was work

for that damned co-op. Everything was for the co-op, for Ramón, Orestes, and Vicenta, the gringo's children, three people who only a couple of years before had been just as poor and humble as everyone else in town. They could remember when Ramón went barefoot like everyone else, when he bought junk fish off the shrimp boats and sold it up the river in his canoe, when he made about twenty-five cents a day selling fish on the river. He had been one of them then. They could remember when Orestes, his mutilated hand so bloody from fishing that he could no longer handle a paddle, had had to beg food from his father for his children; he had been one of them then. And even Vicenta, who quietly stuck to the co-op and received less hatred than the other two, she too had once been one of them. Now she was managing the store and giving or refusing credit, assuming power; she was moving above the town's poverty.

There was one thing for which I was grateful—Orestes had gone to Esmeraldas the day before the fight and was not in town. If he had been at home, and if he had been goaded as they had goaded his brother, there would have been murder that night. Orestes was slow to anger, but brutal when aroused.

In the morning I went down to the *Policía Rural* and put in a complaint, and Carlos Torres and Ramón Arcos were thrown into jail. Then I went up and sat on the store steps. One by one the older people in the town walked up the hill to study the tractor in disbelief and to apologize for the violence of the night. They understood as well as I did, without ever saying it, against whom those machetes had been directed. I wasn't so angry as embarrassed, embarrassed perhaps as a father whose child fouls himself in public.

In a way the town vicariously purged itself that night; it had been a frightful moment of truth for everyone. Ramón visited the jail half a dozen times that day, gradually losing his anger. The prisoners sat in their cement cell and wept and begged forgiveness, and Ramón, the typical Latin who had won but didn't want to win too much, arranged with the *Rural* to release them that evening. He had to continue to live in the town; he couldn't exploit his power and insist that they be sent to Esmeraldas.

But I'm not a Latin, and I was leaving the town. I never spoke to Carlos again. A week later when Ramón Arcos began to visit me as though nothing had happened, sitting comfortably at the table and making jokes, I felt as though I were losing my mind, it was so outrageous. Finally, I made some sarcastic reference to the beautiful way he handled a machete, and he smiled lightly, forgiving my bad taste, and said, "No, no, don't talk about that night; it never happened."

◻◻

My last weeks in Río Verde were punctuated by screams. By then I was pretty sensitized to screaming, and I sat up in bed early one morning, shortly after the big jamboree around the tractor, straining to hear, glad that the door was locked. These were women's screams, and they came from Vicenta's house. They were very loud and piercing, and somehow shattering to the nerves for being consciously ritualistic, the opening lines in the drama of death.

Vicenta was gone from town; I realized this with a feeling of relief. A few days before she had received a half-insulting notice on the Esmeraldas radio from a son-in-law in Muisne instructing her to come immediately and dispose of two pigs which she had entrusted to her daughter there to raise for her. The husband was tired of feeding the pigs. And now from her house, where her two daughters had entered their stepfather's bedroom to waken him, the screams of his discovered death. He was a man of eighty, crippled for years and tired of life, and there was no reason to feel grief at his passing. In all the time I had been in Río Verde I had never spoken to him more than a dozen times, but now, pierced by those screams, I found myself for about ten seconds beginning to lose control, beginning to cry. It was easy to feel that the old man's death would be a blessing and a relief for Vicenta; at the same time I felt for a moment the burden of her grief. But it wasn't just that. I wanted to cry for everything.

All day the dead man's children arrived in canoes from their farms along the river. With each arrival, more screaming. Ramón sent six candles to the house; the cooperative sent fifteen; I sent a package. All day the people of the town visited the house, and the next day, shortly before the funeral, Vicenta herself—the star—terrible in black, entered the house, and the final, climactic screams of the united family and her friends rang through the town. The priest refused to cross the river, and the procession, led by Vicenta's sons carrying borrowed shovels and a crowbar from the cooperative, slowly picked its way through the dead weeds in the town square and marched up the hill behind the school.

Three or four days after the funeral, an interval which was just barely decent, Orestes asked for a special meeting of the co-op. That night Orestes, Vicenta, and Ramón met upstairs in the house. We left the door open, and the candle brought some of the kids, as well as Aladino, Goya, and Pancho, who came in like moths.

Twenty-year-old Aladino was leaving town the next day. He had been a *socio* for a while but had faded away like the others, refusing to be bossed by Ramón. Now, jealous of a younger brother who was, Aladino insisted, his father's favorite, he was determined to leave the town forever. "That Alfredo," Aladino told me bitterly. "He just uses my father; he doesn't have a deep emotion for him like I do. He's just a spoiled kid, but everything he says delights my father. His eyes dance when he looks at Alfredo. For me—nothing, or a sarcastic remark. No, to hell with it. I'm going to Quinindé and stay with my sister's husband and look for work. To hell with Río Verde."

And this was about what Orestes wanted to say, too. "Ramón and I have talked this all over," he said. "We will stay here for one more year, plant and harvest one more crop, and then we want to leave the town."

"What about all your work here?" I asked him.

"That's what we want to talk about," Orestes said.

"What about you, Vicenta? Are you committed to the town?"

"But no one is committed to the town," Vicenta said. "We are prisoners of our poverty. There's no one in town, except perhaps Don Julio, who wouldn't leave if he could."

"You'd like to leave then if you could?"

"If it is God's will, yes, I would like to leave the town."

"Well, then," I said, "let's figure out how to do it."

"Don Enrique feels," Orestes said, "that if this tremendous interest in cotton continues for another year we would have no trouble selling the farm and the tractor. Don Enrique has talked to many people in Esmeraldas; everyone is looking for cotton ground."

"And we could take this money," Ramón said, "and buy a small farm on the Esmeraldas River with pigpens near the river with clear water by the pens always. Water for the house, for the chickens, clean water to wash in. A man would have a chance there."

"Do you want to do it together as a *cooperativa?*" I asked.

"For God's sake, Martín," Ramón said, while Vicenta sadly shook her head and Orestes violently shook his.

"Did Enrique say how much he thought you could get?"

"We mentioned the 140,000 sucres that you said the farm was worth, and he said that that was cheap."

It would mean after prorating their hours of work that both Ramón and Orestes would have twenty-five hundred dollars apiece and Vicenta about two thousand. "Would forty thousand sucres," I asked Vicenta, "be enough to begin a new life in a new place?"

"But that is a richness beyond comprehension," she said. "Who has ever had this much to start a farm?"

"Well, then, why not keep working together for one more crop year?" I asked them. "And after that if you still want to dissolve the cooperative or if the rains don't come again, do it. I agree that Río Verde is a hard place, and I don't think it will be here in another ten years. But don't sell it suddenly, accepting the first offer that comes along. Start now to find a buyer."

We talked for another half hour. Aladino, to whom we still owed six dollars, wanted to know if we could pay him so he could leave town. It was almost more than we had, but we sent Vicenta down to the store to rob store funds. Pancho had something on his mind, but he didn't speak until the meeting was breaking up.

Pancho was a delicate and unknown factor at this point. Earlier we had been very good friends, but a couple of years before I had had to take two Heifer pigs away from him, and he was just beginning to be easy with me again. A year later Ramón had had Pancho thrown in jail for a day for drunkenly saying in the street that even the gringo thought that Ramón had stolen the cameras. What I had said was that one of my good friends had stolen my cameras, meaning Alexandro. Later Pancho had apologized to Ramón, and gradually they had become friendly again, to the point, even, that they were talking about farming a little piece of Ramón's ground together as partners. Two men working together as partners; it was incredible.

Pancho stood at the top of the stairs as everyone was leaving.

"You know," he said sadly, "a co-op would work. If you could teach them patience, if the people were serious, if you could find honest leaders. If you could explain the need for direction. . . . Well, good night, sleep with the angels."

It took me a couple of days to figure out what he meant. He had never been in the cooperative, had always stood apart, watching it and scoffing, and it was difficult for me to take seriously his sadness at seeing the co-op die. I talked to Orestes. The more I thought about selling the farm to one man, the less satisfactory it seemed. Just another *patrón* for the village and the village hiring out to him as day laborers.

"But Pancho isn't serious," Orestes insisted. "Pancho will never work with others."

"He's talking about working with Ramón," I said. "Could you have imagined that two years ago? And anyway, if not Pancho, maybe somebody. And if not Pancho now, then maybe Pancho later."

"Well, do what you want," Orestes said. "You know we trust you all the way. But my God, you are innocent; you're like a little child who thinks everyone is good. Haven't you learned yet what the town is like?"

I didn't answer him, but I guess I could have, saying that the town was just people and that the people changed. "Look," I could have said, "how you and Ramón have changed. And now maybe, just maybe, Pancho is changing." And one by one, maybe, maybe, little by little, people would change.

I spent the last days in Río Verde saying good-by and talking with the more serious people in the town—Pancho, Wilfrido, Umberto, Atoniel, Chuco-chuco. I asked them to form a new cooperative and to make an offer to the old cooperative to buy the farm. There was mild and careful enthusiasm, and they promised to discuss it. Pancho, noncommital, had a faraway look in his eyes.

◻◻

I had always had very circumspect relations with the women in the town. It was a Latin community, and I went by the Latin rules. The women of Ecuador lived in the other room; they appeared when it was time to serve you; they were very much the property of their men. Even my relationship with Ramón's wife, Ester, had always been very correct and almost formal. Ecuadorian women were not trained to be companions nor did they know how to carry on a conversation, and Ester, very typical, had always been reticent and shy, always in the background.

Ramón used to kid me about Ester. "Come for dinner tonight," he'd say. "It's not I who is inviting you, it's Ester; she says she loves to watch you eat."

"Watch me eat?"

"Yes, she says it's pretty the way you eat, sitting up straight and eating slow, you know, like a real *caballero*."

"Oh, come on now."

"No, it's true," Ramón said. "You do eat pretty, you know. This has always been a great sadness to me, that we have been too poor to have you eat with us every day."

It was the last day; I was all packed. The tide was beginning to ebb, and the truck across the river was honking its horn, getting ready to get ready to leave. I climbed the hill for the last time with Ramón for a last cup of coffee and to say good-by to Ester. Ramón was just completing a new house which sat on the top of the hill at the edge of the co-op farm. It had a tremendous view of the town and the beach and the river and the shrimp boats slowly moving across a thousand miles of ocean. He was going to make the front of his house of boards so that the whole town, every time it looked toward the hill, would see his wooden house, the only one in thirty miles. He wanted to paint it blue or yellow; he said it would be a monument to the Peace Corps. He wanted to make a sign to hang outside the house by the gate—"Luz de America," the Light of America. Ah, Ramón, proud, black prince, how you could play Othello.

So I drank the coffee, and Ramón told Martita, six months old by then, to say good-by, pretending outrage because she was smiling, and then I said good-by to Ester, and everything was under control, everything like a dream. But as I stepped down off the porch to leave, Ester screamed, and I turned to see her, her face contorted and the tears streaming down her cheeks. We hugged each other, and Ramón rushed from the house and stood on the brow of the hill looking down intently into the town.